THE ART OF THE

Puppet

BY BIL BAIRD

Special Photography by Arie de Zanger

THE ART OF THE PUPPET BY BIL BAIRD

A Ridge Press Book

The Macmillan Company, New York / Collier-Macmillan Limited

CONTENTS

With Cora

FOREWORD

This book is designed to tell people about puppets and how they differ from each other and how they are alike. It is not written for the specialist, but for everybody. It is my hope that the following pages will be of help in creating a more thorough understanding of puppetry as a performing art and to define it in relation to the other performing arts.

I do not pretend to offer a history of puppetry. The subject is too vast. Rather, whatever historical events are outlined here are set down in order to explain the nature of puppetry and how it operates, from the point of view of a member of the craft.

It is only recently that I have stopped long enough to formulate any ideas about my occupation (and preoccupation). Most of the time has been spent just doing. So it is from a background of forty years of practice in a profession that has given me the greatest satisfaction that I voice the viewpoints set forth in this book. In addition, I have accumulated information, stories, ideas, and pictures from many other sources.

Of all the people who have helped me in putting together this book the most generous has been Otto Kunze, who has made available his lifetime collection of clippings, notes, and observations on puppetry and music, plus his considerable library. These are only equalled by his intense enthusiasm for puppetry.

Probably more than anyone else it was Welthy Fisher and Tom Noonan who started the complicated machinery that brought our company to India and to the roots of puppetry. And it was Kamaladevi Chattopadhyay and Mrinalini Sarabhai who showed us that puppetry and helped us to understand it.

I am indebted to many people for their backstage hospitality and conversations. To Devilal Samar and Malu Ram for special performances. To Sergei Obraztsov, Leonora

Shpet, Eugene Speransky, and Jan Malik for much information and many kindnesses.

To Roberto Lago, Henryk Jurkowsky, Carl Schroeder, and Jan Bussell for informative letters and many photographs. To Som Benegal for color transparencies from India. To Ludwig Krafft for the hospitality of the Munich City Museum's Puppet Collection and for many excellent transparencies—and to Dr. Hadamowsky for making the Teschner material available to me. Dr. Hans Purschke has been of invaluable help in supplying me photographs from Germany. To Margarita Niculescu for her correspondence over a number of years. Dr. Ota Popp sent me the Skupa pictures, while Vaclav Havlik supplied those from the Divine Comedy. I also wish to thank William Duncan, Don Sahlin, Jean Loup Temporal, Michael Meschke and Dr. Deszo Szilagyi for photos and correspondence.

A belated salute to Paul McPharlin for having so carefully researched and annotated the goings and comings of American puppetry—and to his wife, Marjorie Batchelder, for having almost singlehandedly represented her countrymen at the international meetings.

There are some who have indirectly contributed as much to the fabric of the book as those already mentioned. In addition to my old bosses, Tony Sarg and Mat Searle, there are Russell Markert, Julius Monk, Max Liebman, and Fred Waring, who put us to work and helped us to get started on our own. There is our own permanent wandering company, especially Frank Sullivan and Franz Fazakas. And Louis Miller who left behind twenty-two years of woodcarving, philosophy, and German sailor songs.

There are Yip Harburg, Fred Saidy, Burt Shevelove, Arthur Birnkrant, A. J. Russel, and Sheldon Harnick, who are among those artists who have understood the special nature of puppetry and who have written and composed for it.

No book of words and pictures can compete with actually sitting in an audience and seeing a live show in action, but if these pages can in some measure intrigue more such artists to create for puppetry, and as a result to intrigue more people to see it, they will have served their purpose.

—BIL BAIRD

WHAT IS A PUPPET?

1

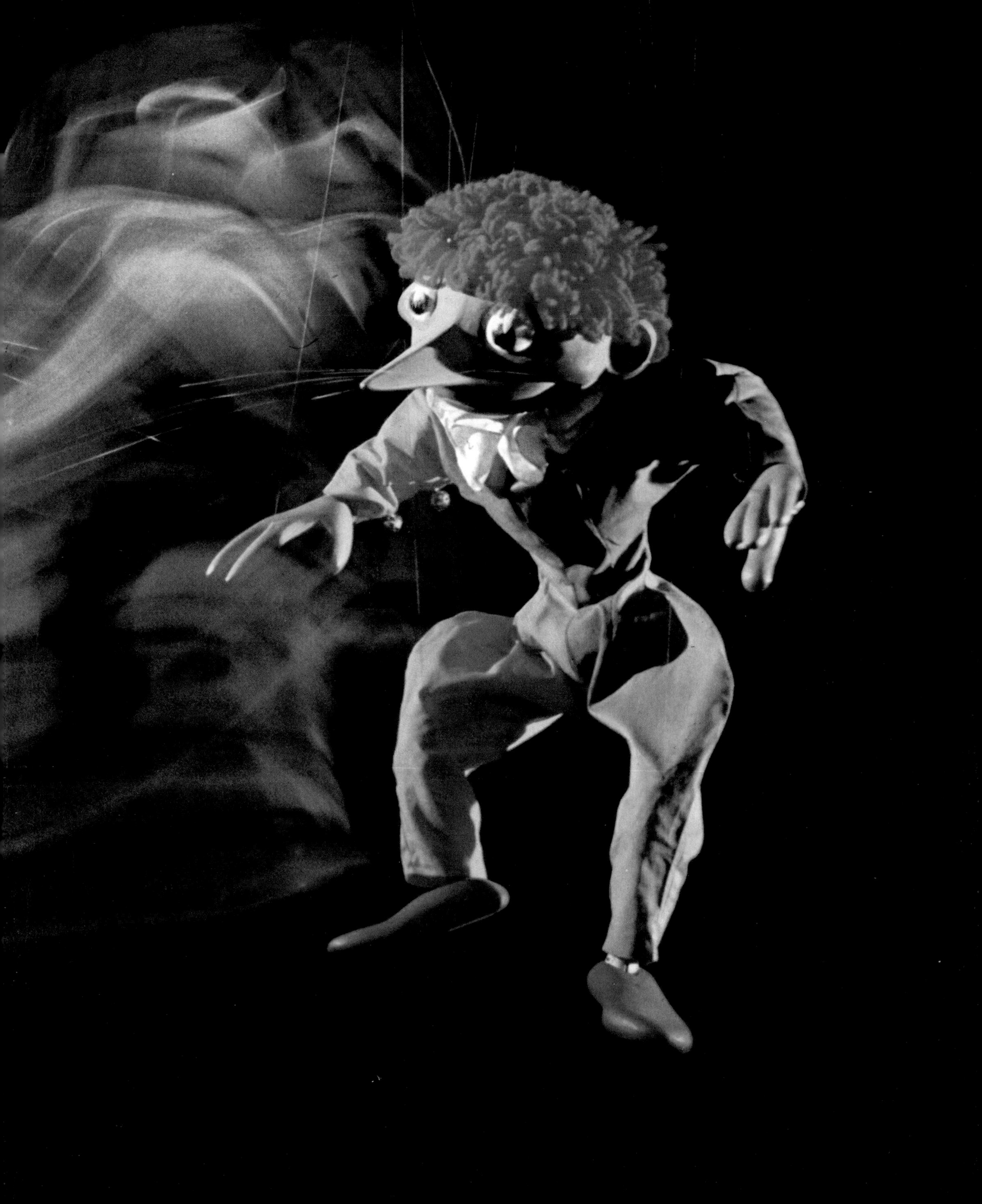

Preceding pages: Multiple-exposure
photograph conveys impression of marionette motion.
Above: Shadows of fan-shaped *genungan* and
rod-operated leather figure were
photographed during actual Indonesian play.

A puppet is an inanimate figure that is made to move by human effort before an audience. It is the sum of these qualities that uniquely defines the puppet. Nothing else quite satisfies the definition. A puppet is not the bowing saint in the cathedral clock or the mechanized display figure in the store window. These are machines. It is definitely not a doll. When somebody plays with a doll, it involves an intimate action which never extends past the two of them. The player supplies the life for both of them. In no sense is that show business.

There are hundreds of thousands of puppets in the performing companies of the world today. They are of many shapes and sizes and operated in an astonishing variety of ways. In Jakarta, Indonesia, where the puppet theater has been known for hundreds of years, someone is creating a puppet. It might be a highly stylized figure of a prince, cut in profile from very thin buffalo hide, intricately pierced, and subtly colored and gilded. Its arms will be articulated at the shoulder and elbow with joints of thread and controlled by two long rods. The entire figure will be mounted on a spike of buffalo horn which has been split and bent to give support from both sides. This is a shadow figure. When the master puppeteer holds his prince against a lighted screen, the royal shadow will be seen in all its delicacy by a rapt audience.

In Munich, San Francisco, or Shanghai, the figure might be of wood, metal, or plastic, sculptured in the round, and jointed in fifteen or sixteen places. It will be carefully balanced and motion will be imparted to it by strings. These will be fastened at one end to a moving part of the puppet and at the other to a wooden controller from which he is suspended. Such a figure is a marionette.

In Moscow or Budapest, the figure might be a rod puppet, whose sculptured upper torso is pierced vertically by a rod which allows the puppeteer to control the movement of the head. The articulated arms will be controlled from below by two other rods. The legs may be made of softer stuff, or merely suggested beneath a skirt or a kilt of cloth. This figure bows at the waist as the operator's wrist is bent.

In Sydney or Calcutta, it might be a hand puppet built to fit the shape of the human hand, with one or more fingers supporting the head and the thumb and another finger inside the cloth arms. This probably will be a smaller figure than the marionette or the rod puppet, and will usually be visible only from the waist up, although sometimes hand puppets are equipped with legs.

And somewhere someone is building a puppet that resembles nothing human or animal at all. It may be an abstraction or a piece of furniture. It may be operated in any one of a number of ways, but it will still be a puppet.

The urge to make puppets is nothing new. People have been creating them for thousands of years. And why? What is the fascination of puppetry? Why have artists like George Bernard Shaw, Paul Klee, Josef Haydn, Wassily Kandinsky, Gian-Carlo Menotti, and George Sand, to name only a few, expressed themselves through puppetry? It is a part of man's ancient urge to re-create life that results in this many-layered art. More diverse than painting, sculpture, dance, song, or story, puppetry has something of all of them. It is also a means of communication, an extension of human expression.

13

How does a puppet come into being? It happens when someone sees an image of himself, or some aspect of the world, in the crooked glass of his imagination and gives it form, movement, and sound. Someone has the urge to bring his drawing to life and make it move and talk. Or maybe he thinks of a sound first and gives it shape and movement. Or it may be an intangible, like the force of the wind, that inspires him and he gives it a shape and character. The primitive urge still applies.

So when a person finds in the world around him a man, an animal, a shape, or a situation, and something strikes him as funny or frightening or sad or awkward about it, he picks out the essence and builds it into a puppet. Certain features inevitably will be emphasized, others diminished or omitted. Always the figure will be a simplification.

The first requirement of a puppet is that it move, however. A fine figure isn't always necessary to create good entertainment. A skilled puppeteer can pick up a handkerchief or a necktie and give it motion and life. Many a veteran Punch character, who has been so beaten and scarred in his daily battles as to be almost featureless, puts on a fine show. It is his style and movement that make him live.

Equally important to the illusion is sound. A very great part of the puppet is the music he works to, or the voice he emits. And his voice can be as much an invention as his movements. Aside from the hundreds of word languages that people use, a puppet can speak with sighs, roars, coughs; through buzzers, poundings on the floor, bells on the ankles of the operators, and the sounds of instruments. In Rajasthan, India, puppet voices for centuries have been the eloquent wordless shrills of a bamboo and leather reed. A special expressive type of orchestration used with animated cartoons today (and called "Mickey Mousing") had its antecedents in ancient India

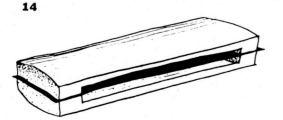

and involves the deft use of the reed and the drum.

There have been so many of us at different times and places looking at the world through our own personal crooked glass that there have been countless styles of puppets. There probably are more puppets in the world today than there are human actors.

Whatever the end result, puppets are not little men, women, or animals. A puppet must always be more than his live counterpart—simpler, sadder, more wicked, more supple. The puppet is an essence and an emphasis. For only in this way does a puppet begin to reflect the truth. When puppeteers try to copy the human animal, they fail. Live actors do it much better. The mechanical copy of life may be amazing, curious, or even frightening, but it doesn't live, whereas the *suggestion* contained in a puppet may be full of life.

But whether a puppet has the aspect of a human being, a grasshopper, or an armchair, it has been created to perform, to entertain, to make a statement. By a motion that is like something we know, yet stronger; by a shape that suggests the living, yet is simpler or more emphatic; by a sound that is understood, yet in some way is exaggerated, the puppet affects its audience as does no other means of communication.

When the puppet performs before an audience, he begins to create a kind of life. I say before an audience, because only in the imaginations of an audience does a puppet begin to exist. George Bernard Shaw once commented on this in a letter to Vittorio Podrecca of the Piccoli Theater: "I always hold up the wooden actors as instructive object lessons to our flesh-and-blood players. The wooden ones . . . move you as only the most experienced living actors can. What really affects us in the theater is not the muscular activities of the performers, but the feelings they awaken in us by their aspect. For the imagination

Far left: Rajasthani marionettes of Malu Ram company of Delhi. Sketch of bamboo-and-leather reed held in mouth to produce shrill puppet voice. Next left: Marionettes by Irmgard Sturm, of Stuttgart. Above: Castellet from tiny guignol theater, Lyon. Right: Wayang golek rod puppets of Java.

of the spectator plays a far greater part than the exertions of the actors."

On another occasion he wrote: "I have often suggested that the Academy of Dramatic Art try to obtain a marionette performance to teach the students that very important part of the art of acting which consists of not acting, that is, allowing the imagination of the spectator to do its lion's share of the work."

Further, and perhaps most important, there is the almost magical interaction of puppet and puppeteer. Never get the idea that the puppet stands independently *between* the audience and his manipulator. The puppeteer can feel the response of the audience through this extension, this part of himself, as much as the actor on a stage. He is very conscious of how he's "coming down the strings."

Perhaps a better statement of this complex relationship between puppet and puppeteer is that of the distinguished puppeteer and actor Vladimir Sokolov. "These creations," he writes of puppets, "are characters of human imaginations—those of its creators. Therefore, they should neither reflect man nor reality, but live their own fantastic lives, lives of free beings.

"The idea of creation unifies itself with the subject and its form. Furthermore, the finished product reflects back to its originator, for the marionette takes possession of its leader. Product and producer cannot be separated.

"The marionette is not a mere embodiment of the human will and imagination, it becomes instead animated and commences a life of its own. As man transfers himself into his wooden puppet and makes it obey his orders—so it happens that man submits to the puppet's own being.

"The puppet obeys his imagination and submits to him, and at the same time, by its obedience, he submits to the puppet.

"In art this is an unexampled phenomenon. Here it is so, as if the actor, the instruments, the notes and even the music unite into one entirety. Not even one of these elements may ever be separated from the total complex. It is an ideal harmony, music transformed into visible, animated form."

It has often been said that the art of puppetry constitutes an international language. I believe it does. But I believe its roots go far deeper than the Babel of words we superimpose on it. Ages ago man learned to differentiate between other creatures' bodily attitudes and facial expressions in order to survive. Opening the eyes in surprise widened man's vision of an approaching danger. A snarling lip revealed a threatening tooth. Beetling the brows thickened the protection over the eyes. The expressions of the body or face, according to Charles Darwin, are as old as the race.

Man has been working with forms and motions and rudimentary grunts and sounds for so long that there are gambits that everybody understands. Gesture, music and even accented gibberish are, therefore, part of the puppets' international language. We have found that our three singing frogs get a laugh anywhere in the world. They sing in English, to be sure, but the words don't matter. It's the intonation. They could keep the same intonation and sing in Swahili. Here it is the combination of the funny (superhuman) face with the funny sound that brings a laugh. Sometimes it's a combination of a ridiculous face with a dignified sound that does it, and sometimes vice versa. The point is that puppets can go to extremes.

Above: Military array of Polish rod
puppets from modern play, *Captive in Tiutiurlistan.*
Below: Percy Press, known as "the
uncrowned king of English Punch men," poses
behind playboard with Punch and clown.

Nor must we think primarily of facial expressions in puppets. The whole body in movement often says more than a face. And there will be occasions when the puppeteer's reflection of reality produces a puppet with no face or no body.

Many puppets have belonged to small companies of wanderers, who have set up a light, portable booth outdoors or in the shelter of some large building and played to any audience they could attract. One wanderer would operate the puppets, another would play an instrument out front or talk to the small performers. Today there are still such shows, only they wander over greater distances.

Other troupes are far more elaborate. They may number hundreds of marionettes. They may have repertoires of dozens of plays written by top playwrights. Special music is created for these puppets by popular composers. The best directors find a new dimension in themselves and increase their understanding of theater by directing puppets. One permanent theater has a staff of two hundred and twenty human motivators to manage its invented population of over a thousand. Some large companies in the tropics play only out of doors at night. Their plays, lasting until dawn, and taken up again the next evening, may continue for six months.

Between the largest and the smallest of these puppet companies there are hundreds of kinds of puppet theaters. Many have their permanent buildings and steady audiences and are constantly building new repertoires. Some are specialized, with actors who handle the puppets and speak

Large mask on live actor (above, left) is
popular puppet technique in modern Poland. Above, right:
Necktie puppets by Tournaire and Gouge, Paris.
Below: Devil by Carl Schroeder. Opposite: Geometric
marionettes by Baird, after Buckminister Fuller.

for them, while other people direct, paint, construct, promote, write, or have ideas. In some companies all the human members are versatile enough to combine many of the skills and duties. Some companies make only motion pictures of puppets; others work live in theaters, television, night clubs, and commercial advertising. Almost all the companies travel to some extent. But no matter what their size or geographical location, the results are diverse, more diverse than any other form of theater.

In the case of the lone operator, the puppeteer has to be a sculptor, actor, playwright, dancer, political commentator, and stagehand. In a two-man company the partner may undertake the complementary duties of carpenter, electrician, singer, or lion stuffer.

If a puppet is an extension of the puppeteer,

Above: A famous team at the height of its popularity on American radio—ventriloquist Edgar Bergen and irrepressible Charlie McCarthy. Yes, Charlie is a puppet. Opposite: Beguiling child figure by Albrecht Roser.

or an instrument in his hand, then what is the puppeteer? Here is no ordinary actor, even granted an actor is something special. A puppeteer should be in some ways more than an actor. His activity is as diverse as the styles of his puppets. Suppose we sit in the audience of a night club and suddenly out of total blackness a cello appears, floating in the air, bowed and fingered by disembodied hands. To the left is a beshawled and bespectacled figure who conducts the music of the cello. Then a frenzied flock of colored notes and butterflies appears, fluttering to the tempo of the music. Backstage it is the Georges Lafaye company, pioneers in the "black" technique of puppetry. Dressed in black leotards and masks, and backed by a black drape, they are virtually invisible. As they lean forward, all we see are their white, gloved hands, holding their colorful "instruments" into a narrow curtain of light across the front of the stage. The butterflies are on black wire springs. In the darkness, the operators must sense each other's presence by looking at the puppets.

Next, let us sit in a theater and watch a couple of purely geometric characters fold, collapse, twist, and writhe to a modern jazz tune. Now two elastic rubbery dancers appear with crazy, excited, invented faces. A little man in a white suit pulls a cage on stage and locks the dancers in it, but they rock-and-roll right through it. Backstage, high up on two aluminum bridges, stand four puppeteers. The two who hold the wooden controllers of the dancers, contort their own bodies in an inane pas de deux and their faces are gleefully twisted in an imitation of those of the marionettes. In the limited space behind any puppet stage the ballet of the puppeteers is fascinating to watch. The choreography is just as strict as anything that's happening on stage.

During the tango in Sergei Obraztsov's *Unusual Concert,* we see two skillful dancers burlesque the Argentine tango. In a whirlwind finish the man swings his partner around his neck as she holds on with both hands. It seems a relatively simple effect, yet below stage there are not two, but seven puppeteers. One puppeteer oper-

Opposite: Backstage view during shooting of
Rufus and Margo Rose Company production of the story
of coffee, in 1937. This was first full-length
industrial film to use marionettes.
Above: Georges Lafaye with symbolic figures
created from folded newspaper. Right: Sketch shows
one method of "black technique." Figure is
thrust into curtain of light (shown here in cross
section) which obscures black-robed
puppeteer operating behind it. Audience sees only
the seemingly unsupported figure.

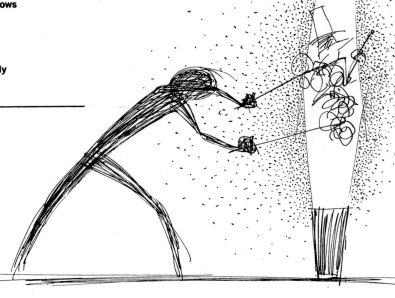

ates the body and head of each dancer with hands inside the costume, while another facing him, manipulates a pair of hand rods. And three other puppeteers dart in and out to lift a knee here or substitute a special figure there. In the limited space under these two rod puppets, the seven operators must govern their movement with perfect timing. They work so closely together that a false move may mean a fall. Again, the puppets have transformed the puppeteers.

There are no fat puppeteers, I can tell you. The work is too strenuous. Even a large one is at a disadvantage; there's not enough room for him backstage. If a hand puppeteer is too short, he raises himself on high cork soles. Special muscles come into play depending on what one is holding and how. We learn to talk and sing in a bent-over position while manipulating heavy marionettes. The lifting muscles in the arms of rod puppeteers become very strong—I know from personal experience. During an impromptu dance at a party at my studio, I swung one of the ladies of the Moscow Central Company over my shoulder. In a few seconds she smilingly lifted me over her head.

Puppetry thrives on diversity. Unlike human actors the range in relative sizes of puppets is enormous. Size is no criterion. The Poles today are working with larger-than-life puppets, and there is one permanent theater in New York whose thirty-six-inch wide proscenium is sufficient for its hand-puppet actors. But design and consequent style of action are often determined by the human operator. A human finger can move only so far in relation to its hand, so that the motion a finger imparts to a two-foot figure may become more limited in one a foot taller.

Controls or levers must be devised to extend the effect of the finger.

One hand of the puppeteer is required to control the hand of a large rod puppet, although the same motion requires only a finger in a small hand puppet. In operating giant figures, the puppeteer may have to run ten feet just to raise the tremendous arms in a long, impressive curve, as was the case with Remo Bufano's figures for the production of *Oedipus Rex*. A giant parade balloon may require fifty or more handlers. Or a cleverly devised multiple control may govern a whole chorus line of marionettes.

Some shows may require the operators to use tons of equipment. On the other hand, I have seen a puppeteer create drama with just his imagination and his own two hands. One time in South India, at a fair, I saw two rudimentary figures perform an exciting battle, seeming to demolish each other with blows from a heavy piece of metal which they tossed into the air and caught again. Later these two wooden-handed creatures opened a pack of cigarettes, pulled one out, inserted it into the one mouth that they had between them, opened a tiny match box, and lit the cigarette. During this show there was a constant exchange of banter between the puppets and the audience. The puppets supplied the rhythm and the story. The audience filled in whatever nonexistent features (costumes, scenery, expressions) they individually felt were needed. It was complete. All alone backstage was an extremely dextrous fifteen-year-old boy.

Whatever the size, style, or action of his puppets, each puppeteer must work out the best system for himself. Many have expressed preferences of one type over another. Some even argue heat-

Antique puppet from Uzbekistan (left) has gourd
head, is held and operated by child inside. Avant-garde
rod puppet (right) was created by
Fred Schneckenburger of Zurich, who conveys illusion
of life through use of moving symbols.

Obraztsov's famous tango couple (top) requires
seven operators. The Standwells perform in New York's
smallest permanent puppet theater—25 seats—run
by Francis Peschka and W. Gordon Murdock. High cork soles
help Budapest puppeteer (right) reach playboard.

edly about whether strings are superior to rods, or hand puppets, or shadows. It is an empty argument. (About as valid as classical ballet versus the twist.) Each method is best for a special purpose. Even tomorrow someone may bring forth a totally different approach.

I use many styles and would hate to be restricted to one. If I need a big mouth and relatively little perambulation, a rubber-headed hand puppet may do the job. My long-legged dancer, however, needs strings but no face.

What a dull craft puppetry would be if all the shows had to move or look the same, or adhere to the proportions of human actors. Each puppeteer must find his own ways to emphasize or compress the truth so that we can understand it.

Since a puppet lives only to make a statement in the hands of the puppeteer, it is not constructed to last forever. Often it is made of the most supple and transitory materials and will outlast its maker by a few generations at the most. By then it may be just a historical landmark, or happily a collector's item, reflecting its times or the original idea that brought it into existence. The greatest pitfall for the puppeteer is his reluctance to part with the tangible material he has built and his tendency to work with it as long as possible. When an idea no longer reflects the times, it dries up. The forms and gambits must be commentaries on the immediate moment. Although human actors age, they don't change much from generation to generation. But the puppet, the superactor, who may appear forever young, or old, quickly becomes dated as life changes and his targets change.

In each generation, man looks on his world with different eyes than those of his grandfather. The values change. But as long as he can look at himself in the funny glass or the sad one, and laugh, he will go on making puppets.

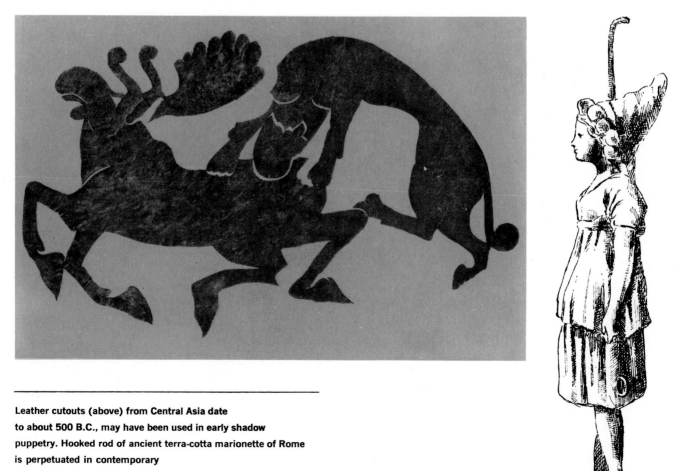

Leather cutouts (above) from Central Asia date to about 500 B.C., may have been used in early shadow puppetry. Hooked rod of ancient terra-cotta marionette of Rome is perpetuated in contemporary Orlando figures of Sicily and Belgium.

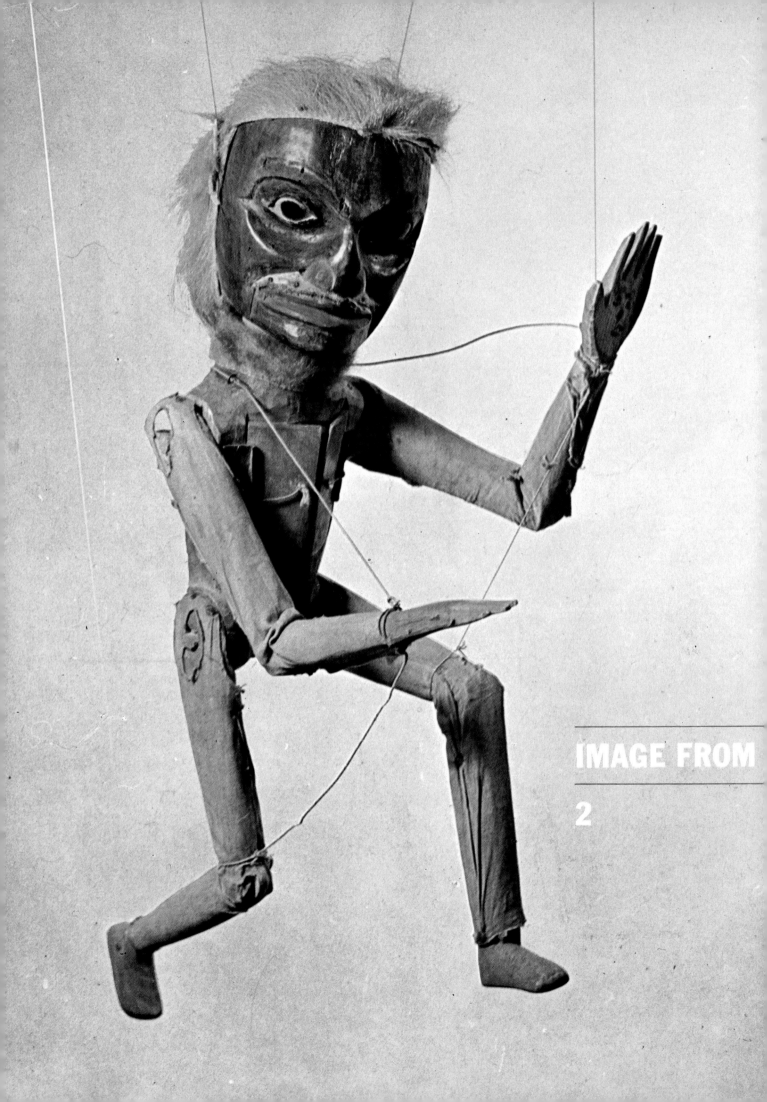

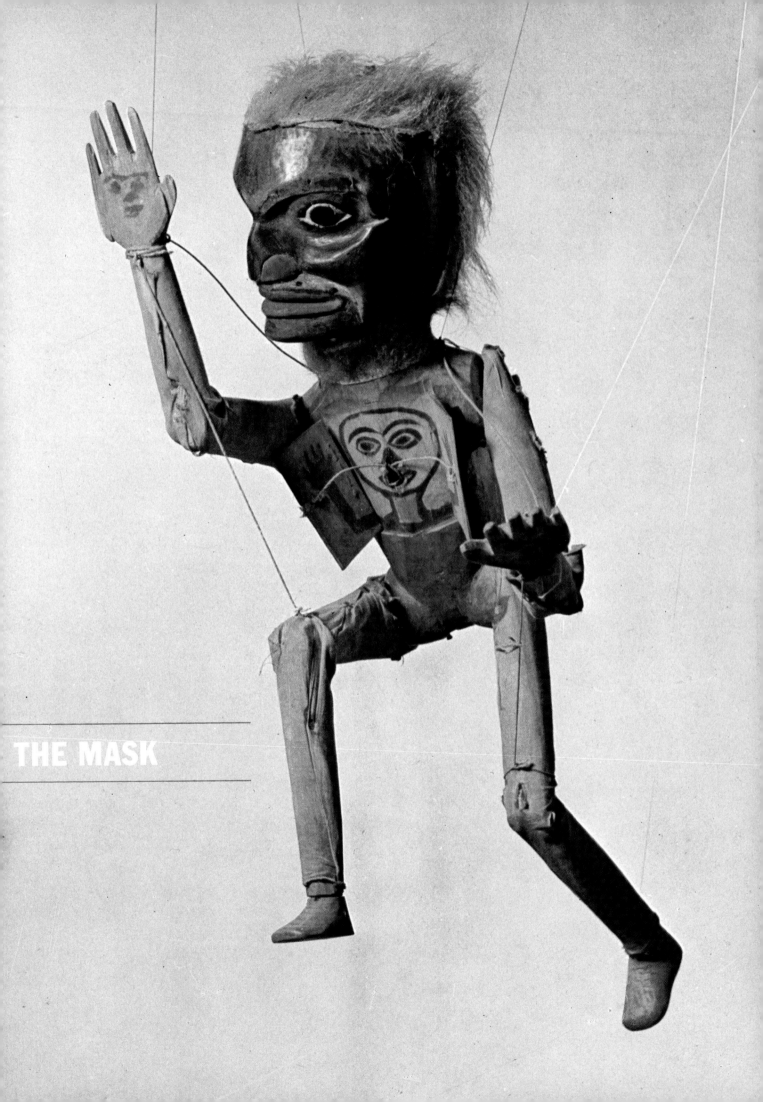

THE MASK

It is fifteen or twenty thousand years ago. In the dim recesses of a cave, a shaman, or witch doctor, is bent over the skull of a cow, which he is holding between his feet. High on the stone walls surrounding him are pictures of animals drawn in warm earth colors. In the flickering light of the crude lamps fueled with reindeer fat, they seem to move, an eerie procession of bison, deer, cows, horses, and gigantic bulls.

The shaman, who can read the meaning of signs and portents, and interpret the deities and demons of the unseen world, is drilling a hole near the jaw socket of the skull with a flint. For a long time the skull has been his mask in a hunting ceremony; now he is hinging the jaw with a thong to make it articulate. He finishes his task and inspects his handiwork with satisfaction. Tomorrow he will emerge from the deepest shadows of the cave and join the ring of squatting hunters tensely awaiting his guidance. The bleached horned skull, flanked by human hands, will be the first thing to appear, and even as the hunters watch, the jaw will move and strange, eerie sounds will issue from it.

Impressive? Effective? Certainly. And as long as the shaman appears to intercede successfully with the powers and the elements, and brings food or rain or springtime, his mask and his magic will be feared and respected. When the magic ceases to work the hunters will probably chop him up and get a new shaman.

It is a reasonable assumption that the mask originally was a disguise, perhaps a skin or a pair of antlers worn to conceal the approach of a hunter moving in the manner of his prey. The success of the masquerade gave it an aura of magic; the mask itself took on a quality of divinity. Masked dances became an important part of the ritual that attended food getting. It was believed that dancers enacting a successful bear hunt could, by sympathetic magic, assure the success of the real hunt.

Masks, particularly hinged and jointed ones like the shaman's, are just an evolutionary step or two away from the puppet. When a single masked dancer began to appear as a performer before the rest of his group, it was the beginning of theatrical performance and a stepping-off place for the mask to become a puppet. Gradually, in the course of centuries, the hinged and jointed mask moved upward, off the head, and was held in the hands in front of the body. Later it moved farther away and was made to live by the manipulation of strings.

Among the totemistic societies of the Northwest Coast Indians of North America—highly artistic, so-called primitive societies which gave us "totem poles"—there has been widespread use of the articulated mask in dramatic religious ceremonies, and clear evidence of an eventual transformation into puppetry. By totemistic is meant a society whose groups associate themselves with specific animals or plants. An individual born into the killer-whale group regards the spirit of the killer whale as his ancestor, and derives strength and comfort from his identification with it (as contemporary societies rally to the American eagle, the British lion, the French fleur-de-lis). The killer whale is his badge, his decoration, his totem, and the dances and ceremonies of his group are performed to propitiate its spirit.

The Northwest Coast Indians were blessed with an abundant food supply that gave them time to develop their talent for carving. They were blessed in addition with fine cedar to carve. Many of the complex and beautiful masks they created took the form of a totem animal which could be opened, by pulling strings, to reveal a human face representing the spirit of the man in the totem. The shaman who wore the masks and directed the ceremonies was the possessor of a great amount of power. He settled problems of weather, toothaches, or family disputes—and when he called the spirit of an ancestor down to earth to help out it appeared as a mask. One mask in the process of leaving the face and becoming a puppet was a figure, jointed like a marionette, worn on the head and operated from below.

Robert Bruce Inverarity, anthropologist and puppeteer, says in his book on these Indians that "the use of puppets controlled by strings was very common. The string sometimes ran over the great beams of the house (the clan residence) and were pulled by hidden manipulators who received their cues from the songs. The sisiutl, a mythical snake, would be conjured up, the dancer concealing it in his palm and releasing it during the dance. The sisiutl would then fly about, pursued by the dancer until he suddenly caught it. Then the dancer, by sleight of hand, would put the sisiutl in his mouth and begin to vomit and spit blood, as if trying to rid himself of the spirit. In this performance there were two sisiutls: one made of tubes that could be collapsed in the dancer's hands and the other controlled by strings which held it in the air. A small bag, filled with blood and held in the dancer's mouth to be bitten by him on cue, created an illusion of reality."

Among the Hopi Indians of the American Southwest, ritual puppet dramas were performed with a variety of animal and human figures. One,

also involving masks, and also played indoors where the dim light would heighten the illusion, was a corn ceremony. A single human performer, wearing a mask danced in front of a brightly decorated cloth curtain hung at one end of the kiva, or lodge. Behind the curtain another player created a frightening roar by blowing on a gourd. On the floor, small cornstalks, held upright on little clay pedestals, represented a field of corn.

Through apertures in the cloth, six large serpents then appeared, their eyes goggling, their mouths gaping, their hawk-feathered crests waving. They extended themselves full length, some five feet, swaying above the corn in unison to the rhythm of the moaning gourd, a sort of reptilian ballet to the singing behind the cloth. Suddenly the heads dipped down and knocked over the cornstalks. The roar of the gourd intensified, and at the height of the excitement the spectators began to shout, pray, and throw corn meal at the snakes. The snakes' heads were suddenly withdrawn through the curtain and this part of the ceremony was over. The puppeteers packed their equipment and made way for another group.

As a practicing puppeteer, I think it likely that neither the Northwest Indians nor the Hopi knew how the snakes were activated, or suspected, for that matter, that they were not real spirits. The quality of the illusion and the audience's acceptance of it were such that the strings supporting the dancing snakes could have been an eighth of an inch thick without anyone's noticing. Just to make sure, of course, there was the masked dancer. Besides dancing with the snakes, he was probably there to make sure that nobody peeked backstage—a kind of secrecy that haunted all puppet shows until recently.

31

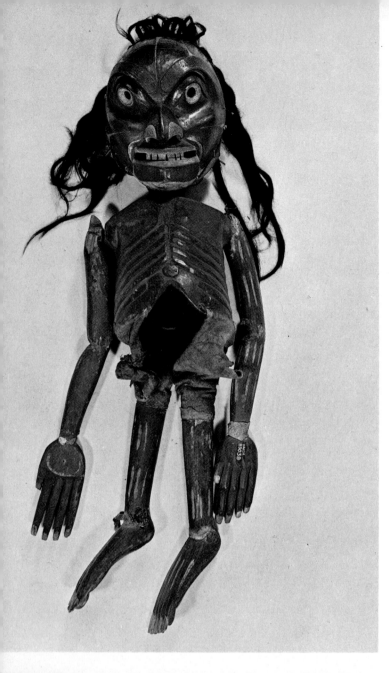

Indian artifacts of British Columbia: Grimacing
wooden figure (top) was worn on head of Haida tribe operator,
marks transition as mask leaves face; crab and
fur-clad puppets of Tsimshian tribe (above) have movable limbs;
articulated masks (right) were worn in medicine dance.

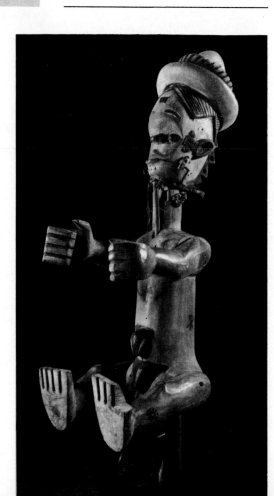

Above: Cannibal of the
Mountains, a Northwest Coast
Indian mask with articulated jaw
worked by hand, and forehead
that is raised and
lowered by strings. Below:
African rod puppet of Ibibio
tribe has jaw that opens
when wire is pulled. Left:
Harrappa monkey model.

Another Hopi ritual features a highly realistic pair of string-operated girl marionettes grinding meal. The figures are not immediately seen by the audience, for they are carried into the kiva wrapped in blankets. In the semidarkness of the room they are set up before a screen which conceals their manipulators. When the music begins, the kneeling figures bend their bodies backward and forward in time to it, apparently grinding meal on the small stone slabs in front of them. Their movements are astonishingly lifelike, even to the extent of rubbing powdered corn flour on their faces, as Hopi maidens do. While they labor, two bird effigies walk along the top of the screen and birdcalls fill the kiva.

This progression from masks to puppet masks to marionettes appears to be a logical one that has occurred, independently, in a number of primitive societies. In *The Golden Bough,* Frazer speaks of a sacred grove attended by priests and of certain trees worshipped as symbols of power and ancestry "at first roughly hewn out as an idol. . . ." This is very much in the character of the masks carved into living trees by the present-day Iroquois Indians and then cut from the tree and worn with the life still in them.

It is strange that the Central Africans, the most prolific mask makers in the world, have made few puppets. Maybe these demonstrative people have found it more exciting to wear the mask and to become the puppet. Egypt, on the other hand, has a long record of puppetry, and the fantastic animal heads of the Nilotic gods suggest a masked totemic ancestry.

Puppetry seems always to have had its genesis in religious ceremony, as an adjunct to priestly power. In its beginnings it has been used as a means of communication and to influence people. There is an old belief in India that puppets are little divine beings who have been sent down to earth to amuse and educate man. One Hindu legend provides a charming account of their touch of divinity.

The Lord Shiva and his wife Parvati passed a carpenter's shop one day, so it is said, and saw therein some doll-like figures the carpenter had made with jointed limbs. Shiva and Parvati were so intrigued by the figures that they permitted their spirits to enter them and set them dancing to the amazement and delight of the carpenter. When Parvati tired, the gods left the figures and resumed their walk. The carpenter ran after them, pleading, "Why do you leave my figures now that you have given life to them?" Parvati replied: "You made them, so you should give them life, not I." The carpenter pondered and finally arrived at the idea of moving his creations with strings. Hence, the marionette.

India's acquaintance with puppets is of long standing. In a museum in New Delhi there is an ancient little terra-cotta monkey that I believe was once operated by a string. He is not more than three inches high and he has an eccentric hole running vertically through his clasped hands and feet. Today he stands on a stick, but originally—about four thousand years ago—I believe a string ran through the holes. If such a string were held loosely, the monkey would climb (or slide) down it. Pulling it taut would stop him.

The monkey was found in the ruins of Harrappa, on the Indus River, a site yielding some of the earliest evidence of Indian civilization. If I am correct about the string, this tiny simian could well be the oldest existing ancestor of the profusion of Indian string puppets performing today.

For the monkey's survival, incidentally, we can be thankful that he was made of a material even as substantial as terra-cotta clay. Jointed puppets are made of perishable, pliable materials, and they tend to be short-lived—one of the difficulties in establishing the sequence of events in puppet history. The knockabout life of the traveling troupe, the constant packing and unpacking, and the fighting, dancing, and generally abrasive action on stage eventually erode the hardiest of figures. Very few have come down to us that are more than two hundred years old.

Animated figures such as the Harrappa monkey are quite rare. Contemporary with the monkey is a little Indian bull with a jointed neck, which was found at Mohenjo Daro; the Louvre has a very old terra-cotta head of a jackal from Egypt with an articulated jaw. As more ancient sites are uncovered and more jointed figures come to light, we may be able to fit them into their proper places in the jigsaw puzzle.

Some of the evidence we have to consider is most tantalizing. What, for instance, are we to

make of the tiny marionette theater, the first ever found, which was discovered at Antinoe, a city on the Nile built by the Roman Emperor Hadrian in the second century A.D.? The theater actually is a cabin mounted on a wooden Nile barge. Two ivory doors open to reveal a stage. Inside, two pillars support a rod across the front of the stage. Small cords still hang from it—undoubtedly used to operate the small, jointed ivory figures found on the cabin floor.

Size alone would indicate that this was for private use, not for public entertainment. A tiny stage often suggests a magic or religious rite. Mortuary paintings on the cabin walls concern Osiris, the Egyptian god of the Nile, the creator and benevolent judge of the dead, and indicate that the miniature theater was part of the paraphernalia of a ceremony devised to celebrate the cycle of fertility, the annual death and rebirth of growing things.

Could this ritualistic use have been the only purpose of the tiny stage? Or might it have been a model of a larger puppet theater operated by priests in the temples and sacred places of Egypt's deities? One thing suggested by the sacred writings of the time is that all theater, spectacle, and religious ceremony was firmly in the hands of the priests.

Our earliest authority, Herodotus, writing in the fifth century B.C., refers to figures operated by strings or wires as of great antiquity, but cites as an example a fertility figure he observed being carried in a procession of Egyptian women during a celebration of the Festival of Osiris. The figure, the earliest recorded mobile statuary, stood about twenty inches high and had a phallus of similar length, which could be erected by a string.

The Leningrad Hermitage Museum has a terracotta fertility figure from about the same time that might well have been used in the same Osiris ceremony. About nine inches high, in his right hand he holds a stylized sun and in his left a sheaf of grain. Under his robes at the back are fastened his jointed legs and curved phallus while above the joints are pierced holes for the strings to control the members.

Lucian, a Greek writing some six hundred years after Herodotus, describes a performance of the oracular god Jupiter Ammon at Heliopolis. Invasion, occupation, and cultural overlays had by then mingled the deities of Egypt and Rome. Ammon originally was Ra, the sun god, whose cult was centered at Heliopolis, the "sun city." Then the all-conquering Romans made him a suffix to their own Jupiter. When the image of Jupiter Ammon wanted to speak, it moved by itself—or so the people believed. If the priest didn't question the oracle, it moved again to gain attention. In any event, the image of Jupiter Ammon, placed on a litter supported on the shoulders of eighty priests whom he directed by the turning of his head, was carried several times around the hall of the Temple of Apollo and then questioned by the head priest. If the god were disposed to answer affirmatively, his image drove the carriers forward. If the answer were negative, they backed up. The figure finally rose to the vault of the temple. "I saw it," says Lucian, "with my own eyes."

The ancient puppeteer inside the litter, or next to it, probably experienced a thrill of power—or had a good laugh. The Romans even had a name (*adytum*) for the control room behind the statues, where the priests stood to pull their secret

Iroquois mask was carved from the wood of a living tree, thus preserving the "life" of the tree in it. Masks like this one from American Indian Heye Foundation, N.Y., were often used in dance to cure illness.

wires and to speak through tubes, concealed in the masonry, that carried their voices to stone mouths sometimes quite a distance away.

In addition to the moving statuary some quite marvelous automata had been constructed. Petronius mentions a silver doll that could move like a human being; eastern caliphs were diverted by trees adorned with mechanical birds that sang and flapped their wings, powered by water. Our best source of information on automata, however, was a Greek contemporary of Lucian's, Heron of Alexandria. Heron was a mathematician and natural philosopher, and he probably understood exactly how Jupiter Ammon was induced to move. He has explained the mechanics of such animated figures as the statue of Bacchus, which poured milk, water, or wine over the figure of a panther, while Bacchantes danced automatically in a circle around the two figures. Heron is credited with having a theater in which a mythical tale of vengeance, fire, storm, and shipwreck

Ancient altars employed mechanical devices for religious effect. Above: Egyptian shrine with doors that opened by steam from heat of sacrifice. Right: Greek shrine of Bacchus poured wine and milk, turned hydraulically.

was played entirely with automatic mechanisms. The Greek fleet returning home from Troy was lured by false beacons onto the rocks and was destroyed. This must have been a fascinating miniature spectacle—anything larger would certainly have had people running it.

If the golden statue of Apollo at Heliopolis could nod its head and fly, the Biblical "golden calf" may well have switched its tail. There is no doubt that the use of the animated figure was a practical thing in early religious ceremony, and attempts to stamp it out were not very effective.

The first reference to puppet theater as such seems to be Xenophon's in his account of a visit, in 422 B.C., to the house of the Athenian, Kallias. Host Kallias had hired a traveling Greek showman from Syracuse to entertain the guests with his puppet theater. But one man, Xenophon reports, was not interested and would not pay attention—Socrates.

Some of the best verification we have of the popular knowledge and awareness of puppetry in classical times is found in the widespread use of puppet similes in literature. Listen to Aristotle, in the fourth century B.C., explaining how simply the Lord of All controls the universe: "All that is necessary is an act of his will—the same as that which controls the marionettes by pulling a string in order to move the heads or the hands of these little beings, then their shoulders, their eyes and sometimes all the parts of their bodies, which respond with grace."

Apuleius, some five hundred years later, translating Aristotle, describes how "those who control the movements and gestures of these little wooden men have only to pull a string to move this or that limb—to bend the neck, to lean the head, to give the eyes a searching look, or cause the hands to do anything necessary; in fact, the entire body seems to be graceful and alive."

Galen, the physician, compares the marionette's strings to men's muscles. Plato sees them as men's passions, pulling them this way and that. Horace, in his satires, compares man's lack of free will to the marionette's subservience to the whim of the manipulator; so, later, does the contemplative emperor, Marcus Aurelius.

Not until the third century A.D. do we finally encounter a puppeteer by name. And then it is a bad notice. Athenaeus, fondly regarded by scholars for his revealing recital of Greek manners and customs, remarks with some disgust that the Athenians have permitted Potheinos, the "string puller," to play the theater of Dionysus, where once the noble tragedies of Euripides were performed.

Unfortunately, Athenaeus does not explain his objections, whether he despises all puppetry, or simply Potheinos. Probably it is puppetry. Compared to the likes of Euripides, Athenaeus no doubt felt it among the humbler forms of entertainment.

What kind of show was Potheinos putting on for the Athenians? We can only speculate. He was an operator of marionettes, for Athenaeus called him *neuropastos,* which derives from *neuron,* meaning a cord made of sinew. Hence, "string puller."

Evidence would indicate that most of the Mediterranean and Aegean puppets of this period were string—not hand—controlled. The early puppeteers must have felt that their illusion was made more successful by using strings instead of a more obvious hand type of operation—this despite the

fact that the farther away from the operator, the more difficult a puppet is to handle.

What were the string-puller's figures like? The theater of Dionysus is neither small nor intimate, but is not hard to imagine as a proper setting for the puppet stage. The actors who played in the Greek theater wore masks with mouths shaped like megaphones to carry their voices to the huge audiences. Having been sired by the mask, the puppet is also at home in the repertoire of the early Greek masked buffoonery. Puppetry and the Greek theater make use of the same kind of impersonal dramatics.

Possibly Potheinos played to a fairly small audience using figures like the Paladins of Sicily who enact the heroic legend of Orlando. If so, they were probably like the early Roman figures two

PLINTHIO O' CASSETA.

to three feet high—held by a hooked rod to the head, assisted by a cord or two to the hands.

Most disappointingly, we have no clue to the content of his show. No doubt, it was neither elevated nor serious, or Athenaeus would not have been so disapproving. It could have been a parody on Euripides himself. But whether it was a series of vaudeville turns, or political and social satire, or a popular marionette *genre* now lost to us cannot be said. In all of Greek and Roman literature not so much as a scene or a paragraph survives to tell us what the puppet theater was like.

One of the characteristics of the puppet theater, however, always has been a liberal trade of ideas with its live counterpart. The puppet theater at least has always felt free to lift plots and stories from the live theater and to parody the most serious efforts. And many a playwright and producer has borrowed the fantastic and outrageous aspects of the puppet theater.

The most likely source to borrow from would have been the so-called Dorian mime, a form of folk entertainment whose beginnings are buried in a dim past, but which was well known in the fifth century B.C. Mime was not dramatic in the sense of the great classical plays. It was rude, full of slapstick, a boisterous caricature of the life of the times. It was antic, highly obscene, refreshingly topical, and uproariously funny. Padded comics beat each other with huge comic phalli, undoubtedly borrowed from earlier fertility rites. Masks and extreme costumes were liberally used. From it emerged the earliest of stock characters: the clever slave, the doddering old man, the slow-witted rustic, the sharp-tongued hunchback. Although illiterate, the cleverest of these actors became quite famous for their inventiveness and

for their portrayal of special roles.

From Greece, and the Greek cities of Sicily, mime inevitably spread to Rome. To Rome, that is, by way of Atella. For it is at this little city, between Naples and Capua, that the Roman form of the mime first flowered and flourished. Rome welcomed these comedies and called them *Atellanae*—the Atellan farces.

Atella itself no longer exists; the modern town of Aversa is built on its site. But its farces persisted for many hundreds of years and contributed elements still discernible in the live, and puppet, theaters of today. They were played before appreciative audiences on the many festival days that dotted the Roman calendar and were part of the games and entertainment in the Roman arenas.

However much they elaborated on their Greek foundation, the farces always retained their rustic spirit and a loose framework, permitting lively improvisations. Singing and dancing were woven into the patomime and the character sketches. Dialogue was minimal, but there were jokes and quips and daring, sharp digs at the fallibility of emperors or other harsh truths of the times.

By the fourth and fifth centuries A.D., and the approaching extinction of imperial Rome, prominent characters had evolved, principally two buffoons, Maccus and Bucco. Maccus had a crooked nose and a prominent stomach, and was an insolent, energetic, witty, and slightly fearsome fellow. Maccus's friend, Bucco, was a conceited braggart, a coward, and a thief. Yet probably not unattractive. Another character, Manducus of the frightful teeth, was the scourge of children. Each character's mistakes and mischances, beatings and defeats were only too familiar to the peasant audience, and the occasional outrageous,

Fertility was hoped-for effect of ritual use of these primitive puppets. Top: Ancient Greek figure holds sheaf of wheat and sun, had movable phallus operated by string. Figure shown is reconstruction of orginal in Hermitage Museum, Leningrad. Left: Hopi puppets did corn dance.

lying, cheating triumphs were warmly welcomed.

To what extent the Atellan farce was mirrored in the puppetry of the time, or to what extent it may have appropriated the puppets' style, can only be guessed at. But there would seem to be no doubt that they so closely parallel each other that it would be far more unusual for them to have had no interchange than for them to have had a great deal.

When the highly organized Roman spectacles crumbled with the fall of the Empire, it is certain that the puppeteer moved on, carrying his small

Highly conjectural 19th-century engraving depicts
possible use of planchette-type figures found in Roman ruins.
Bearded operator manipulates them at right.

world with him, to perform in a barbarian world unsung and unpublicized. The farceurs found the same road. Through barbarian neglect and the active hostility of the Christian church, the Roman theater of elegant comedy and high tragedy was suppressed, along with the excesses of the arena. But the Atellanae and the puppets evidently were too commonplace to bother with. Each continued to play, whenever and wherever occasion offered. Each contributed its measure of imaginative and preposterous humor. Each survived.

3

A visit to a traditional village puppet show in India is like stepping back into history. Although modern India is well on its way to new techniques, those who watch over India's culture have been wise enough to preserve the old traditional performing arts, and that is the kind of puppetry I shall discuss in this chapter.

According to ancient mythology the Adi Nat, or first puppeteer, was born from the mouth of Brahma, the Creator. That is about as venerable a beginning as is accorded any puppet culture. It is also believed that puppet drama preceded the live drama by a long time. In ancient times it was considered taboo to impersonate someone else. It presaged sure death if one pretended to be or acted out the part of another; thus the theater of actors was unthinkable. The non-personal puppet was not so restricted. In the live Indian theater the expression for stage manager or director is *sutradahr*, or controller of strings, another bit of evidence that the puppets were there first.

From its beginnings in antiquity Indian puppetry took many forms. It is sometimes difficult for us in the West not to think of India as a cultural unit. But even today, after the many princely states that were once India have been united, there are eleven different scripts in use, and cultural differences still thrive. The kind and style of village puppetry depends on where you are.

In the state of Rajasthan, for instance, which is in the northwest, string marionettes predominate. They are operated by members of a centuries-old subcaste of entertainers known as the *kathputli bhats*—the "wooden-puppet perform-ers." The *bhats* number some fourteen thousand people, nearly two thirds of whom are active in puppetry today.

Indian village puppet shows are played most often at night. The puppeteers work on the ground, standing behind a brightly colored cloth backdrop stretched between two poles, or perhaps between two upended *charpoys*—wooden bed frames. In front of the cloth, lined up elbow to elbow, is the cast of marionette characters, an assemblage commonly called the *durbar*, or court, the most important part of the Rajasthan setting. Their strings are wound around a length of bamboo at the top of the back cloth, and unwound when it is time for a particular character to go "on stage." Oil lamps placed at either side light the figures. The audience is fanned out in front, seated on the ground. (The sight lines improve if the show happens to be played on the steps of a temple, or if the audience is able to range itself on a natural slope. But the raised bridge of the western operator doesn't seem to have occurred to the Indians.)

All literary references to strings on the fingers of the puppet master are true in Rajasthan. The *kathputli* have only two strings. One running from the top of the head over the puppeteer's fingers and back to the puppet's waist supports it and allows it to bow and whirl. The other continuous string moves the hands. Such a simple control suggests simple results, but a *sutradahr* can be most eloquent. The warrior brandishes his sword and shield, the dancing girl delicately lifts the hem of her dress with the aid of pins at the tips of her fingers.

Furthermore, the way the marionette is constructed gives it a considerable degree of built-in activity. The head and body are carved from a solid piece of wood, often mango. The downward-curving arms are made of stuffed material that is quite springy, and, therefore, very good for the puppet's fast fighting actions. No legs are needed. A pleated skirt, the marionette's proudest garment, can suggest any manner of walking, running, or dancing. It is rather like a kilt, but longer and extremely full. It is made of light, thin material weighted with borders of gold or silver cloth. The kilt has a life of its own, and a skilled operator can whirl it, spin it, spread it flat on the ground, or fill it with air like a balloon.

Among the Rajasthani *bhats,* it has been the custom to put a new kilt on top of the old one when a marionette passes from father to son. In time, the history of the marionette and the fortunes of the puppeteer could be read in the successive layers like the rings of a tree trunk: rich days, poor days, dusty days, gold. Even so, after four or five kilts the old spring leaves the arms, and the stylized face with its large eyes becomes chipped and battered. And when the marionette has thus reached the end of its useful life, it is floated down a holy river with a prayer. The longer the figure floats, the more kindly are the gods judging its actions and experiences on earth. It is a curious and touching ceremony. Even in this simulated death there is the quality of a tiny god—a devotional link to a remote past when, as the Rajasthanis believe, the *kathputli* were little celestial creatures sent to earth by the gods for man's amusement.

Certainly there is an element of the divine in the *kathputli* language, a wordless vocabulary of sounds that seems most appropriate for the small (eighteen- to twenty-inch) figures. This simple, effective language is produced by the head puppeteer with a bamboo-and-leather reed which he holds in his mouth and articulates by blowing through it and shaping his lips. Other later puppet cultures have attemped to improve on this technique by articulating real words through a "Punch whistle"—called "swazzle" in England and "pratique" in France—but the Indians accept it as a puppet language and let it go at that. Actually, I think the high, reedy, vibrating voice is better than words for these tiny characters, and I never had any difficulty understanding what was going on in any of the shows I saw in India. A sharp or tremulous action is emphasized with a staccato piping sound. A slow, down-curving tone, together with a turning away of the body, conveys disgust with great expressiveness. Spluttering anger becomes a delightful thing to hear. In short, many of the devices the makers of animated movie cartoons have learned about emphasizing action with music or sound effects have been known to the Rajasthanis for centuries.

India's early marionette theater concerned itself largely with the two great Sanskrit epics, the *Mahabharata* and the *Ramayana.* Longer by far than the Bible, these ancient stories teem with gods, heroes, villains, wars, loves, human frailties, and great deeds. There are elephant gods, buffalo demons, gods with horses' heads, representing the powers of humanity and of nature.

The *Mahabharata,* probably a compilation of the work of many poets, was composed somewhere between 200 B.C. and 200 A.D., and consists of some ninety thousand couplets. Its story tells of a dynastic struggle and civil war that occurred about the ninth century B.C., in the kingdom of Kurukshetra, near Delhi.

Above, left to right: Puppeteer
with Gangar figure; Kuchi
horse and rider; trick rider
who swings under horse's
belly; musicians with typical
instruments. All
marionettes are Rajasthani.

Leila (far left) and Khadbad Khan (left) are marionette characters in the play, *Amar Singh Rathore.* These two figures are from the collection of the New Delhi Theater Museum.

The five sons of Pandu—the Pandavas— claim the throne, but are opposed by the hundred treacherous sons of Dhirtarashtra—the Kauravas. It is a lovely story, and complex as only something that takes ninety thousand couplets to relate can be. Included in it, incidentally, is the Bhagavad-Gita, a dialogue between the god Krishna and Arjuna, one of the Pandavas. Today it is one of the principal devotional and philosophical works of the Hindu religion.

The *Ramayana* is equally old, although considerably shorter. Here Rama, a beloved prince, goes into exile with his wife, Sita, after his throne has been usurped. Sita is magically kidnapped by Ravana, the ten-headed ruler of Ceylon. Sugriva, the monkey king, offers his help to Rama, but then procrastinates. His son, General Hanuman, however, builds a bridge to Ceylon, rescues Sita, and defeats the witch demons of Ravana.

These are very thin sketches of two very important religious epics, but enough to show that they are the stuff of which great marionette shows are made.

And so, too, are the plays about the life and achievements of King Vikramaditya, monarch of Ujjain, in north central India, in the distant past. He lived splendidly both as a warrior and as a connoisseur of art and literature, and his many good deeds were advertised throughout the kingdom by hundreds of marionette companies.

Living kings began to recognize the public-relations value of this fascinating and entertaining type of live newspaper, and more and more epics of these monarchs' lives began to appear in the repertoires of the *bhats*. One such patron was Amar Singh Rathore, of Nagpur, in central India, who exalted the *bhats* to an im-

portant status during his lifetime. The play about him survives today in debased form.

In one episode, for instance, a *dhobi*—laundry-man—and his wife bring their donkey, laden with clothes, to the riverbank. There is some amusing byplay with the stubborn donkey, who is then led away by the wife while the *dhobi* wades into the stream to wash the clothes. Now the *dhobi* is attacked by a crocodile and yells for help. The wife returns and jumps about on the riverbank, screaming, until the poor *dhobi* is pulled under by the croc. (Remember this is all spoken in the tiny puppet language of the reed.) In human terms it is a tragedy, but with struggling marionettes uttering unearthly squeals it is high comedy. The audience howls with laughter.

Next, the grieving wife runs to the Mogul court for help. The emperor is unfortunately of too high a caste to speak to her, but he sends an aide. The audience, well-acquainted with the story, knows that when the attendant leans toward her he is suggesting that she forget her late, lamented husband and marry one of the palace guards. This gesture and the alacrity with which she accepts brings another roar from the audience.

In Udaipur, in the state of Rajasthan, there is on one of the main streets a huge mask standing some four stories high. It is the doorway of a building—the Lok Kala Mandal—and people enter through the mask's gaping mouth. The Lok Kala Mandal is an institution devoted to the perpetuation and development of India's performing arts, and in Udaipur its facilities include a large outdoor theater and a puppet playhouse and museum. It is a new center, one of many that India has established since achieving indepen-

dence to revitalize her many folk arts and crafts. Its director, D. L. Samar, a dancer and choreographer, as well as a puppeteer, has been continuing the old Rajasthani style of puppetry, while adding new, more modern elements and techniques learned in Europe and new choreography. Before a puppet show in Udaipur, a wooden figure of Gangar, a symbol of love and beauty, like Aphrodite, is dressed and carried on the head through the city to attract an audience.

Among the effective acts we saw at the Udaipur theater was a ballet performed by a group of Kuchi horses. These are very simple marionettes with only three strings and two jointed parts. One continuous string supports the horse and rocks him fore and aft. The other string is attached to the head of the rider and as long as it is taut the rider, jointed to the horse at the saddle, sits straight up no matter what his mount does. The horse's neck is loose. The horse is

sculpted from wood, down to the point where the legs would normally join the body. From there on down to the road, the marionette wears a full, pleated, cloth skirt, like a medieval war horse, and his legs are left to the imagination of the audience. This is a great part of his charm. The drum supplies the sound of hoofbeats and one can imagine all kinds of complicated steps as the kilt sweeps and swings with the jumping and whirling. Think of a dozen little horses doing an impossible ballet. At one moment they are all in line, at another they are whirling, rearing up on their "hind legs," or trotting rhythmically in two parallel lines.

India has saved for us these more than human dancing shapes. These legless little horses and their accomplished riders pack an enormous amount of suggestion. And this is puppetry at its best—when the audience has to work a little, to imagine. This is the "make" part of make-believe.

Members of Ganpath Bhurra marionette troupe display their portable theater. Sutradahr stands at right. Cloth curtain cut with scalloped arches is known as "Taj Mahal." Note style of head carving.

A selection from vast variety of Indian puppets.
Top row: Orissa marionettes from play, *Kansabad,* include sentry,
(left), a flower seller, and Kansa, uncle of
the Lord Krishna. Bottom row, from left: Two Bengali rod
puppets — a queen (in red) and a king; Andhra
marionette Naika (the Heroine), companion of Naik seen on pages
44-45. Note shadow of circular control.
Directly below is the popular character Sugriva,
monkey king of the epic poem, *Ramayana.* Here he is seen as
a two-dimensional tholubomalatta shadow-play
puppet of Andhra. All of these puppets
are from the New Delhi Theater Museum collection and
were photographed there by Madan Mahatta.

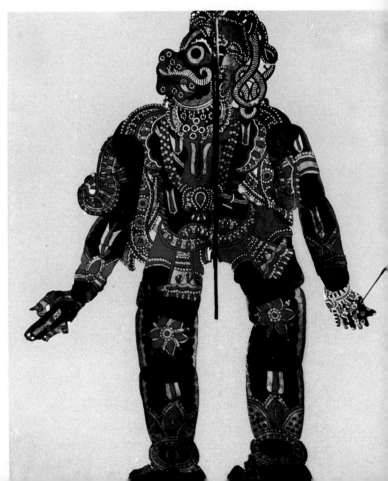

Another number, probably hundreds of years old, concerns the young man in pursuit of a beautiful girl. He is an idiotic looking clown, one of the few Rajasthani marionettes I've seen with moving legs. He leans toward the girl, then turns away, and in an instant the girl flips upside down and becomes an ogress. The lover flees. She chases him. He hides his head in fear. She flips again and becomes once more the gorgeous girl. This occurs several times, with variations, the squeaky voice purring invitingly as the lover approaches and shrieking as he runs. It is uncanny, beautifully timed, and entirely believable.

(The girl-ogress, of course, is made up of the upper halves of two ladies, joined at their waists, with a free-falling skirt, so that while one is visible, the other is hidden beneath the skirt. Just two strings for each head reverse the figure.)

Usually, a female member of the puppet company sits in front of the show with a drum. She sings the story—she is reputed to understand the celestial language of the reed.

Early during our tour of India I got the first intimation of what we had inherited from this ancient showmanship. The Ganpath Bhurra troupe had watched our show for three nights in Hyderabad and after the performance came bursting up onto our stage and insisted on giving us a show. They had brought their *kathputli* in bags, and we supplied a backcloth over a pole, and lights. They settled for our bass drum and the action started. It slowly dawned on us that we were being charmed with the building blocks of our own profession. Dance steps we thought we

Hero (left) and two demons confront each other in a Balinese performance of *wayang kulit* shadow figures. *Dalang's* operating rod can be seen supporting hero's hand under flickering flame in background.

had invented; rapid humorous rhythms; horse throws rider—almost; snake bites man; double takes: they were all there. It was quite a jolt to experience the complete entertainment they were creating with two and four strings compared to the fourteen to twenty-odd we use.

Our heritage from the East is a diverse one, for there is virtually no kind of puppetry that some region of India has not tried and developed.

In Tamil Nad, the country around Madras in southern India, there are the descendants of a highly refined puppet culture known as the *bomalattam*. These are lavishly costumed and decorated wooden figures controlled from above by strings and also by rods to the hands. A head control consisting of a circle of cane is worn by the puppeteer like a hat rim. To it are attached the head and shoulder strings of the *bomalattam*. The puppeteer nods his head and so does the marionette. A bow of the head, a turn, an upward look—no problem. But what about the legs? They are moved by kicking them through the backdrop.

In Orissa, setting of the magnificent temples of Konarak and Bubaneshwar, three types of figures have been developed. String marionettes, including one style with legs and another without, are in the majority, but hand puppets and shadow figures are also to be seen. Religious themes seem to dominate the repertoires of both professional and amateur groups.

In the state of Kerala, in southwestern India— what was formerly the Malabar Coast—the principal puppets are one-piece leather shadow figures called *pavaikoothu*. They are large and are pierced for decoration, but, of course, have no moving limbs. Kerala also has string marionettes called *pavakali*.

Perhaps the most interesting of the south-Indian puppet types for me, however, were the *tholubomalatta*—the articulated, leather, shadow puppets—which are the probable ancestors of Indonesia's *wayang*. The Indian puppets are less delicately designed than the Indonesian, but are brilliantly colored and intricately pierced. They are extremely large: four or five feet is not an unusual height, although there are smaller ones. The figure of a king or a god often is made from deerskin, which is considered to be holier and more noble than ordinary leathers, such as buffalo hide, and thus more fitting to the character. *Tholubomalatta* are made of "nonviolent leather," meaning that the skin comes from an animal that has died a natural death rather than one that has been slaughtered.

The figures are held in a vertical split cane. Two other canes animate the arms and hands. The legs swing freely from the knee. The heads are mostly in profile and often may be detached and interchanged.

Most often the plays derive from the *Mahabharata* and the *Ramayana,* and the shows frequently are given in the temple grounds.

A typical shadow screen of a *tholubomalatta* show is constructed of two thin white *saris*. The *saris* are stretched, one above the other, and pinned together with date-palm thorns, making a screen of some seven by twenty feet. The bottom is knee high from the ground. This would be sufficient for a quite large audience. A single oil lamp suspended high in the back behind the screen creates the shadows.

The show lasts all night, and the puppeteer's craft is a highly athletic operation. He emphasizes the action by dancing and stamping on sounding boards below the screen, often shaking the bells on his ankles. His play may last for several months, literally. I wondered what kind of society could stay up all night for weeks on end watching a shadow play and get any work done, but I found that the magic of play and festival are just as much part of the village Indian's life as his work. The audience comes and goes, tends its children, and eats its meals as the play proceeds. Everyone knows all the stories by heart, anyway.

No one knows how old the Indian shadow play may be, although references to string controlled puppets in the *Mahabharata* indicate that it must date at least to 200 B.C. In any event, as Hinduism spread in Asia the puppet theater went along. And in Indonesia both religion and puppetry took a special hold. It is certain that the puppet theater was well-established in Java, and probably Bali, by the eleventh century, and it survived the transition to Islam that occurred with the Moslem invasion of 1475. Today the *wayang*, or shadow, theater exists in two principal forms. Bengal had created a rod puppet style which I believe moved eastward with Hinduism and became the *wayang golek*, performed with three-dimensional wooden figures that are manipulated with rods. More popular is the *wayang kulit*, which uses flat leather figures, like those from south India.

Miguel Covarrubias, the eminent anthropologist-illustrator, told me about the *wayang* in Bali, where it has retained its purest form. The *wayang* plays retain a ceremonial, mystical aspect which suggests that originally they may have been a religious ritual performed by the head of the family to invoke the aid and advice of ancestral spirits. To the members of the family, the spirits then appeared in the form of shadows. Gradually, the headman's function was taken over by professional *dalangs,* who acted as mediums between family and spirits, and in time supplemented spiritual advice with their own philosophical and moral preachments.

Today the *wayang* still is an important element of the celebration of milestone events—marriages, anniversaries, birthdays, coming of age. And the *dalang* has become a deft combination of spiritual teacher, storyteller, and dramatist. Before he may perform, he must be ordained by a priest, who writes the mystic syllable "Ongg" on the dalang's tongue with the stem of a flower dipped in honey. He must also remember the endless complications of his plays. And he must have the wit to improvise comedy based on local personalities and situations.

As in India, the play is an all-night affair. The *dalang* sits cross-legged behind his screen, which is supported by a bamboo frame and measures five feet high and from ten to fifteen feet wide. An oil lamp hangs above his head, casting a single shadow. Along the foot of the screen is a piece of banana stalk into which the *dalang* sticks the ends of the main control handles of his figures when they are not in use. At his left is a chest containing his puppets.

Some figures are believed to be imbued with magical power and are kept apart from the others and wrapped in special cloth. Between the toes of his right foot, the *dalang* holds a piece of horn with which he hammers on the chest in order to signal the orchestra, or *gamelan* (usually four metallophones).

In Java, the men sit behind the screen with the

Sculpted wood *wayang golek* puppets (left) are elaborately painted and dressed. Two of the many characters are red-faced Rahwana and blue-faced Bradjamusti. Team of two-dimensional *wayang kulit* heroes and helpers ranged below includes (from left) the popular Arjuna, Semar, Petruk, Gaveng, and Bagong. These gilt figures are shadow puppets, the *wayang golek* are rod puppets.

dalang, watching the puppets, while the women sit in front, watching the shadows. In Bali, the men may sit behind the women and see the shadows, if they prefer.

At the beginning of the show, the orchestra begins to play. It is strange, delicate music, yet quite sympathetic to western ears. On the screen appears a leaf-shaped shadow (in Java, the *genungan;* in Bali, the *kayon*) which represents a tree, or may be symbolic of the heart. It has many functions. It opens and closes each act when placed slantwise in the middle of the screen, and can create a mood, suggesting by its movement or position a storm, danger, fire, sickness, mountain, or ocean. It sways, it floats to the rhythm of the music, and by its mood indicates to the audience the tempo of the scene to follow.

The *wayang* is itself symbolic of life, with good and evil arranged at the right and left hands of the *dalang,* who in this instance is God.

The *genungan* disappears and the showman introduces his characters, one by one. Princes, gods, and kings are placed on the right. Witches, villains, giants, and demons are at the left. Good characters—those with noble, refined, self-disciplined natures—are slender. Their eyes are almond-shaped, their lips thin, their noses and foreheads run together in a straight line. The evil ones are broader and coarser and have round eyes.

One indication of the superimposition of the

Hindu culture on the older Javanese base is shown in the design of the figures. Javanese art displays a great love of the grotesque and this is evident in the design of the clowns, who are supposed to belong to a time before Hinduism came. Some of that grotesque design has been transferred to the Hindu characters of the *wayang* and can be seen in the elongated arms and shoulders of the heroes and in the shapes of the demons, but the Indian gods and heroes have managed to retain the pointed noses of the Indian people. Actually, the pointed noses are a Javanese caricature of the Indian ideal by a people with much flatter noses.

The piercing and decoration of the leather, the various modes of dress, and the kinds of turbans worn, all have a meaning. Cutting the eyes involves certain ritual; it is done last, bringing life to the figure. The angle at which the head is set is also significant. A downward glance suggests modesty, a high chin arrogance. A red face connotes physical strength and is characteristic of giants and heroes. A white face goes with a fiery nature. Black is the color of restraint.

The figures range from twenty to twenty-four inches. Arms are joined at shoulder and elbow with a knot of string, and the arm movements are controlled by rods of horn attached to the hands.

Once the characters have been introduced, they are removed from the screen and the play begins. Often the plays are the same as those seen in India. Hanuman, the monkey general, is a very important character in Bali, as is Arjuna, the warrior hero who debates the Bhagavad-Gita with Krishna in the *Mahabharata*.

The Hindu characters in Indonesia enact the struggle between good and evil, each personifying his virtue or vice without shading or complexity. The pre-Hindu characters the Indonesians have added are almost entirely comic. In Java, it is the ancient clown Semar, and his sons Gaveng, Bagong, and Petruk. They are fat and mischievous, and the *dalang* uses them to extemporize a funny commentary on current events. In Bali, the additions are the *parekan,* the sly, clever, or amusing servants of the serious characters in the play. Twalen, a fat, black monster, and his son, Merdah, are the servants of gods and heroes. Twalen is intelligent, as well as monstrous, and through his understanding of magic is often able to

Droll Javanese trio of *wayang golek* puppets (left) includes one-toothed Semar, blue-faced Buta Terong, and mustachioed Tjitrayuda. Above: A Malayan shadow-figure hero (center) encounters two demons.

Dagger-bearing Siamese rod puppet (above)
and Siamese *nang* figure (right) are both in the
Munich City Museum collection.
Nang figure is held aloft by dancer to the
accompaniment of music and narration.

come to the hero's aid. It is a role somewhat comparable to that of Sancho Panza in *Don Quixote*.

On the sinister side is a fat, red monster called D'elam, who is loud, bawdy, and almost—but not quite—the equal of Twalen as a magician. Covarrubias felt that these popular subordinate characters are possibly ancient Indonesian gods, dwindled and degraded to the status of retainers. This also is said of Ireland's leprechauns: old gods shrunken in the path of a new religion.

Whatever their source, the shadow figures of Indonesia have an established place in the lives of the people. Despite the predominantly Moslem character of the nation as a whole, and despite the political changes of recent years, efforts to change the fundamental Hindu character of the *wayang* have met with little success. The old stories have the most power and the most influence. They are an inheritance from the past that the present cannot alter.

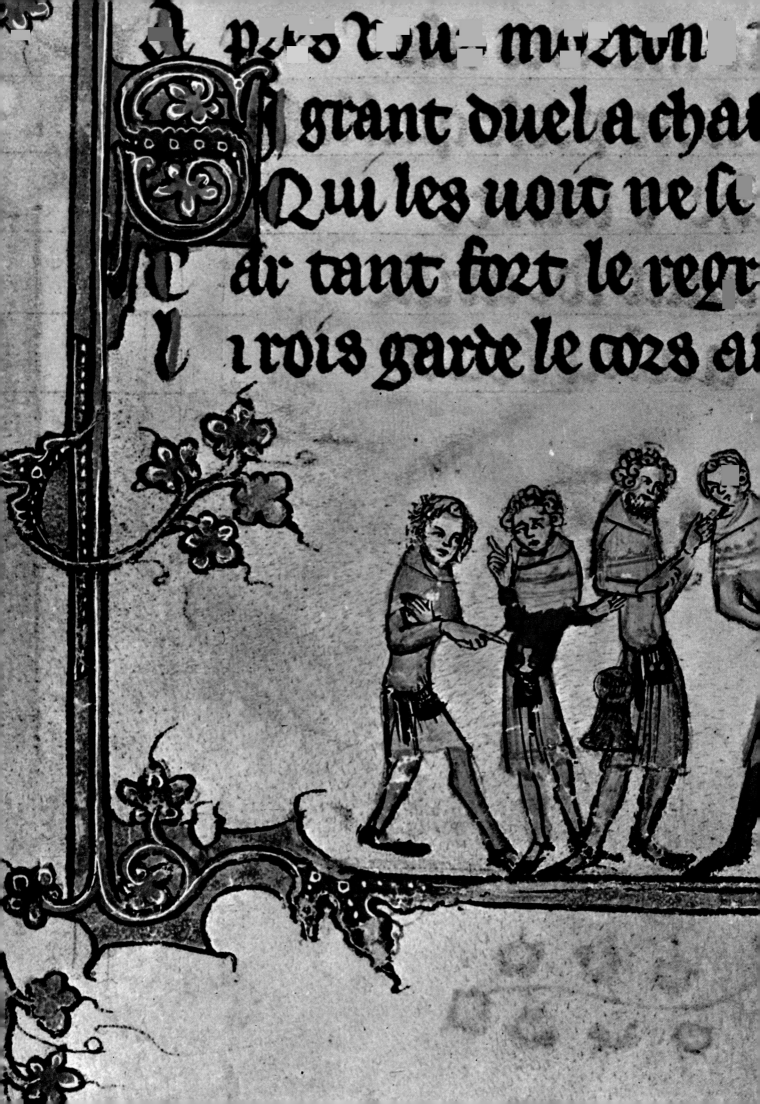

p̃ꝑ Yoꝰ· m̃ æun

grant duel a chat

Qui les uoit ne li

Ar tant fort le regr

i rois garde le cors a

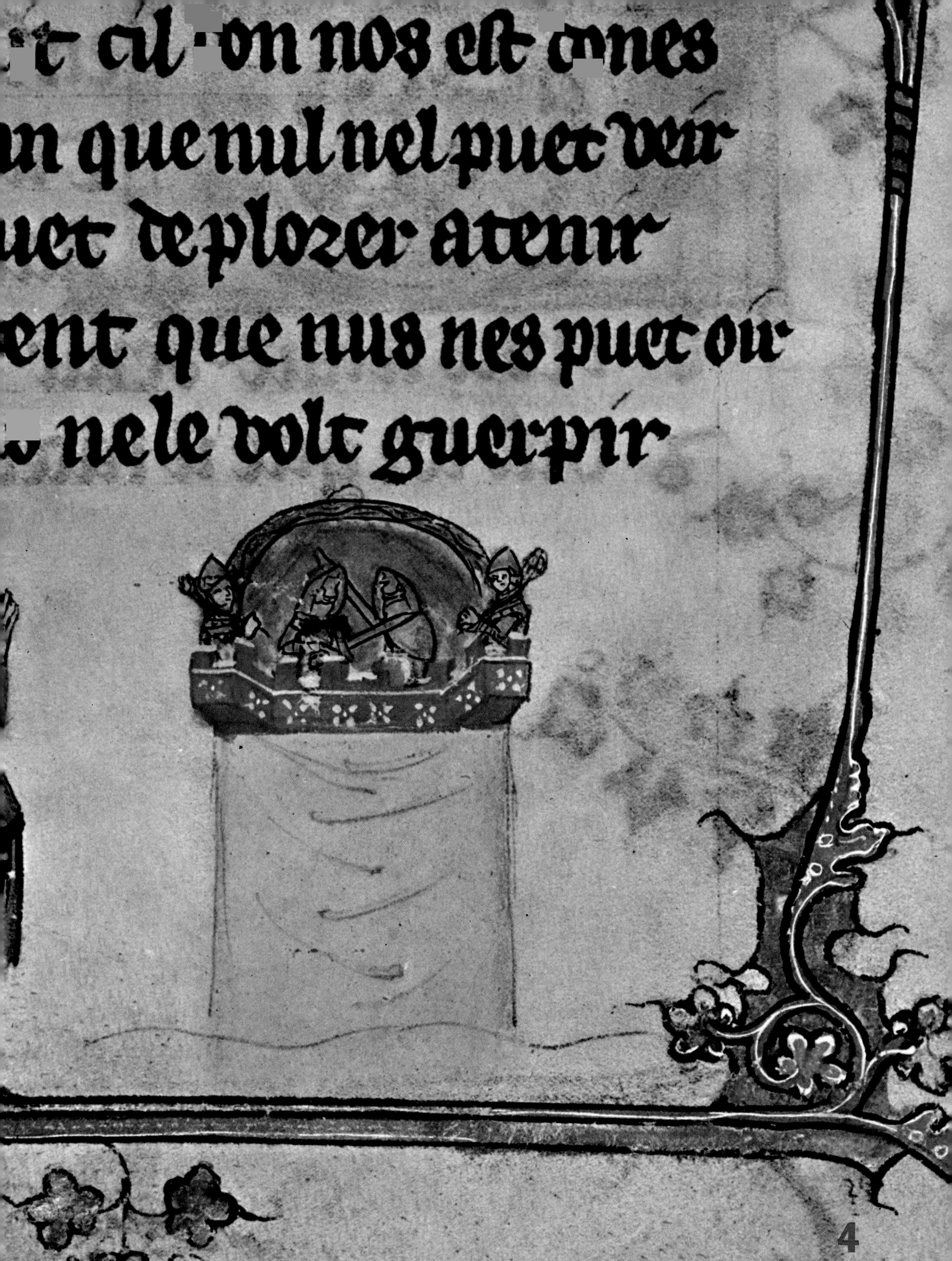

t cil · on nos est omnes
in que nul nel puet veir
uet deplorer atenir
ent que nus nes puet oir
o nel e volt guerpir

ANGELS, DEVILS & EVERYMAN

The year is 1443. In the Church of St. James at Dieppe, on the channel coast of France, a mass known as the "Mysteries of Mid-August," which celebrates the Virgin's Assumption into heaven, is taking place. A stage has been set up across the choir of the church, extending to the ceiling. High up in the vault, under a ceiling spangled with a golden sun and crystal stars, flights of angels surround the throne of God. The Lord is seated on a cloud—a venerable old man dressed as sumptuously as a king and wearing a crown.

Two angels, leaving His side, make a majestic descent to the foot of an altar where the tomb of the Virgin rests. They raise her to the feet of God; she lifts her arms and moves her head in supplication. The Lord gives her His blessing as another angel places a tiara on her head, and then she floats off gracefully behind a cloud.

This masterpiece of medieval showmanship was performed entirely by marionettes and moving statuary. The only human beings involved were the operators—priests and laymen—plus a mechanic or two stationed at different levels behind the scenes.

The mass of the "Mysteries" was only one form of the religious theater of the Middle Ages, but it was a particularly notable one and its fame drew pilgrims to Dieppe from many lands. The mass, or play, lasted an hour and a half, and unless the old chroniclers were simply dazzled by their faith, the figures were marvels of inventiveness. "Iron wires cleverly hidden controlled all the movements," one of them explains, "and people cried out with joy to show their admiration."

Four life-size angels beat their wings in time to the music of the organ and the voices of the choir. Two smaller ones sounded an Ave Maria on little bells to signal the end of each office, accompanied by two huge angels blowing trumpets. Below and at either side were angels holding large chandeliers ablaze with wax candles to light the scene. When the service was over and priests came to snuff the candles, these angels would quickly dodge from side to side to prevent it, and bring a laugh from the congregation.

There was even a marionette clown. During the play he ran about making monkeyshines. He opened his arms in surprise and clapped his hands as the figure of the Virgin arrived at God's throne. He lay down at full length, playing dead, then climbed to the vault and skidded under the Lord's throne, leaving only his head in view. The people knew this comic character as Grimpesulais, and his impudent antics, aping the action of the play, were thought to be hilarious. The children screamed every time he appeared.

The presence of puppets at the altars and in the ceremonies of the medieval church occurred slowly, however, over a span of centuries, and not without opposition.

When great Rome toppled under the assaults of the barbarians, the humble art of puppetry dropped from sight. For some several hundred years there is no documentary evidence of any sort—official records, literary references, pictures—to give even the slightest hint of its fate.

We know nothing of the invading Goths' and Vandals' taste for puppetry, but its remaining Roman patrons were either too poor to afford the entertainment or too disorganized to write about it. To the emerging, once-underground Christian church any kind of show or idolatrous image was abhorrent. Too many of the faithful had been butchered as props and actors in the theatricality of the Roman circus.

Under the circumstances, the puppeteers probably lived by their wits. The individual artist doesn't stop the vibrating process of creation when the big show closes. We can be sure he was a part of the restless movement of people traveling over the rude highways of Europe in that tumultuous age, finding an audience wherever he could in the streets and taverns along the way.

It was not until somewhere between the seventh and ninth centuries that we hear of puppetry again. By that time it had been put to the service of the steadily growing Christian religion. It was not until the end of the seventh century that Jesus was represented as a man. Until then, he had been referred to and represented as the Lamb of God. Moving statuary was introduced into the churches—holy images rolled their eyes, nodded, and even bled, with the pull of a wire. Still later puppets appear to have performed in pantomimes while someone standing in front of the stage or booth recited a Bible story. The practice must have been effective and must have spread in the face of its detractors. But by the eleventh century an abbott of Cluny was denouncing puppets as smacking of idolatry, and by the thirteenth century, even the Pope was inveighing against them—but apparently without success. By this time, puppets had slipped into the educational pattern of the church. While this kind of theater was gaining a foothold in the church, we can be sure that the tribe of wandering showmen scattered over Europe was still busily engaged. Around the hearth in great halls and lowly taverns, mountebanks, jugglers, and

mimes varied their turns with puppets.

These were undoubtedly hand puppets, since they are easy to carry and in no way as bulky as the heavy marionettes of Rome.

The earliest picture we have of medieval puppetry is the famous twelfth-century woodcut (page 66) showing two boys maneuvering armored figures in battle on a table. This is documentary evidence that at the time figures were being operated by strings and that swordplay and violence were standard puppet fare.

In two illuminations (pages 62-63, 67) we see hand-puppet booths with castle turrets on either side and a crenelated wall between—in short, the traveling puppet booth known to this day as a *castelet, castillo,* and *castello,* in France, Spain, and Italy.

In northern Europe jugglers used to bring puppets known as "kobolds" or "tattermen" out from

Ludus monstrorum

Saludo monstrex designat vania quanitat

GILBERT

under their cloaks to surprise the rusties and amuse the nobility. Kobold (after cobalt) was supposedly a mischievous little earth sprite, who inhabited the mines and who we may be sure many people believed actually were alive. But relatively little mention was made of ordinary, everyday puppetry. It is the puppet's entry into the church and his eventual expulsion from it that become the major part of his story in the Middle Ages.

From pantomime for a recitation to a starring role in a mystery play was a long step only in time. For the early church, while it frowned on the vulgarity of live actors, was fully aware of the educational value of the theater and the arts "to elevate the common people to knowledge and to show in some palpable form the eternal truths." In order to have the one without the other, it welcomed the puppet. And despite occasional grumbling in high places puppetry became an integral part of medieval religious drama.

The Assumption of the Virgin, celebrated in mid-August and played then at Dieppe, was a typical mystery—or miracle—show, and a performance in 1443 would have been at the height of popularity of such plays. They began in France at quite an early date, caught on somewhat more slowly in England, and reached their fullest development in the fifteenth and sixteenth centuries. At first they were simply enactments of episodes from the Bible or from the lives of the saints to celebrate a particular church holiday.

Above: Earliest picture of medieval puppetry is 12th-century woodcut of youths playing with double planchette figures.
Right: Nameless ancestor of Punch wields club in 14th-century hand-puppet booth.

But, eventually, in England, there evolved great cycles of plays, ranging from the Creation to the Last Judgment.

Sometimes the plays would be performed by human beings, but many were the exclusive province of the marionettes. The story of the Nativity was played by puppets before it was ever entrusted to human beings; in fact, somewhere along the line the wooden actors became so closely associated with the Nativity as to acquire the name of marionettes, or "Little Marys."

Medieval Poland called its Christmas puppet play *szopka,* or manger, and performed it on a stage resembling a cathedral. The simplicity of the structure permitted different playing levels, and slots in the floor at each level enabled small puppet figures to be moved about from the back. These *szopki* were stationed in front of the altar, or carried outdoors and placed on a table, where musicians played and priests or puppeteers told the story.

Old Russia also knew the *szopka.* In the Ukraine, in Byelorussia, where it was called *bertep,* meaning Bethlehem, and in other provincial areas, the puppets performed in brightly painted wooden cathedrals with golden domes, like their churches. Often the play was on three levels to represent Heaven, Earth, and Hell.

The *szopka* performances survive to this day in Poland with the handsome structures placed in the churches and streets on religious holidays.

With the success of puppets in the church, their clowning got the upper hand. The frolicking that so endeared Grimpesulais to the congregation at Dieppe eventually was his undoing. There was so much buffoonery in the service that the shows had to be moved out into the churchyards, and, finally, into the public squares. Here the guilds took over from the monks, each assuming responsibility for one episode or another. The bakers performed the Last Supper, the butchers the Crucifixion. And always the crowd followed.

Hence the gradual transition from religious to secular drama.

It is difficult to maintain the solemnity of a service if you're getting laughs. Little by little the comic characters and scenes, injected to lighten the miracle plays, became more boisterous and more outrageous. The shepherds of the Nativity play became rude comics and buffoons. Noah's wife became a shrew. New, ludicrous devils were invented to carry screaming sinners into the fire. The extraneous clowns and jesters wandering through the plays became coarser and their pres-

ence more distracting.

The advent of the morality plays in the fifteenth century paralleled the problem. The morality plays were dramas in verse, which substituted personified abstractions of Gluttony, Vanity, Lechery, Perverse Doctrine, Covetousness, and Vice, or Old Vice, as he came to be called, for the Biblical characters of the miracle plays. These were fat parts, and actors, monk and puppet, made the most of them. Old Vice, in particular, was a comical rogue and sinner, a roisterer, a quarrelsome braggart, and a coward. In the end, he was usually carried away by the imps of Satan, howling as he went. Audiences enjoyed him hugely, and though later he slipped into Elizabethan drama as a buffoon, his origins had been to teach a moral lesson.

When the puppets were thrown out of the church it was not because they weren't getting their messages across. It was because they were too theatrical or too vulgar. It didn't happen everywhere and not all at once, of course. But here and there a show reached too low for laughs and puppetry was expelled. Henceforth, it was to play the streets, the fairgrounds, the inns—and when it had gained status once again, theaters of its own.

The puppet shows of Shakespeare's England were called "motions" and their operators "motion men." Mostly these were the banished moralities, still emphasizing the slapstick and bawdry that had brought about their expulsion. Sodom and Gomorrah, Jonah and the Whale, The Burning of Nineveh were typical motions, and to catch the eyes and ears of their audiences, the motion men mixed local allusions, leering songs, fisticuffs, fireworks, and floods into their shows, as well. In a monstrous, two-century anachronism, Marlowe's Tamburlaine was shown fighting with the Duke of Guise, an instigator of the terrible St. Bartholomew's Day massacre of the French Huguenots. Julius Caesar pops up in one play, Guy Fawkes in another.

Presumably the performers were hand puppets, for the descriptions we have of what went on in the shows—fighting, throwing things, hitting the man outside over the head—are logical hand-puppet activities.

Playbills advertised the motions, and performances were signaled by running up a banner while drum beat and flageolet played, just as in the live theater. Admission prices varied. It was perhaps a tuppence for the wealthy, a penny for others.

Bartholomew Fair, about which Ben Jonson

wrote a play (1614), was a favorite place to pitch a motion. It was in Smithfield, a district in the west of London, and was open country that had been used for markets, jousting, and executions since the twelfth century. Everybody went to the fair—lords and ladies, merchants, peddlers hawking their wares, thieves and whores, and gawky farm lads in from the countryside to sell a pig and see the sights.

Jonson's play also includes a puppet play, one of the few of the period that has been preserved. The play is presented by a showman named Leatherhead, who stands before his stage and announces *The Ancient Modern History of Hero and Leander*. It mixes characters and plots from history indiscriminately, offers a full measure of bawdy slapstick, and incidentally shows Leander being rowed in a boat instead of swimming the Hellespont. Leatherhead, standing in front of his "motion" and conversing with the puppets, may have been a hangover from times when an interpreter stood in front of a foreign setup providing "subtitles." Or indeed, he may have merely interpreted the unearthly voice of the reed if it was in use at that time.

By 1573, Italian puppetry had invaded England. "Italian marionettes," says an order issued that year by the Lord Mayor of London, shall "be allowed to settle in the city and to carry on their strange motions as in the past and from time immemorial." Immemorial or not, this is the first we hear of them.

In Italy puppetry had thrived, developing approximately at the same time and in the same direction as the *commedia dell' arte*. Like the rest of Europe, Italy had its religious mystery plays, but in addition it was evolving a comic tradition of farce, burlesque, improvisation, and, most important, of character. With the passage of time, the clowns of the Atellan farces had become Scaramouche, Pantalone, Pulcinella, Arlecchino, and each had acquired a certain cluster of exaggerated characteristics that governed his actions completely. Yet within these limits there was great flexibility and diversity. All told, the *commedia* was a perfect theatrical style for puppetry. It was a perfect theatrical style for both media.

In Arezzo, Italy, there is a festival held twice a year in which armored citizens on horseback tilt at a quintain. This is a dummy that swivels on a post and strikes back when its shield is hit by the horseman's lance. The object is to duck. The dummy is called Burratto, after a Saracen king who once sacked the town, and townfolk

Puppets were everywhere in medieval Europe. Top: 16th-century
drawing by Magnasco shows crank-operated peep show.
Above: Earliest picture of Russian puppets dates from 1636, is
probably of Petrouchka buying a horse from a gypsy.
Right: 17th-century mountebank sells with aid of hand puppets.

commemorate the event by riding ceremonially against their former oppressor. If "Burrato" has become synonymous with "dummy," then we may have here the origin of "Burrattini," or little dummies, as hand puppets are called in Italy. Italian marionettes were warmly received in France and later in England, where, as we shall see, they influenced the evolution of Mr. Punch.

By the first quarter of the seventeenth century, motion men were traveling all over England, along with tinkers, beggar gypsies, and ballad singers. Vagrancy acts aimed principally at thieves occasionally caught the wanderers in their nets, although some troupes were lucky enough to have noble patronage or a royal license, permitting them to travel and perform without hindrance.

However, motions were a relatively small part of the English theater and generally ignored officially. When Cromwell and his Puritans achieved the Commonwealth in 1642, the theaters were locked tight, but as in old Rome the puppets kept on playing because they did not seem important enough to ban.

For eighteen years, the only theater in England was the puppet theater. Live actors petitioned; theater owners and managers complained. Puppets, they raged, were more depraved than ever. It was to no avail. The Roundheads couldn't be bothered.

The Lord Mayor of London once tried to banish puppet shows from Bartholomew Fair during this period, but he died the next year and the shows returned, irreverent as ever, with the Lord Mayor reappearing as a puppet. The Devil probably carried him off.

In Germany, meanwhile, the greatest puppet play of the western world was coming into being. This was the story of Johann Faust, the learned doctor who denied his better nature and bartered his soul to the Devil for wealth and power. There was, in fact, a Dr. Faust, a wandering scholar and magician, in the early sixteenth century, but the story that has grown up around his name is now deeply rooted in German legend and folklore. Other sources put the tale a bit earlier, saying that old ballads related the tragedy of Dr. Faust about the time of Gutenberg's invention of movable type (1436-37). By coincidence one of Gutenberg's partners at Mainz was a Johann Fust, and it is thought that this may have given rise to the version of the play which credits Faust with the invention of printing.

The first printed version of the play appeared a century later, in 1587, in the *Folksbook* published at Frankfurt am Main. Its title was *The History of That Everywhere Infamous Black Artist and Conjurer Dr. Faustus Compact with the Devil, Wonderful Walk and Conversation and Terrible End.*

Within a year the *Folksbook* had reached England and the Faust story had inspired Christopher Marlowe to write *The Tragical History of Doctor Faustus.* Before another year had passed, English players were performing it in Germany. The English had been the chief purveyors of the drama to Germany since the fifteenth century, when touring companies went abroad with a repertory of miracle plays. By Elizabethan times they were all over the continent—even appearing at Elsinore, according to Shakespeare. Many of these troupes carried marionettes with them to play the devils, monsters, and flying animals.

Marlowe's tragedy underwent many changes

after it was transplanted to Germany, and others when the puppets took it over for their own. The largest was the introduction of a comic character who had no connection with the original play, but was added for laughs. The Germans called him Hanswurst in both the live and puppet plays. Later on with the terrible depletion of Germany's population during the Thirty Years' War, theater companies were forced to use marionettes to replace missing actors.

Hanswurst started out fairly modestly as an assistant to Dr. Faust's faithful servant, Wagner. But being Hanswurst, he soon elbowed his way into a prominent role. His earthy wisdom and indecent antics made him extremely popular; after all, the players were more often entertaining at fairgrounds and town festivals than at the castle, and the language and the action of the play were tailored to the quality of the audience.

In time, Hanswurst became a counterpart of Dr. Faust and conducted a running parody of the serious play. Eventually, he so dominated the stage that the serious play was ruined.

To restore order, and also to escape the censor, Hanswurst was booted out of the live play, although he stayed on with the puppets, where he blithely engendered a tribe of comic and indecent devils to counterbalance the sinister Mephistopheles. Somehow a puppet's indecent outrages are more acceptable than a human being's.

What was the puppet play like? There were many versions and the beginnings are obscure, but enough pieces have been found—a bit of manuscript from a monastery, another from a cloister library—mostly from the neighborhoods of Ulm, Augsburg, and Strasbourg, to put together a script from the period of 1668.

Here is the prologue:

The scene is in hell. The backdrop is a forest with rocks at the right and hell at the left. Charon, Ferryman of Hell; Pluto, Prince of Hell, and supernatural spirits make up the cast. A terrible wind is blowing. Lightning, thunder, then silence. Charon (on his boat, rowing in) calls,

CHARON: Pluto. (*Echo:* Pluto.)

PLUTO (*from without*): Hey. (*Echo:* Hey.)

CHARON: So. (*Echo:* So.)

PLUTO: What so? (*Echo:* So?)

Pluto appears with thunder and lightning.

(*Pause.*)

CHARON (*loud*): I don't want to remain your slave any longer.

PLUTO: My slave?

CHARON: Yes, your slave, your hellish galley slave. Raise my wages or I won't sail anymore.

PLUTO: What? Charon, you beast of hell and slave? Haven't I raised your salary from one penny to two. For each soul you have brought me? Therefore I say to you: SAIL!

CHARON: Well then. I'll sail. But your lazy devils will have to bring me more souls. Send them on earth among the people to teach them evil-doing, so that I can bring you more souls.

PLUTO: You faithful servant. I'll call all my devils and furies and send them out. They will bring you a famous man, whose soul is of greater value than a million of souls, Doctor Johannes Faustus.

CHARON: Mighty King of Hell. My gratefulness has no end.

(*Change of mood!*)

PLUTO: Hey . . . Hey . . . you lazy devils. Where are you?

DEVILS (*murmering from without*).

PLUTO: Have you forgotten your duties? Are you asleep?

DEVILS (*murmering again*) (*snoring*) (*a moment of silence*).

PLUTO (*loud*): You spirits of Hades, appear! (*The supernatural spirits appear with thunder and lightning moving around muttering.*)

PLUTO: Silence! Listen to me and do as I tell you.

DEVILS: Do not doubt our willingness, mightiest Pluto.

PLUTO: Go up on earth and teach people to do evil. To lie, to steal and gamble. To turn things upside down so that they will suffer confusion, and easily be condemned. Let penetrate among the women. Let them become haughty whores and prostitutes—and let them practice unchastity, lead men into bankruptcy and desperation. Penetrate into the schools of learning and teach them to live in excess and gluttony. Let them quarrel and feel the spell of evil magic. Let them beat each other.

DEVILS: Do not doubt our willingness, mightiest Pluto!

PLUTO: Now go. And do as I have told you. And here is my blessing: BAH, BAH, BAH.
All disappear. Thunder and lightning.

CURTAIN.

Efforts to censor the puppets were generally unsuccessful. The companies moved too fast. Germany was a patchwork of some three hundred princely states in these times, each with its own notion of what to censor. Yet there were no printed versions of the plays. The puppeteers simply learned them by heart, and extemporized as the spirit moved them. Censorship often arrived on the scene after the curtain had been rung down.

Puppets survived (again) the strictures of the Reformation in Germany, and by the eighteenth century Faust was as basic and essential to German puppetry as Punch or Polichinelle or Orlando or Karaghioz to their own countries.

Goethe's *Faust*, the classic version of the play, had its beginning in the poet's boyhood, when, it is known, he saw marionettes perform Dr. Faustus in Frankfurt. He probably also saw it at the fairs in Leipzig, and by 1770, when he was twenty-one, he had decided to raise the legend to epic height. "The thoughts of this marionette play," he wrote, "echoed and hummed about me in every key . . . and it delighted me in my solitude, without my ever writing anything about it."

The idea gestated a long time. The first part of *Faust* did not appear until 1808, and the second until 1832, the year of Goethe's death.

But there was great excitement in Europe when the masterwork by Germany's foremost poet appeared. It was taken up and produced in every possible theatrical form—opera, ballet, pantomime, and shadow play. Even the puppets, which had been responsible for starting the whole thing, prospered. Whereas puppet shows had formerly been for the very rich in their homes (or castles) or for the very poor anywhere, now the entire status of the art was elevated and puppetry was swept off the streets and into the theater.

Several intelligent puppeteers capitalized on

this new enthusiasm and toured the capitals of Europe with considerable success. In deference to the sensibilities of their newly found, high-toned audiences, however, they cut the crude indecencies that traditionally peppered the serious parts of the show.

It must have been about this time that Hanswurst was finally replaced by Kasperle, the clever little Austrian peasant whose name now stands for a specific form of puppet theater in middle Europe today. Poor Hanswurst. He was a hopeless vulgarian. He was not without background,

springing from the same line as Pickleherring and Jan Posset and other rustic boors, but he was spoiled by success.

So here came Kasperle. If he is sly and greedy, he is also nimble bright and joyous. The old puppet play kept alive the idea that the search for wisdom was sinful and the work of the devil. The church had taken the horned god of the cave shaman and turned him into the devil for their new religion. But Kasperle turned Old Nick into a comedian. The devil never got Kasperle—Kasperle didn't believe in him.

Every age has invented its comic to poke fun at authority. For centuries it was Karaghioz, the shadow puppet who was the best loved clown and principal theatrical figure of the Ottoman Empire. Since the sultan's dominion once stretched from the gates of Venice to the borders of India, and encompassed the Balkans, the Middle East, and North Africa, the boisterous chronicle of Karaghioz's adventures enjoyed a vast audience. Indeed, he is the first hero to give his name to a style of theater.

In more recent years Karaghioz has suffered a decline in Turkey, his ancient home and the scene of his greatest triumphs. In Greece, however, where he was planted during the Ottoman occupation, Karaghioz has remained full of life, even emigrating to America with his countrymen. Finally he is staging a comeback with the blessing of the Turkish government, which belatedly has acknowledged that an authentic folk hero should not be permitted to pass away.

Karaghioz has often been referred to as an ancestor of Punch, whom he precedes by several hundred years. Although no direct line can be established, the similarities are certainly there. Like Punch he is a roisterer and a rogue. He is a libertine, impetuous, vain, violent, with no respect for authority and determined to have his own way. Seen in profile, as shadow figures usually are, he has a large, bald head with a bearded chin and one large dark eye. His name *Karaghioz* means "dark eye." The outlines of both legs can be seen clearly, for one is attached to the torso in front of the other. One arm has shrunk to no more than a hand which emerges from the chest. The other—the active arm—has acquired a third joint and a useful, apelike length. In the bawdy cafe entertainments of old Constantinople, Dark Eye was also endowed with a prodigious phallus. He was no beauty, but he was designed for action. Karaghioz was a puppet of violent action—the first requirement of a puppet to give it life.

All too often, people assume that a beautifully made, carefully finished figure must be the best. Yet delicacy of form or features may only satisfy a small audience. A beautiful figure may be too limited in the actions it can perform, or too detailed to project well in a large theater. A puppet designed for a large audience, on the other hand, may seem crude up close, although when seen from a distance it will come fully to life. With Karaghioz the distortions have been made for a purpose. He has not been made to be studied like a photograph, but to be seen as a colored shadow, often in dim light, often through a less than perfect screen. I believe that Karaghioz has evolved from necessity into the eloquent simplicity of his present form.

All the permanent characters of the Karaghioz troupe likewise have been reduced to simple, symbolic forms that are instantly identifiable when they appear on the screen. Hachivat—the other principal character, who is Karaghioz's best friend, foil, and straight man—sports a pointed turned-up beard. Celebi, the dandy, is one of the few whose clothes and style have changed to match the current fashion. The bellowing, bullying Tusuz Deli Bekir always has a scimitar or a pistol in one hand and a jug of wine in the other. Tiryaki, the bearded opium smoker, can readily be identified by his pipe, his fan, and a huge humped shoulder. The many foreigners who turn up in the various plays are distinguishable by the style of their dress. In one collection from the classic theater, the

company contains some thirty characters. There are three figures of Karaghioz—one wearing a turban, one a hat, and one dressed as a woman. And there are two of Hachivat. Others include three Turkish women, two Jews, the son of Karaghioz, the son of Hachivat, a naked girl, a fisherman, a baby, an old beggar, the sultan of the palace, a Persian on horseback, a Persian on foot, a tambourine player, a night watchman, a Kurd, a Negro, a bather in a Turkish bath, wrestlers, two Albanians, and a public broker. Each has been reduced to a symbol. There is no mistaking one for another.

The action of these figures has dictated their shapes. Each of them has a hole somewhere in the upper part of the body into which the control rod may be snugly inserted from either side. The hole is reinforced with a leather socket and the rod, held at right angles to the plane of the figure, casts a hazy shadow upward on the screen from a low bank of lights. It is the manipulation of these rods plus an occasional hand rod that gives Karaghioz his distinctive action and, hence, his shape.

His movement is entirely different from that of the Indian, Indonesian, and Chinese shadows. Since the latter are supported by a vertical rod, they can do a quick flip and face in the opposite direction, and use their hands to embellish their speech. Karaghioz can do a complete somersault with a twist of the rod, and that is precisely the reason he and his tribe alone behave the way they do. A quick bow, bending almost double, lying on the back, and swinging the legs are manipulations easily accomplished. Karaghioz talks with his head or his whole body. Moreover, the Karaghiozis of Greece, whose rod is attached to a hinge at his back, is able to do an about-face quickly, as well.

The classic repertoire numbers about forty plays, of which the average showman of days gone-by would know at least twenty-eight, one for each night of Ramadan, the Moslem Lent, when Karaghioz was most frequently played. The plays always have been handed down orally, from father to son, and the showmen stick closely to the traditional script. Attempts to update the stories have failed for the most part. It is a somewhat rigid framework within which to operate, but the showmen were virtuosos who managed to develop individual styles of puppet handling.

The atmosphere and flavor of a Karaghioz performance have been delightfully caught in the childhood reminiscences of a distinguished Turkish historian, Sabri Esat Siyavusgil. For some days before Ramadan, he recalls, the windows of the tobacco shops were peopled with funny little brightly colored cardboard cutouts of the Karaghioz characters, their limbs and parts strung together with knotted cord. These figures, and marvelous big posters, were a foretaste of the fun

and drolleries to come.

Every evening at sundown the boys and girls would hurry to the cafe with their fathers and uncles. The youngsters sat down in front on little stools so they would not be in the way of their elders, and ate sherbets. The adults, seated on benches that ringed the room, smoked the narghile and drank coffee.

In one corner of the room there was a rectangular screen of thin, translucent muslin, illuminated from behind and bordered by colorful rugs. In the middle of the screen, a colored, ornamental set piece was displayed until it was time to start the show. "Sometimes," says Siyavusgil, "it was a galley whose oars, lit up by the flickering candles behind it, seemed to move in space and give the impression that it was about to depart. Sometimes it was a vase of flowers which might excite the

imagination of contemporary abstract painters; or again it might be a marvelous seraglio which only awaited the love of the odalisques or the anger of the eunuch."

At last this figure was removed and a love song was played—a sign for the entrance of Hachivat, who, with rolled-up sleeves and a tobacco bag at his belt, advanced to the middle of the screen and called for divine protection for the show. He described the universe as a great screen and its people as fleeting shadows, like the characters who were about to appear.

At this a cry of joy arose from the children, for they knew the formalities were ended and that Karaghioz would soon appear from the right. Although there is no scenery, everyone knows that the locale of the play is the Place Christeri, one of the classic quarters of Istanbul, and that

A master Turkish puppeteer manipulates a
Karaghioz figure on the front of a backlit screen.
In an actual performance, the
puppets are placed in front of the light and
their shadows cast onto the screen.

Karaghioz's house is on the right, as Hachivat's is on the left.

Hachivat now demands to speak with someone able to converse in Arabic, Persian, and Turkish, someone who understands science, appreciates poetry, and is possessed of distinguished manners. Karaghioz, who has not yet made his entrance, although his head can be seen, presumably looking out his window, protests that he can't measure up to all that. Hachivat says, "Nonsense," and requests the noble presence of his friend.

At this point Karaghioz leaps from his window and gives Hachivat an unmerciful beating, as the children in the audience shriek happily. Hachivat flees, returns, is beaten again, flees, returns, and eventually is allowed to stay. Now come the references to local affairs. They may satirize local events, retail gossip of the quarter, or take pot shots at the government or minor officials, a thing that only a puppet would dare to do under such strict rule.

After this somewhat extemporaneous opening, Karaghioz goes home to await the formal play.

Unfortunately Professor Siyavusgil, like the showmen, has left us with no written script. For a detailed recital of a formal play, we must rely on a French traveler, Gerard de Nerval, one of the first Europeans to offer a friendly understanding to the Karaghioz theater and to report it accurately. It does, to be sure, require understanding —or a degree of tolerance, at least—of those who are not used to it. For the humor is quite gamy and sexual episodes are not only numerous, but breathtakingly candid. Western observers, particularly the Victorians, have watched the shows from start to finish with the dedication of the devoted censor. Karaghioz, however, is in the comic tradition that inspired the Atellan farces, and the classic Greek comedy of Aristophanes. Even in Turkey, there seemed to have been two kinds of Karaghioz shows. The workingmen and middle classes demanded and got a rough and rowdy show about the daily life of the city.

In the sultan's palace, however, the behavior of Karaghioz was more circumspect. Here his performance was directed by cultivated showmen with all the literary, philosophical, and musical knowledge of the time. Their shows were in keeping with the ancient moral codes and religious traditions; at the same time they were satirical. They were keyed exactly right for their sophisticated and socially elevated audiences.

De Nerval, writing in 1851, describes a play he saw in a cafe. He is somewhat surprised by Karaghioz's crudities, but even more fascinated by his freedom of style.

An orchestra in a high gallery begins to play, he tells us, and when the music ends the lights of the hall are extinguished and a joyous cry of expectation bursts from the audience. Now is heard a rattling sound—as though "a number of pieces of wood were being shaken in a sack"—which is the customary signal for starting the show.

Suddenly, a spectator, probably a part of the show, cries out: "What are you going to give us today?"

"It is written over the door for all who can read," comes the reply from behind the screen.

"But I have forgotten what the *hodja* taught me." (The *hodja* teaches children to read and write at the mosque.)

"All right then," says the showman. "It is about the illustrious Karaghioz, victim of his chastity."

"How can you justify that title?" the spectator

jibes, continuing the game.

"I count on the intelligence of people of good taste," answers the showman, imperturbably, "and in imploring the aid of Ahmad (Mohammed) for our Dark Eye."

"You speak well. Let's see if you can put the show on!"

"Don't get upset," says the showman. "My friends and I are worthy of the critics."

The orchestra plays again, and then on the screen appears a palace in Constantinople with a fountain and houses in the background. Passing in front of it are figures in bright, strong colors.

Soon a Turk comes out of a house, followed by a slave carrying a traveling bag. "Karaghioz, Karaghioz, my best friend," the Turk cries. "Are you still asleep?"

Karaghioz puts his head out of the window and is greeted with delighted cries. He withdraws and reappears in the street to embrace his friend.

"Listen," says the Turk. "I am going to ask a great favor of you. I have important business that takes me to Brusa [now Bursa]. You know that I have a very beautiful wife, and I confess that I feel very uneasy about leaving her alone. I haven't much confidence in my servants. Well, now, my friend, I have had an inspiration. I shall make you guardian of her virtue. I understand your sensitivity and the deep affection you have for me, so I am happy to give you this honor and proof of my esteem."

"You fool!" exclaims Karaghioz. "Look at me. Just look at me."

"All right," says the Turk. "What about it?"

"Don't you understand," replies Karaghioz, "that once your wife has cast eyes on me, she won't be able to resist the desire to possess me."

The audience loves this.

"Not at all," says the Turk. "She loves me, and any fears I have of her being seduced certainly wouldn't be from your direction. No, my good friend, your honor assures me of that. And finally, by Allah, you are unusually put together. I trust you."

He leaves.

Karaghioz alone continues: "Blindness of men! Hah, hah—Me, unusually built! Ha, ha! Very handsome, very seductive, very dangerous, eh? Well my friend has made me the guardian of his wife. I must be worthy of his confidence. So let's go into his house as he wishes and lie down on the divan. Oh, no, no, no! His wife, with a woman's curiosity, would want to see me, and the moment she laid eyes on me she would be lost in admiration and abandon all resistance. No. I'll stay here in the doorway, like a sentinel. After all, a woman is such a trifle, and a true friend is so rare.

"What to do?" he asks. "Watch at the door, wait for my friend to come back. That's it. But no —the woman can see me here through the grille. And then again she might be tempted to leave the house with her slaves and go to the bath. No husband, alas, can prevent his wife from leaving the house for this reason. And if she did she'd be able to admire me at her leisure. Oh, my foolish friend, why did you give me this watchman's job to do?"

In succeeding scenes, the humor turns on the fact of Karaghioz's large phallus. To camouflage himself from the woman, he lies on his stomach, propped up by the phallus, pretending to be a bridge. People, horses, dogs, a military patrol walk back and forth over him. He jumps up just in time to save himself from a heavy wagon pulled by oxen.

Then he rolls onto his back and pretends to be a post. Some laundresses returning from the fountain tie a clothesline to him. Next some slaves enter leading a group of horses, and meeting some friends, they decide to go into a tavern. But where can they tie up their horses? They find their solution in Karaghioz, still lying there. Soon, happy songs are heard from the tavern. The

horses become excited and begin to pull in all directions. Karaghioz howls for help. The crowd delivers him and sets him back on his feet. The audience is convulsed.

Now the friend's wife comes out of her house to go to the bath.

"Oh, you handsome man!" she cries. "I never saw anyone so beautiful!"

"Excuse me, madam," says Karaghioz, very properly. "You're not allowed to speak to me. I'm a night watchman."

"Then how is it that you're here in the daytime?"

Karaghioz claims he has been carousing and was left drunk in the street. When she tries to take his hand to help him he cries in terror, "Don't touch me, madam. I am impure. I have just touched a dog!"

The woman eventually leaves, but cannot refrain from telling the other women at the bath about the beautiful, well-made stranger. Accordingly, a crowd of bathers follows her home. They set upon Karaghioz, tearing at his clothes, mussing his hair, and otherwise roughing him up in an excess of passion. He is just about to give in when the French ambassador passes by in his

Set pieces and characters of Karaghioz puppet drama: Garden, snake, and buildings (opposite) are often shown on screen before play begins. Above: His form and costumes may vary, but Tiryaki, the opium-smoker, can invariably be identified by such props as fan and pipe.

coach. Karaghioz begs his protection, the ambassador fends off the women, Karaghioz jumps into the coach and disappears, leaving behind a wailing disappointed crowd.

The husband returns and is reassured to find that the chastity of his friend has preserved the purity of his wife. End of play.

Karaghioz seems never to have had a human counterpart. As far as we know, he derives from no one. Turkish historians claim he was an entertainer turned philosopher. I would suggest that anciently Karaghioz was a nomadic herdsmen's fertility deity turned clown. He is unique. His origin is obscure, although it is certain that he gained his name and popularity among the nomadic tribes of Central Asia, where the tradition of the shadow theater is old. For nomads have animals and, therefore, leather. They have tents and fire and, therefore, a lighted screen. A shadow show of fifty actors packs into a small saddlebag. It is known that the Scythians of the third and fourth centuries B.C. made handsome silhouettes of leather. And in burial grounds among the Altai Mountains near Outer Mongolia, along the old trade route between China and Russia, there have

been found cutout leather animals, one a moose that could well have been a shadow figure.

The Turkish tribes that wandered Asia before 1000 A.D. are known to have had a theater called *kogurcak,* which is translated as "figures that the makers of shadows cause to appear behind a curtain."

This, of course, does not prove that the shadow theater was a Turkish invention, or even that the Turks introduced it to the Moslem world. Turkish authorities attribute the origin of the shadow play to India—I am inclined to agree. The first Arabic writings about the shadow show, however, coincided with the entrance of the Turkish tribes into the Middle East.

An ancestor of Karaghioz may very well have traveled with the armies of Genghis Khan. For in the Mongol tongues also his name means "dark eye." He certainly had a cousin in Persia by the name of Katchel Pehlavan—the "bald roisterer." But it's doubtful if the clan ever got very far into India. The competition there was too strong.

All we can say for sure of the Mongols is that their emperors knew the shadow play. For of Ogotai, the son of Genghis Khan, it is said that

once, while attending a shadow play, he observed the figure of an old Moslem being pulled across the stage with his white beard tied to the tail of a horse. This so infuriated Ogotai that he reprimanded the puppet operators severely and had them thrown out.

There are allusions in very old Arabian religious plays that compare the universe to the shadow theater to illustrate the doctrine of creation and the relationship between divine and earthly beings.

So much for history; the mythology is more fun. Popular legend paints a more attractive beginning for both Karaghioz and Hachivat. They lived in Brusa in the fourteenth century, Karaghioz a mason, Hachivat a blacksmith. They met and became friends on a construction project, the building of a mosque for the Sultan Orhan. The two evidently were natural comedians and eventually held up work with their continual clowning. The other workers would drop their tools and gather around whenever the two jokesters began such sessions.

When word reached the sultan, he flew into a royal rage and had the pair arrested and executed. Later he regretted this cruel and hasty action. A courtier, a certain Sheik Kusteri, wishing to console the sultan, put up a screen in a corner of the palace and by using his slippers to cast the shadows imitated the antics of the two departed clowns. Today, wherever Karaghioz is played, even among the Greeks, the name of Sheik Kusteri is mentioned with respect in the prologue, as though he were, indeed, the creator of Karaghioz and the patron saint of their showmen's guild.

One showman was reputed to have a repertoire of three hundred plays. He is said to have been able to conduct a dialogue between Karaghioz and Hachivat for fifteen hours. On one occasion a sultan became so excited by the shadow play of a sea battle between a galley and a merchant ship near some dangerous rocks that he wanted to make the showman an admiral in the Turkish navy. The showman accepted a double fee, but wisely declined the promotion.

Today, although no longer the principal dramatic star of the Middle East, Karaghioz still has friends there. In Algeria a far milder Karaghioz shares the screen with such stories as that of Aladdin and the Legend of the Seven Sleepers. In Athens, Eugenios Spatharis operates as the descendant of a long line of Karaghioz performers. Besides playing special shows for children, the Greek Karaghioz plays at festivals and fairs the entire year round. The satiric essence of the "dark-eyed one" is fully appreciated by the Greek people. In everyday speech they use his phrases as proverbs. They speak of "a shack like Karaghioz's" or "a Karaghiozis marriage." His companion's name comes out Khatsiavatis. The plays are not based on the classics of Ramadan. They have much more to do with recent Balkan history. And, since puppetry is no stranger to politics, Karaghiozis on one side of the Aegean often takes a swing at Karaghioz on the other side.

In Turkey, after a lapse of many years, Karaghioz is due for a revival. A permanent, full-time Karaghioz theater has been opened in Ankara for children, and folk-art companies are reappearing in the countryside. Once again his impudent shadow will be the delight of Ramadan, and once again the cycle is complete, from the temple, to the people, to the children.

Paper cut-out puppets are a popular Greek version of Karaghioz. Figures may be mounted on cardboard and used in improvised shadow plays. Many sheets are available. This one has devil, monk, soldier, urchins, and props.

PUNCH & JUDY: THE FIRST FAMILY

6

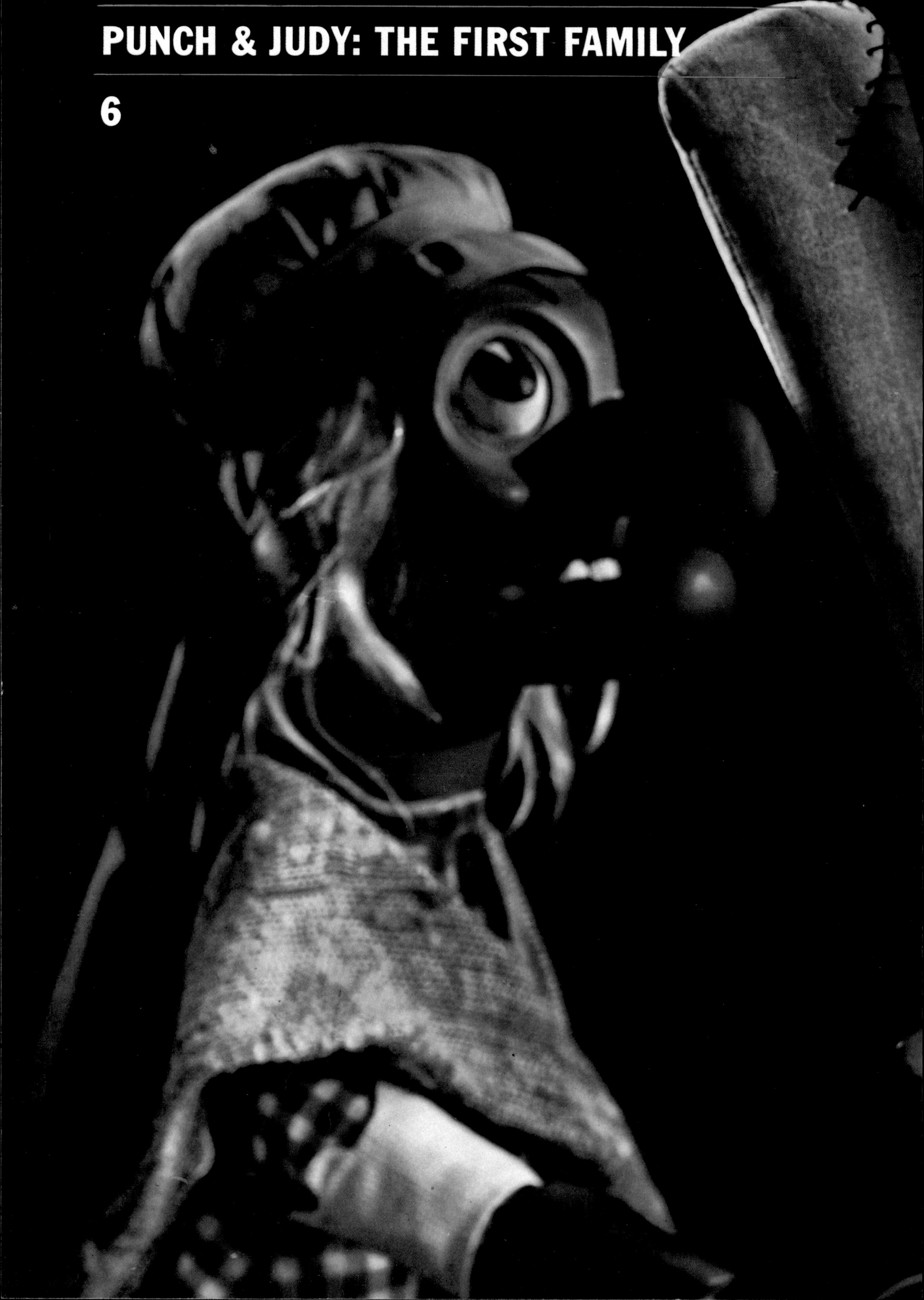

THE TRAGICAL COMEDY OR COMICAL TRAGEDY OF PUNCH AND JUDY

Enter Punch—after a few preliminary squeaks, he bows three times to the spectators; once in the centre, and once at each side of the stage, and then speaks the following:

PROLOGUE

Ladies and Gentlemen, pray how you do?
If you all happy, me all happy too.
Stop and hear my merry littel play;
If me make you laugh, me need not make you pay.

Exit.

ACT I

Punch is heard behind the scene, squeaking the tune of "Malbroug s'en va-t-en guerre"; he then makes his appearance and dances about the stage, while he sings to the same air. He continues to dance and sing, and then calls

Judy, my dear! Judy!

Enter the Dog Toby.

PUNCH: Hollo, Toby! Who call'd you? How you do, Mr. Toby? Hope you very well, Mr. Toby.

TOBY: (*Snarls.*) Arr! Arr!

PUNCH: How do my good friend, your master, Mr. Toby? How do Mr. Scaramouch?

TOBY: Bow, wow, wow!

PUNCH: I'm glad to hear it. Poor Toby! What a nice good-tempr'd dog it is! No wonder his master is so fond of him.

TOBY: (*Snarls.*) Arr! Arr!

PUNCH: What! Toby! you cross this morning? You get out of bed the wrong way upwards?

TOBY: (*Snarls again.*) Arr! Arr!

PUNCH: Poor Toby. (*Putting his hand out cautiously, and trying to coax the dog, who snaps at it.*) Toby, you're one nasty cross dog: get away with you! (*Strikes at him.*)

TOBY: (*Seizing Punch by the nose.*) Bow, wow, wow!

PUNCH: Oh dear! Oh dear! My nose! my poor nose! my beautiful nose! Get away! get away, you nasty—I tell your master. Oh dear; dear!—Judy! Judy! (*Punch shakes his nose, but cannot shake off the Dog, who follows him as he retreats round the stage. He continues*

to call "Judy! Judy, my dear!" until the Dog quits his hold and exits.)

PUNCH: (*Solus, and rubbing his nose with both hands.*) Oh my nose! my pretty littel nose! Judy! Judy! You nasty, nasty brute, I will tell you master of you. (*Calls.*) Mr. Scaramouch! My good friend, Mr. Scaramouch! Look what you nasty brute dog has done! *Enter Scaramouch, with a stick.*

SCARA: Hollo, Mr. Punch! What have you been doing to my poor dog?

PUNCH: (*Retreating behind the side scene, on observing the stick, and peeping round the corner.*) Ha; my good friend, how you do? Glad to see you look so well. (*Aside.*) I wish you were farther with your nasty great stick.

SCARA: You have been beating and ill-using my poor dog, Mr. Punch.

PUNCH: He has been biting and ill-using my poor nose. What have got there, sir?

SCARA: Where?

PUNCH: In your hand?

SCARA: A fiddel.

PUNCH: A fiddel! What a pretty thing is a fiddel! Can you play upon that fiddel?

SCARA: Come here, and I'll try.

PUNCH: No, thank you. I can hear the music here very well.

SCARA: Then you shall try yourself. Can you play?

PUNCH: (*Coming in.*) I do not know till I try. Let me see! (*Takes the stick and moves slowly about, singing the tune of the "Marche des Marseillois." He hits Scaramouch a slight blow on his high cap, as if by accident.*)

SCARA: You play very well, Mr. Punch. Now let me try. I will give you a lesson how to play the fiddle. (*Takes the stick and dances to the same tune, hitting Punch a hard blow on the back of his head.*) There's sweet music for you.

PUNCH: I NO like you playing so well as my own. Let me again. (*Takes the stick, and dances as before; in the course of his dance he gets behind Scaramouch and with a violent blow knocks his head clean off his shoulders.*) How you like that tune, my good friend? That sweet music, eh? He, he, he! (*Laughing and throwing away the stick.*) You'll never hear such another tune, so long as you live, my boy. (*Sings the tune of "Malbroug" and dances to it.*) Judy, Judy, my dear! Judy can't you answer, my dear?

JUDY: (*Within.*) Well! what do you want, Mr. Punch?

PUNCH: Come upstairs: I want you.

JUDY: Then want must be your master. I'm busy.

PUNCH: (*Singing to tune, "Malbroug."*)
Her answer genteel is and civil
No wonder, you think, if we live ill,
And I wish her sometimes at the Devil,
Since that's all the answer I get.
Yet, why should I grumble and fret,
Because she's sometimes in a pet?
Though I really am sorry to say sirs,
That that is too often her way, sirs.
For this, by and by, she shall pay, sirs.
Oh, wives are an obstinate set!

PUNCH: Judy, my dear! (*Calling.*) Judy, my love— pretty Judy, come upstairs.
Enter Judy.

JUDY: Well, here I am! what do you want, now I'm come?

PUNCH: (*Aside.*) What a pretty creature! An't she one beauty?

JUDY: What do you want, I say?

PUNCH: A Kiss! A pretty kiss! (*Kisses her, while she hits him a slap on the face.*)

JUDY: Take that then: How do you like my kisses? Will you have another?

PUNCH: No; one at a time, one at a time, my pretty wife. (*Aside.*) She always is so playful. Where's the child? Fetch me the child, Judy, my dear.
Exit Judy.

PUNCH: (*Solus.*) There's one wife for you! What a precious darling creature? She go fetch our child.
Re-enter Judy with the Child.

JUDY: Here's the child. Pretty dear! It knows its

papa. Take the child.

PUNCH: (*Holding out his hands.*) Give it me— pretty littel thing. How like its sweet mamma!

JUDY: How awkward you are!

PUNCH: Give it me. I know how to nurse it so well as you do. (*She gives it to him.*) Get away! (*Exit Judy. Punch nursing the Child in his arms.*) What a pretty baby it is! Was it sleepy then? Hush-a-by, by, by.

(*Sings to the tune of "Rest thee, Babe."*)
Oh, rest thee, my baby,
Thy daddy is here:

Mr. Punch

Engraved by George Cruikshank
from an original miniature
_____

Thy mammy's a gaby,
And that's very clear.
Oh, rest thee, my darling,
Thy mother will come,
With a voice like a starling;
I wish she was dumb!

Poor dear littel thing! It cannot get to sleep: by, by, by, by, hush-a-by. Well, then, it shan't. (*Dances the Child, and then sets it on his lap, between his knees, and sings the common nusery ditty.*)

Dancy baby diddy;
What shall daddy do widdy?
Sit on his lap,
Give it some pap;
Dancy, baby, diddy.

(*After nursing it upon his lap, Punch sticks the Child against the side of the stage, on the platform, runs up to it, clapping his hands, and crying, "Catchee, catchee, catchee!" He then takes it up again, and it begins to cry.*) What is the matter with it? Poor thing! It has got the stomach ache, I dare say.

CHILD: (*Cries.*)

PUNCH: Hush-a-by, hush-a-by! (*Sitting down, and rolling it on his knees.*) Naughty child! Judy! (*Calling.*) The child has got the stomach ache. Pheu! Nasty child! Judy, I say! (*Child continues to cry.*) Keep quiet, can't you? (*Hits it a box on the ear.*) Oh you filthy child! What have you done? I won't keep such a nasty child. Hold your tongue!

PUNCH: (*Strikes the Child's head several times against the side of the stage.*) There!—there! there! How you like that? I thought I stop your squalling. Get along with you, nasty, naughty, crying child. (*Throws it over the front of the stage, among the spectators.*) He, He, he! (*Laughing and singing to the same tune as before.*)

Get away, nasty baby;
There it goes over:
Thy mammy's a gaby,
Thy daddy's a rover.

Re-enter Judy.

JUDY: Where's the child?

PUNCH: Gone—gone to sleep.

JUDY: What have you done with the child, I say?

PUNCH: Gone to sleep, I say.

JUDY: What have you done with it?

PUNCH: What have I done with it?

JUDY: Ay, done with it! I heard it crying just now. Where is it?

PUNCH: How should I know?

JUDY: I heard you make the pretty darling cry.

PUNCH: I dropped it out at window.

JUDY: Oh, you cruel, horrid wretch, to drop the pretty baby out at window. Oh! (*Cries, and wipes her eyes with the corner of her white apron.*) You barbarous man. Oh!

PUNCH: You shall have one other soon, Judy, my dear. More where that come from.

JUDY: I'll make you pay for this, depend upon it. *Exit in haste.*

PUNCH: There she goes. What a piece of work about nothing! (*Dances about and sings, beating time with his head, as he turns around, on the front of the stage.*)
Re-enter Judy with a stick; she comes in behind, and hits Punch a sounding blow on the back of the head, before he is aware.

JUDY: I'll teach you to drop my child out at window.

PUNCH: So-o-oftly, Judy, so-o-ftly! (*Rubbing the back of his head with his hands.*) Don't be a fool now. What you at?

JUDY: What! You'll drop my poor baby out at window again, will you? (*Hitting him continually on the head.*)

PUNCH: No, I never will again. (*She still hits him.*) Softly, I say, softly. A joke's a joke.

JUDY: Oh, you nasty cruel brute! (*Hitting him again.*) I'll teach you.

PUNCH: But me no like such teaching. What! You're in earnest are you?

JUDY: Yes, (*hit*) I (*hit*) am (*hit*).

PUNCH: I'm glad of it: Me no like such jokes. (*She hits him again.*) Leave off, I say. What! You won't, won't you?

JUDY: No, I won't. (*Hits him.*)

PUNCH: Very well: then now come my turn to teach you. (*He snatches at, and struggles with her for the stick, which he wrenches from her, and strikes her with it on the head, while she runs about to different parts of the stage to get out of his way.*) How you like my teaching, Judy, my pretty dear? (*Hitting her.*)

91

Cruikshank engravings show action of Act
Two: Punch calls for horse, canters briefly (top, left),
is thrown. He calls for doctor (top, right),
who gets kicked in eye while examining him. Doctor
beats Punch with stick, is beaten dead in
return by Punch, who throws body away. Servant
comes to complain of noise (middle, left),
is also killed. Punch subsequently does away
with a blind man, a constable, an officer,
and finally hangs hangman (middle, right), in
between times singing of his love for
pretty Poll. At last Devil appears and Punch
begs for mercy. Fight ensues,
ends with Punch whirling Devil on staff (right),
crying, "Huzza, huzza, the Devil's dead!"

JUDY: Oh, pray, Mr. Punch. No more!

PUNCH: Yes, one littel more lesson. (*Hits her again.*) There, there, there! (*She falls down, with her head over the platform of the stage, and as he continues to hit at her, she puts up her hand to guard her head.*) Any more?

JUDY: (*Lifting up her head.*) No, no, no more.

PUNCH: (*Knocking down her head.*) I thought I should soon make you quiet.

JUDY: (*Again raising her head.*) No.

PUNCH: (*Again knocking it down and following up his blows until she is lifeless.*) Now if you're satisfied, I am. (*Perceiving that she does not move.*) There, get up, Judy, my dear. I won't hit you any more. None of your sham-Abram. This is only your fun. You got the head-ache? Why, you only asleep. Get up, I say. Well, then, get down. (*Tosses the body down with the end of his stick.*) He, he, he! (*Laughing.*) To lose a wife is to get a fortune.

> Who'd be plagued with a wife
> That could set himself free
> With a rope or a knife,
> Or a good stick, like me?

(*He throws away the body with his stick.*)
Enter Pretty Polly.

PUNCH: (*Seeing her, and singing out of the "The Beggar's Opera," while she dances.*)

> When the heart of a man is oppress'd with cares,
> The coulds are dispelled when a woman appears,

PUNCH: (*Aside.*) What a beauty! What a pretty creature! (*Extending his arms, and then clasping his hands in admiration. She continues to dance, and dances round him, while he surveys her in silent delight. He then begins to sing a slow tune and foots it with her; and, as the music quickens, they jig it backwards and forwards, Punch catches the lady in his arms and kisses her most audibly, while she appears "nothing loth." After waltzing, they dance to the tune of "The White Cockade," and Punch sings as follows:*)

> I love you so, I love you so,
> I never will leave you; so, no, no:
> If I had all the wives of wise King Sol,
> I would kill them all for my pretty Poll.

Exeunt dancing.

END OF ACT I

The name of this famous dramatic team is a household expression throughout the English-speaking world—Punch and Judy. Theirs may even be the world's best-known puppet play. The above text is a notable one. It dates from 1828 and represents the laudable effort of an otherwise unremembered English publisher, Mr. Septimus Prowett, to preserve a contemporary London street performance of the Punch play.

The show he chose was that of an elderly Italian puppeteer named Piccini, and was by all accounts the best then playing in London. To sketch the scenes of Punch's adventures, Mr. Prowett engaged George Cruikshank, an excellent and noted illustrator. To set down the text, he enlisted John Payne Collier, a student of the drama who would one day be a notorious literary forger.

Cruikshank tells us that arrangements were made with Signor Piccini for a morning performance in the clubroom of the King's Arms, a low public house in Drury Lane, where Piccini lived. (Piccini, like many another performer of his time, would die in St. Giles workhouse.) Piccini's theater frame was not collapsible and evidently too big to pass through the King's Arms doorways. A first-floor window sash had to be removed so the booth could be hauled into the clubroom.

"Mr. Payne Collier, the publisher, and myself formed the audience," Cruikshank relates, "and as the performance went on, I stopped it at the most interesting parts to sketch the Figures, whilst Mr. Collier noted down the dialogue; and the whole is a faithful copy and description of the various scenes represented by this Italian, whose performance of 'Punch' was far superior in every

respect to anything of the sort to be seen at the present day."

The Piccini play, probably the best known, was and is only one of many published versions.

Since Piccini's time, the framework of the English Punch and Judy play has remained very much the same, with individual "professors," as they are known, varying the performance to suit their own personal styles and to please a particular audience.

But Punch was not always the character he is in the play recorded by Collier. Punch had been evolving over a period of many centuries. Today's Punch is now a hand puppet, and that fact more than anything else has shaped his character. He is the child of his own activity. He is who he is because of the way he behaves. Long before he had his present form or name, some ancestor of Punch was fighting, beating, picking things up and throwing them, as only a hand puppet can do. Finally, it was the audiences that picked the character of their protagonist from among all the jovial, horrendous, or outrageous creations which leaned out of the castelets of the wandering showmen. The audiences formed the character—but never froze the form.

Another group of ancestors may have given our hero his name and his shape.

He may have inherited his hump and his hooked nose from a Roman clown. These two characteristics turn up later in the make-up of Pulcinella—the creation of a professional comedian, Savio Fiorillo (whose work dates to about 1600), in the *commedia dell' arte*. Pulcinella was a braggart and a coward both in the live and puppet theaters, and, of course, the type traces back to the first days of the Atellan farces. Though never a leading character in the *commedia,* Pulcinella became a highly successful marionette, and before long he crossed the Alps into France with troupes of puppet players. By 1630, he was playing under the name of Polichinelle in Paris, where he made quite a reputation for himself. Or several names.

Like all foreigners in a strange land, Pulcinella had trouble getting the natives to spell his name correctly. It was rendered variously as Pollicinella, Punchanello, Polichinello, Polichinelli, and finally the English boiled it down to Punchinello.

The first reference to him in England is dated May 9, 1662, and noted, appropriately enough, by that incurable diarist Samuel Pepys. On that date he saw an Italian puppet play at an alehouse in Covent Garden and found it "very pretty, the best I ever saw." He also informs us that the puppeteer, "Signor Bologna, alias Pollicinella," performed his play before King Charles II and was rewarded with a gold chain and medal. In 1666, the overseers' books of St. Martin's-in-the-Fields acknowledge the payment of a license fee: "Rec'd of Punchinello, ye Italian popet player, for his booth at Charing Cross." It must have been that Pepys saw this show as well, for on March 20, 1667, he records having taken his wife "to Polichinelli at Charing Cross, which is prettier and prettier and so full of variety that it is extraordinary good entertainment."

The performances Pepys saw were not the Punch and Judy shows of later years, but pantomimes with music, dancing, tricks, and transformations. They were performed by marionettes, and rather large ones at that, controlled by strings and a heavy wire to the head. There were

Preceding pages: Street entertainment in 19th-century England was often provided by Punch and Judy. This huge painting, done in 1829 by Benjamin R. Haydon, shows a scene in front of Mary-le-bone Church. In center, an old farmer from the country watches show in fascination as his pocket is picked by boy sheltered in cloak of woman accomplice. Boy is watched by officer with club.

skeletons and dismemberments, jugglers and clowns. Punchinello was short and fat, and was a hundred years away from his present form.

The next thirty-five or forty years, however, were a time of great changes in Punch's development. The style of the Italian shows was quickly adopted by the English, who made it their own, and who enjoyed it immensely. The showmen presented moralities, legends, comedies, and pantomimes. The marionette survived in some shows. In others, the hand puppet was emerging. There are descriptions of Punchinello fighting with old morality figures, such as Want and Weariness; sitting on the lap of the Queen of Sheba, and dodging the representatives of the Inquisition, as well as the Hangman.

Punch, meanwhile, found himself engaged with the likes of Scaramouche, St. George, and his old antagonist the Devil.

Judy, or Joan as she was first known, and the

Baby seem to have appeared in Punch's life sometime after 1688, and by 1700, or perhaps a bit later, Punch was an established comic character of such popularity that few shows could succeed without a major part for him.

By 1710, Punch played a command performance to four visiting Iroquois Indian chiefs, then the toast of London. In this play marionettes reenacted Marlborough's victory over the French. French missionaries in America had been spreading the word that Queen Anne's realm was merely a small appendage of France and the British were anxious to correct the impression.

The favorite Punch show of the early eighteenth century probably was Martin Powell's, which played in Covent Garden, opposite St.

Above: Pulcinella marionette was Italian ancestor of Punch. This one was member of an 18th-century *commedia dell' arte* troupe. Left: Early English puppeteer Powell, dressed as Punch, introduces Punch and Joan.

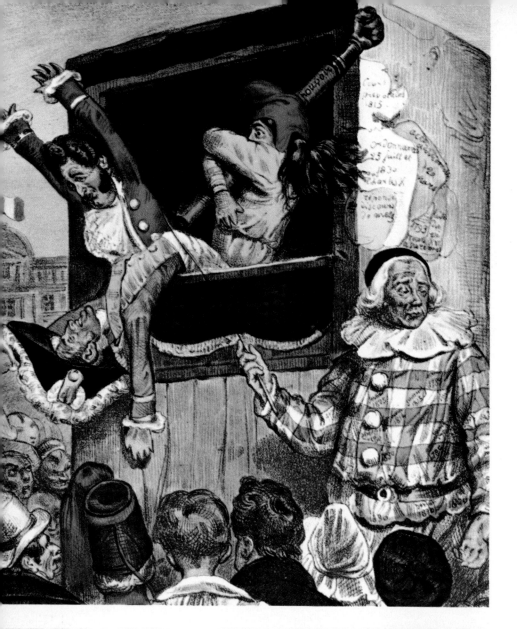

Polichinelle played diverse roles in 19th-century France, as hand puppet (below), cutout toy (right), and character in a political cartoon (left). In cartoon, red-capped Liberty belabors two aristocrats with club labeled "power." They are shouting, "I will have it, you will not have it, I will have it, etc." In street scene below, Polichinelle has disposed of two foes and is about to bludgeon Devil. Polichinelle's dog watches at right.

Paul's Church. Powell himself was small and a hunchback, and he is said to have appeared on his stage to recite the prologue dressed as his main character. The form of this marionette, who starred in every play, may be deduced from the frontispiece of a Powell program, which shows the figure as having a big, protruding belly, while the hump, if there was one, is obscured by a large, Elizabethan ruff.

Powell was so successful that a letter appeared in *The Spectator* of March 16, 1710, complaining that Punch was luring the congregation away from church. Further, since Punch plays were shown everyday from 10 a.m. to 10 p.m., the morning church bells were being taken as a signal that Punch was beginning to show. The letter purportedly came from the sexton of St. Paul's, but is generally attributed to the prolific, humorous essayist, Richard Steele.

Throughout the eighteenth century Punch was in the ascendancy. An engraving of Southwark Fair by Hogarth, which is dated 1773, shows three distinct types of puppetry going on at the same time. Rear center, a pair of hand puppets can be seen fighting with clubs. They seem to be ballyhooing the show inside, for there are cloth signs nearby advertising the story of Original Sin—and Punchinello (with front and back humps) is shown dumping a character, possibly Old Vice, from a wheelbarrow into the flaming mouth of a dragon. In the lower-left foreground of the engraving, a pudgy piper dances his marionette a la planchette with a cord attached to his knee. And in the center foreground a woman with a hurdy-gurdy across her back is performing a gallanty show (from "gallantry") for a single customer. A gallanty was a peep show of battles or great deeds in which silhouettes moved across a shadow screen.

It is Punchinello who interests us most, however. For his humps indicate that he is still a marionette, since a large hump on a hand puppet severely limits the action of the figure's arms. On the other hand, the presence of the hand puppets in the background indicates that perhaps the front hump is on the way out, and the more aggressive Punch on the way in. For as has been noted before, the most important thing a puppet does is move. And the fact that Punch is a hand puppet had more to do with the shaping of his belligerent character than anything else.

By the turn of the nineteenth century, Punch was completely himself, which is to say completely English. He kept just a touch of an Italian accent for comedy. His form was fixed: He had his hunchback and nutcracker nose and chin and he had slimmed down a bit.

His costume changed from time to time—or according to the whim of the individual Punch man. Cruikshank shows him with a kind of admiral's hat, with its wide brims turned up fore and aft. This is entirely English, and at complete variance with Polichinelle's hat and with the curved peaked clown's hat Punch wears on the cover of the magazine bearing his name.

Most important of all, the Punch man by his very resilience and ingenuity has arrived at a unique kind of theater. Let us see how it works.

A performer with a folding screen under one arm and a bag in his other hand arrives at a populated place. He surveys his surroundings, unfolds his screen, and takes out of his bag a number of small cloth and wooden characters, which he hangs inside the screen. He is now ready to com-

municate. Here in the smallest space and the shortest time he has established a theater. He is our Punch man. He has at his fingertips "instant theater." He is often alone and is the author and designer, and the singers and actors for his entire repertoire of plays. In no other theatrical medium is this possible. In no other theater can one person perform so many functions at one time. There is the greatest economy in the telling of Punch's story. One setting serves to represent anywhere in the world. The cast all enter from the bottom of the frame. Zip! And there's an entrance—no time wasted—a technique which preceded the movie cut by a few hundred years.

In addition, theater is composed of two parts—the other part is the audience. When the audience arrives, it gives our Punch man a pattern around which he invents a performance: something special to fit the butcher, baker, and candlestick maker that are attending that particular day.

Hogarth engraving of Southwark fair shows four scenes of puppetry: poster (1) has Punchinello dumping Old Vice into Hell; (2) tiny hand puppets fight with sticks; in foreground (3) a bagpiper works planchette figures with toe; (4) galanty-show operator works with hurdy-gurdy on back.

Herein lies the special power of this branch of puppetry. An entire cast is ready to play a special new drama on the instant. The legitimate theater cannot do it; it must rehearse. The movies cannot do it; they require time, at least, if not many, many people as well. A mime approaches it.

Of course, in the past, there has always been a proportion of the hand-puppet performers that chose only to entertain, and varied their shows solely to amuse their audiences. But the very natures of the heroes they developed tells us that the audiences demanded more.

Punch—and by Punch I mean Polichinelle, the German Hanswurst, the Russian Petrouchka, the Czech Kasparek, Vitez Laszlo from Hungary, and all the rest—was created by natural selection. He is rough, brutal, and vindictive. He is vain, lecherous and deceitful, yet he is of the people, and that is why he remains popular. He is a commoner at odds with his surroundings. His adversaries are the landlord, the judge, the hangman, death, the devil, the policeman—and even his wife. Because he is a puppet, he can carry out our outrageous fantasies—such as hanging a policeman, drinking a barrelful, talking while hanging from the gallows, clubbing his spouse, riding a crocodile. Punch, in flouting petty authority, has been a great spokesman for liberty and many a brave, intelligent Punch man has outwitted all kinds of censors in his audacity. "Triumphant Punch!" cried Byron, "with joy I follow thee through the glad progress of thy wanton course."

The framework of the English Punch and Judy play remained much the same throughout the nineteenth century. Each Punch man introduced his own specialty acts into the performance. Many of them used jugglers. Often a pair of boxers has been effective. Essentially, however, the principal players, besides Punch and Judy, were Toby the Dog, the Baby, the Doctor, the Negro Servant (whose only line is "Shallaballa"), the Beadle (or Constable), the Clown, the Hangman, the Ghost of Judy, Mr. Jones, Hector the Horse, the Crocodile, and the Devil.

Across the channel, meanwhile, Polichinelle was playing with an almost identical cast of characters, and looking a good deal like his English counterpart, Punch. The faces showed the same family traits, but Polichinelle retains his clumsy humps, while Punch has but one, on his back, curled up like a cornucopia.

A handsomely illustrated book of French Polichinelle plays published in 1863 by the Parisian playwright-puppeteer Duranty demonstrates the parallel. The book, called *Theatre des Marionettes du Jardin des Tuileries,* is dedicated to George Sand, a lifelong devotee of puppetry.

Three principal players of the Lyonese Guignol:
Madelon (top, left), Guignol (bottom, left) and Gnafron.
These hand puppets are preserved in
the Musée Gadagne, Lyons. At right is a drawing of *La Mère Gigogne* with a few of her 177 children.

The English Doctor and Beadle appear in France as *Le Medecin* and *Le Gendarme*. The Servant is *Le Negre*, who speaks the Creole patios of Haiti. The Hangman becomes *Le Bourreau*, the Devil is *Le Diable*. Both casts contain clowns. For an equivalent of Mr. Jones, there is an all-purpose character named *Cassandre*, who plays fathers, landlords, and other elderly, solid citizens. A small live dog often was trained to sit on the playboard and be Toby. There was a puppet horse, however.

Polichinelle, unlike his English cousin, figures in a variety of different plots, and, like as not, Pierrot or Harlequin may have a more important part. Polichinelle is not ordinarily married, but sometimes a plot will require him to wed *La Mère Gigogne*, who brings as her dowry a sack of gold and one hundred seventy-seven children. At the wedding Polichinelle tries to pay off the notary with a child, instead of money, and when the offer is refused, Polichinelle throws the infant at the ungrateful man.

There are twenty-four Polichinelle plays in Duranty's book, and a hundred more probably could be found in other volumes of the period. Polichinelle often is on stage with two or three other principals, which indicates that more than one operator was required backstage. Punch, of course, was performed by one operator, plus a "bottler," or front man, who drummed or bugled up the crowd, collected the money, and talked back to Punch.

Duranty's plays were both artistic and witty and had a keen edge of topical satire. He touched on medicine, marriage, alcohol, the law, money-lending, and many other pertinent subjects. Whatever the story, however, Polichinelle always

played himself.

Here is *Le Tonneau* (in English, *The Cask*):

DRAMATIS PERSONAE

POLICHINELLE

NIFLANGUILLE

BAILLENFLÉ

THE SORCERER

THE GENDARME

A SOLDIER

A CROCODILE

SCENE I

POL: Oh, Niflanguille, I'm terribly thirsty! Ever since I was born I have never been able to quench my thirst. This has to end! I must have a big drink.

NIF: All right, Polichinelle, do you want a half bottle?

POL: (*With disdain.*) Oh!

NIF: A bottle?

POL: You're joking.

NIF: A jug?

POL: Pooh!

NIF: A pail?

POL: No!

NIF: A keg, perhaps?

POL: Oh come on!

NIF: A cask, then.

POL: Ah, Niflanguille, that's it! But where will we find a cask?

NIF: Oh, it won't take long. Wait a minute. Hey! Friend Baillenflé!

Enter Baillenflé!

SCENE II

BAI: Well, what do you want?

NIF: Polichinelle is thirsty.

BAI: Let him drink.

NIF: Don't you have cask to give us?

BAI: Yes, but will you pay me?

POL: Certainly!

BAI: Then I'll bring you one right away. (*He leaves.*)

SCENE III

NIF: Now I hope you'll have something to drink.

POL: I can't wait to bust open the barrel.

NIF: Oh! Look! Is he coming back?

Baillenflé re-enters, rolling a cask.

SCENE IV

BAI: Here I am! Here I am! God! This is heavy!

POL: Ah! So much the better. *(Bai. rolls the cask onto Nif.)*

NIF: Hey there! Ouch! My arms! My stomach! My head!

BAI: It's a good cask!

POL: What is it that's squawking inside your cask?

NIF: Get me out from under this!

BAI: Ah! My God! Your friend!

POL: Well, help him, then.

BAI: Oh, the poor man!

NIF: Oh, I'm hurt!

POL: *(Pushing the cask onto Bai.)* Take that!

BAI: Ow! Ooooh! Help, help! I'm being squashed!

NIF: *(Getting up.)* Ah, that's better!

POL: What's the matter, Niflanguille? You're still complaining?

NIF: No, It's that idiot under there. *(Bai. continues to cry out. Pol. and Nif. roll the cask onto his head.)*

BAI: Hey! You're crushing my head! *(Pol. laughs.)* Rascals! *(Getting out.)* You pushed that cask on top of

105

me on purpose! All right, I want my money and you're going to pay me now!

POL: What do you want?

BAI: Money

POL: Don't you know me?

BAI: Why sure I know you and that's why I want my money.

POL: Well, if you know me, you ought to know that I never give any money.

BAI: Well, that's all right with me. This person here, looks respectable. He'll pay for you.

NIF: But I'm not Polichinelle's banker.

BAI: Will you pay me anyway?

POL: No.

BAI: All right then, I'll take my cask away.

POL: No! No!

BAI: This is too much!

POL: Yes, here's a deposit. (*He hits him.*)

BAI: All right. Now you listen! I've been a cooper and I'm going to treat you like a stave! (*He takes a hammer.*)

POL: Well, we'll see about that!

BAI: (*Singing and beating him.*) Tra la la la.

POL: Tra la la la.

NIF: (*With a club, singing and beating, too.*) Tra la la

POL: Eh! Oh! Ah! He! Houm! Ahic! Good-by. (*He leaves.*)

SCENE V

BAI: You better run away too! (*Knocks club out of Nif.'s hands.*) Pif! Paf! Here take this for your cousin!

NIF: I'm not his cousin on the club side.

BAI: It's nothing to me. I'll treat you like a barrel. Pan! Pun! Pan!

NIF: Oh, I'm hooped! (*He runs.*)

SCENE VI

BAI: Ah, these tricksters thought they could put one over on me, but I'm going to amuse them with another surprise. Hey, hey! My brother the sorcerer! Would you please come here?
Enter Sorcerer. They bow.

SCENE VII

SOR: What can I do for you, my brother?

BAI: I want you to enchant....

SOR: Me to enchant?

BAI: Yes, that you enchant this cask so that it will stir up some trouble for Polichinelle and Niflanguille. They beat me up terribly.

SOR: All right. It will be as you asked. Parafini.... Parafino....

BAI: Hey! What are you saying?

SOR: Don't break the spell! (*He hits him with his wand.*)

BAI: Ouch!

SOR: Teribiri, diriboro.

BAI: Do you think that will do it?

SOR: (*Hitting him another blow.*) Quiet!

BAI: The devil! I won't move anymore.

SOR: Ron ton ton tinoto. It's done.

BAI: What have you put into it?

SOR: Don't look inside, or you'll be sorry.

BAI: Ah! Bah!

SOR: Is that all you want?

BAI: Since you guarantee that my cask is enchanted, that's all I ask of you.

SOR: You can give it to them. After such a gift, they'll never walk on the same side of the street with you. Good-by.

BAI: Thank you. Good-by. (*They bow. In leaving, the Sor. whacks Bai.*)

SCENE VIII

BAI: Good! He and his big words! Well, anyhow he has enchanted my cask. Now for some laughs. (*Calling.*) Hey, Polichinelle!

POL: (*From the wings.*) Hey, friend, Baillenflé!

BAI: Hey, Niflanguille!

NIF: (*From the wings.*) Hey, Baillenflé!

BAI: Come quick. Come quick, my friends!
Nif. and Pol. enter.

SCENE IX

POL: What does he mean, his friends?

BAI: Yes, my friends, I've thought it over—I don't want any bad blood between us. I give you my cask!

NIF: I don't get it.

POL: You give us the cask?

BAI: I make a gift to you—do you understand?

POL: That's because it's empty.

BAI: Oh, on the contrary! I guarantee you that it is full.

NIF: Well, we'll soon see.

Three European cousins of Punch are seen above: German
Kasperle marionette by Walter Oberholzer (top, left); Russian hand
puppet of Petrouchka (bottom, left) by Zaitseff;
gaudily dressed French Polichinelle (right) has large wood
head supported by stick, dates from 19th century.

Guignol toy theater cutout was sold in
19th-century France. Characters included audience
and human actors as well as puppets.

POL: Yes, let's open it up.

BAI: Drink to my health, won't you? (*Leaving, he bumps his head.*) Ooops, I slipped! (*He looks attentively at the ground.*)

POL: Well, go on then. (*He hits him and sends him on his way!*)

SCENE X

POL: (*Pol. and Nif. try to open the cask.*) Oh, oh. I can't budge it.

(*The crocodile sticks his head out and grabs Pol. by the nose.*)

POL: Oh! Oh! My nose! The devil! What is it? A fish? It must be water and not wine.

NIF: No, it's a crocodile. We're lost!

POL: No, she is sweet, this little creature. (*Crocodile jumps out after him.*) Hey there, maybe she's hungry. Do you want something to eat? (*He holds out his club. The crocodile takes it down into the cask. Pol. gives him some more.*) Here, take some fishbones. Choke yourself! (*The crocodile appears again with his mouth open.*) What? More? All right, here is Madame Cassandre's broom—Madame Cababuche's frying pan—Monsieur Grippandouille's hat, a mattress from Monsieur Berlingue, two mattresses, three, four, five, six mattresses. (*The crocodile carries them all into the barrel.*) Well, you ought to be satisfied now! (*The crocodile takes Nif.'s wig.*)

NIF: Hey there!

POL: Oh, it's Niflanguille you want! Uh huh, well, here he is!

NIF: No, no, no! Polichinelle! Hola! Hola! (*Crocodile takes him.*)

SCENE XI

POL: (*Laughs and draws near the cask. Crocodile pokes his head out.*) Me too? Oh, no! Not me! (*He shuts the barrel.*) You stay in there. (*He sits on the lid.*) Oh! He's bouncing me! (*He jumps.*) Heh! Wait! (*The crocodile throws him into the air.*) Thief! Stop, thief! Police! Help, police!

Enter the Gendarme.

SCENE XII

GEN: Who called police? Who called police? Oh, it's you, Polichinelle. How come?

POL: Well, it's for the first time in my life, but it's very serious.

GEN: Well, what is it then? What's the matter?

POL: There's a frightful criminal in this barrel.

GEN: Is he a tough character?

POL: I think so. He's already eaten a man!

GEN: Oooh! Then he must be a cannibal.

POL: No, he's a crocobal.

GEN: I wouldn't know. Hey, criminal! Come out of there so that I can arrest you.

POL: (*Mimicking.*) Hey, criminal! Come out of there so that he can arrest you.

GEN: You can't hide from me. I'm a policeman.

POL: (*Mimicking.*) You can't hide from him. He's a policeman.

GEN: Hey, criminal! Come out of there. Oh, a thousand devils. He's getting under my skin. (*Shaking the barrel.*) Do you hear me? (*Crocodile grabs him and pulls him into the barrel.*) Help! Help! Help!

SCENE XIII

POL: Yes, when the crocodile finishes eating, arrest him, since that's your business! (*Crocodile comes out again.*) Oh, he's going to come out for his little walk. (*He caresses the crocodile.*) Oh, how nice he is—how sweet he is—pretty, pretty, pretty! (*The crocodile grabs him by the nose.*) Ouch! My nose! (*He gets away—crocodile gets him by the backside. Pol. yells, dragging everything around the stage.*) Ouch, you're pinching me! (*He gets away and comes back with a soldier who carries a cannon.*)

SCENE XIV

POL: Aim your cannon right there! That's right! Now stay there while I load it!

SOL: But that animal is going to eat me!

POL: No danger. Only take care that he doesn't get away.

SOL: Yes. But hurry up and light the fuse.

POL: Don't move. Ready. Aim. Fire! (*Gun explodes and kills the soldier.*)

SOL: Oh, I'm dead! (*Crocodile takes him.*)

SCENE XV

POL: Oh, the poor man! How generous he is to let himself get killed like that. (*He goes to pick up the cannon and burns himself.*) Ouch, it's too hot! (*He throws it.*) Oh, that crocodile, I wish I could get rid of her. Let's see if there's any wine left! (*Crocodile gets him from behind again.*) Oh, my God! Let go of me! (*They chase*

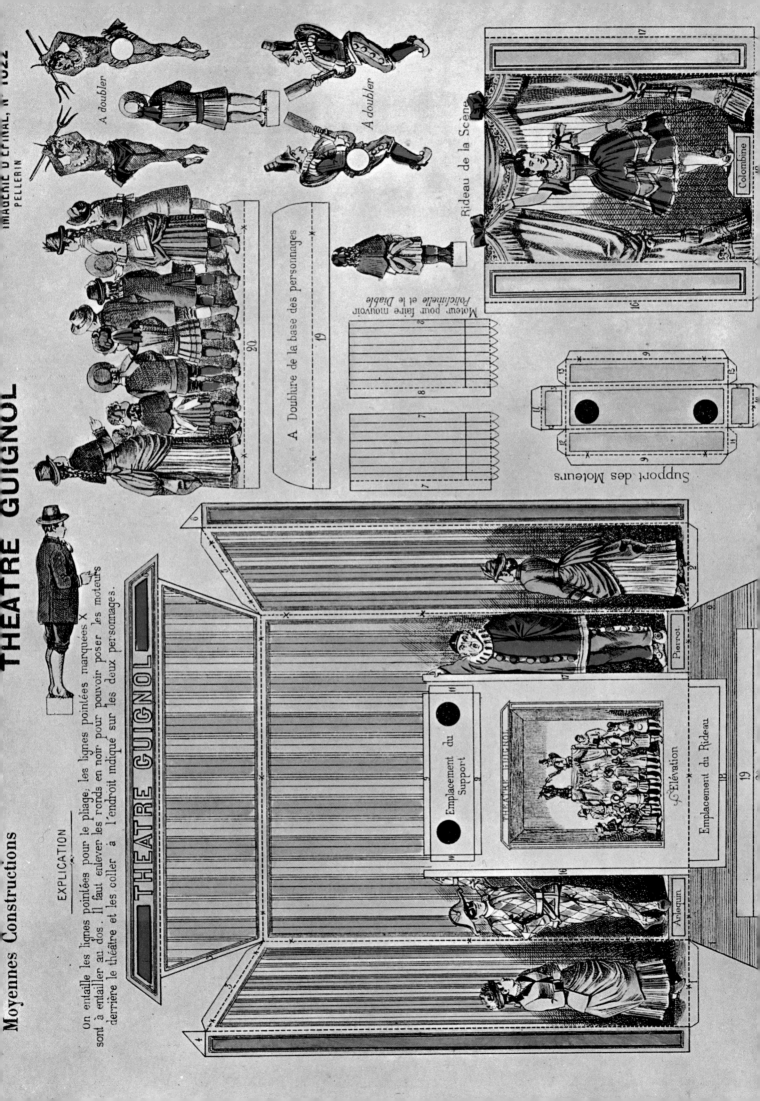

THÉATRE GUIGNOL

Moyennes Constructions

IMAGERIE D'ÉPINAL, N° 1022
PELLERIN

EXPLICATION

On entaille les lignes pointées pour le pliage; les lignes pointées marquées X sont à entailler au dos. Il faut enlever les ronds en noir pour pouvoir poser les moteurs derrière le théâtre et les coller à l'endroit indiqué sur les deux personnages.

A doubler

A doubler

Rideau de la Scène

Colombine

A Doublure de la base des personnages

Moteur pour faire mouvoir Polichinelle et le Diable

Support des Moteurs

THÉATRE GUIGNOL

Emplacement du Support

Pierrot.

D'Élévation

Emplacement du Rideau

Arlequin

around the theater. When they reach the cask, Polichinelle climbs in and sticks his head out. He sings:)
"In my beautiful chateau
My Tantirelirelire."
(The crocodile jumps toward him. Polichinelle hides his head, then sticks it back out, the crocodile being far away.)

"In my beautiful chateau
My friend the croco
Is a drunken so-an-so."
(Same play. Then the crocodile gets into the cask. Polichinelle cries and runs away. The crocodile pursues him and leaves.)
Oh, my God! He's in my house! He'll eat up my wife and children. They haven't got a chance! Help, help! *Enter Sorcerer.*

SCENE XVI

POL: Huh? Another crocodile? Oh, no, it's the sorcerer. The wine seller's brother! I see it all now. You put the crocodile in the cask!

SOR: I put him in there to eat you up!

POL: Well, he ate up everybody except me.

SOR: Drat! I went wrong in my calculations.

POL: If you don't want any more trouble, fish him out with your line.

SOR: Yes, but where is he?

POL: *(Showing him the crocodile, who enters with a ham in his teeth.)* There he is! Still eating!

Backstage at the Josserand Guignol theater in 19th-century Lyons. This picture, dated 1871, shows Josserand family (holding puppets) greeting friends. Note unusually large proscenium, scripts.

SOR: Tiribiri, didiboro, ron ton ton tee no to. (*The crocodile bites Pol. The Sorcerer frees Pol. and captures the crocodile.*) I've got him this time.

POL: You wait here. I'm going to get a gallows We'll hang him. (*He leaves.*)

SOR: Good idea! Hurry up!

POL: (*With the gallows.*) All right, hang him quick! (*He leaves.*)

SOR: So, that's the way you're going to help me, huh?

POL: Oh, but he made such a face at me! (*He hides behind the cask.*)

SOR: But I'll never be able to hang him all by myself.

POL: Are you done? Have you finished?

SOR: Not yet.

POL: You're taking your time.

SOR: It's done.

POL: (*Armed with a club.*) Infamous crocodile! You wanted to eat me, and see! Now you are hanged! (*He is going to hit the crocodile, but he hits the Sorcerer.*)

SOR: Watch out, you cowardly idiot!

POL: Those are high-sounding words.

SOR: You can drink now.

POL: Yes, what's to stop me now?

SOR: Not me. (*He wraps the crocodile around the gallows and leaves.*)

SCENE XVII

POL: Now will I have fun! (*We hear the whistle of the Devil, who appears with his pitchfork*) Oh! The villainous crocodile!

DEVIL: (*He puts Pol. in the barrel and carries him off.*) And that for all thieves and drunkards!

While Punch swept the field and eventually reigned supreme in England, Polichinelle—dear to the hearts of Frenchmen as he was—encountered competition which finally overcame him and banished him from the stage forever. This was Guignol, who has given his name, as Punch and Kasperle gave theirs, to identify the hand-puppet theater of his country.

Guignol occurred, almost by accident, in Lyons toward the end of the eighteenth century. It is said Laurent Mourguet, who operated a hand-puppet theater, heard a friend exclaim, *"C' est guignolant!"* ("It's a scream!") about something that pleased him, and promptly put the words in the mouth of a character who played with Polichinelle. Audiences laughed and called the character Guignol. Mourguet, realizing he was onto something, developed his creation carefully. Guignol wears the simple costume of the Lyonese silkworker. He has a coat of a solid color and an

111

old, beat-up, tricornered hat pulled down at the sides; a long pigtail extends from the back of his head. The expression under the hat is young, gay, and perky. Guignol is a goodhearted citizen, uneducated and inclined to revelry, but natively shrewd. He is not easily surprised or bamboozled.

The Mourguet theater prospered and was handed down through the family. Old Laurent died in 1844 at the age of ninety-nine, leaving behind some two score plays, a few of which are still in the repertoires of today's Guignol theater. The family enterprise continued to flourish under his son Jacques. One of Jacques's daughters married Laurent Josserand, and when *their* son Laurent was married, his father-in-law, Monsieur Dunand, entered the business. It was a lucky stroke, for Dunand is credited with creating Gnafron, Guignol's best friend and constant companion. Between them, young Josserand and his father-in-law not only added substantially to the literature of Guignol, but rejuvenated the works of Mourguet.

Today Polichinelle has disappeared, but Guignol carries on strongly. The traditional theater continues in Lyons. In Paris, Robert Desarthis, a second-generation puppeteer who began to work professionally at the age of seven, offers Guignol for children and more elaborate marionette shows for adults in the Luxembourg Gardens.

A remarkable aspect of modern Guignol is the participation of the audience. The children answer almost as a unit when Guignol speaks to them. They know their Guignol well, and the theater rocks with their responses. It is a fast, happy show.

One very active puppeteer may handle the whole thing—lights, curtain, sound tape, and puppets, which he changes with rapidity. Props and light switches are just below the playboard. At knee height hangs a big piece of sheet metal which makes the crashing sound when kicked, to accompany each bump of a head or blow with a club. An operator frequently finds himself standing on one foot, kicking the metal with the other, and manipulating puppets with both hands!

George Prentice, of California, is an old-timer who has been playing Punch for nearly forty years. A well-knit, sturdy bundle of a man, George works almost continually and travels some fifty thousand miles a year. If anyone travels more or farther, I don't know him. One week George may be in the Arctic, the next in Japan or the Philippines, and after that in London's Palladium (where he has had runs as long as eight months). He appears before the audience with a large suitcase and in seconds has unfolded it into a Punch frame designed to represent a house. Instantly he starts his show; he exudes energy, and his performances move at a swift pace. His Punch has slipped rather far from the basic British routine, but his action is vigorous enough to be in the tradition.

He uses a fiber slapstick, which makes a good sound, but erodes his puppets unmercifully. Every so often he has to pave their faces with sole leather. He uses a skunk to great advantage. When Punch says, "Pussy, pussy, pussy," to the skunk it sounds very well through the swazzle.

When Ed Wynn was starring in *The Laugh Parade* on Broadway in the early 1930s, he had a number in which he appeared dressed as Punch and pushing a booth on casters. He turned the booth so the audience could see backstage, then

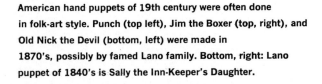

American hand puppets of 19th century were often done in folk-art style. Punch (top left), Jim the Boxer (top, right), and Old Nick the Devil (bottom, left) were made in 1870's, possibly by famed Lano family. Bottom, right: Lano puppet of 1840's is Sally the Inn-Keeper's Daughter.

turned it again, ducked inside, and the little curtain opened on a most amusing Punch play. When it was over, Ed came out with Punch on one hand, the Devil on the other, and a squeaker in his mouth. But it was young George Prentice, unacknowledged and unlisted, who slipped under the backdrop every night to do the show.

There are about fifty professional Punch men active in England today and as many amateur companies. Many of them double in magic. Still,

their Punch is more vigorous than ever, and probably better performed. Percy Press is England's leader in the art. Beginning as a stage player and comedy performer, he took up the cudgel and swazzle in 1933, and in wartime went into uniform with his frame and delighted the troops, as his predecessors had done. (We can be sure Punch traveled with Wellington.) Press is now recognized as Britain's top authority on Punch, as he continues to play in music halls, on TV,

French troopship, on way to Crimean War (above), carried Polichinelle show that performed in horse stall on deck. Troupe, which may have been Lyonese or Parisian, provided show to soldiers' taste. In contrast, polite Victorian gathering at right was probably a Christmas entertainment or children's party in rich home. Note Panpipes around neck of "bottler."

in the cinema, and on the beaches.

On Saturday, May 26, 1962, there was a great celebration at St. Paul's Church in London to commemorate the three-hundredth anniversary of Punch's first performance in England. Forty professors gathered from all over England for a service in the church and then for a mass performance outside. A huge booth had been erected, a large crowd had assembled. Clowns outside the booth played music and beat their drums, cackling and calling for Mr. Punch. Up he pops, bandys conversation with a clown, then bangs the playboard three times with his cudgel. Suddenly a sunburst of Punches appear. The forty professors have crowded their wide variety of Punch figures on stage as a tribute to the progenitor of them all. And on a wall of St. Paul's was affixed a plaque reading: "Near this spot Punch's puppet show was first performed in England and witnessed by Samuel Pepys 1662."

ORLANDO FURIOSO: THE FLOWER OF CHIVALRY

7

The curtain rises on a medieval courtyard. Two knights in shining armor are conversing in flamboyant Italian. The golden one, on the right, is angry and as he speaks he beats his breastplate to accent his words. The other knight, an evil-visaged and mustachioed warrior in black armor, turns to the audience with a whining snarl. This is Gano, the traitor. The audience growls and hisses. The knightly converse becomes more heated. The golden one, Ruggiero, steps forward and back with a stiff-legged regal stride, pounding the wooden stage with his feet. Gano beats his shield with his sword, and then both knights turn and exit at opposite sides of the stage.

Immediately the courtyard backdrop is pulled up to reveal a scarred and battered woodland glade with a castle in the distance. The warriors re-enter and the harsh words resume. Both then lower their visors, pull up their shields, and begin to slash at each other with their swords. They step apart, then clash. Thump, bang, clash. The armor rattles, the stage resounds with the fury of their blows.

They pause. Then comes a long, impassioned speech by Gano. Ruggiero's answer is ridicule, punctuated by metallic breast beatings and foot stampings. They draw back, then fly together, chopping at each other furiously as they meet in mid-air. They drop to earth and continue to fight.

Then, as if in complete scorn of the other's powers, Ruggiero makes a complete turn, showing his back to Gano after every stroke. But Gano is wounded and cannot take advantage of this flaunting challenge. He departs, swearing revenge.

As he leaves, three of his henchmen arrive and engage the golden warrior. Ruggiero is hard-pressed, but after several exchanges one of the newcomers cries out and topples to the ground. Now there are but two. Then Ruggiero's fearsome sword flashes and a soldier's head flies off. The body slumps on top of the first luckless warrior and down comes the head, including the long iron control rod. The third of Gano's men is polished off with one stroke, even as reinforcements arrive. In a few minutes there is a pile of warriors on the stage, most of them headless.

This is a brief description of one short battle in one of the numerous episodes of the five hundred plays that constitute the Sicilian marionette epic, *Orlando Furioso*. Orlando is one of the few durable heroes, along with Punch, Karaghioz, and Kasperle, who has given his name to a distinctive type of puppet show. In this case it is an almost endless tale of medieval chivalry, based in fact, but inevitably embellished and adorned by the poets, troubadours, and puppeteers of several countries and over five centuries.

Historically, Orlando is Roland, an eighth-century Frankish knight who served as a commander on the Breton border of Charlemagne's great empire. In 778 A.D., as Charlemagne's army returned from fighting the Saracens in Spain, the rear guard was cut off by hostile Basques at a pass in the Pyrenees and Roland was killed.

It was the stuff of which legends are woven, and eventually, in the eleventh or twelfth century, it emerged as *The Song of Roland,* one of the *chansons de geste*—literally, songs of deeds—with which French lords and ladies titillated themselves in the so-called "courts of love." By that time Roland had become Charlemagne's nephew, as well as one of his most trustworthy knights, the

Basques had become Saracens, and the fatal battleground the still-existing pass of Roncesvalles.

In outline the story is the same, but the new version palpitates with warm human emotion. Roland—with his magic sword, Durlindana—commands the doomed rear guard, which is attacked by the Saracens through the treachery of Ganelon, count of Mayence and vassal of Charlemagne. Noble Roland refuses to blow his ivory horn to recall his king until it is too late. Roland is the last to die; as his life ebbs he hears Charlemagne returning. The faithless Ganelon is tried and executed.

Several hundred years later, at the height of the Renaissance, the Italian poet Ludovico Ariosto came forth with a remarkable grab bag of history, fantasy, and legend called *Orlando Furioso*. Orlando is, of course, the Roland of old, the invincible and invulnerable knight beyond compare. An important part of the Ariosto poem is Orlando's frustrated love for Angelica, whom he pursues even at the neglect of his duty. When she marries someone else, Orlando goes mad—hence, *Furioso*.

But this is only a beginning. There is Orlando's cousin Rinaldo, who also loves Angelica, but inadvertently drinks from the fountain of hate while she drinks from the fountain of love, and then vice versa, and so on.

And there is Rogero, who is in love with Rinaldo's sister Bradamante, but is loved by Marfisa, a Moorish girl who eventually turns out to be his sister.

Meanwhile, the good knight Astolfo rides the hippogriff to the moon to recover poor Orlando's lost wits.

This obviously is the finest of puppet fare,

and with improvements and additions by generations of puppeteers, it has become—and is today—a great, rich feast of giants, dragons, witches, ogres, eagles, magic swords, intrigues, transformations, heroics, betrayals, loves requited and unrequited, and deaths noble and ignoble. One complete version set down in the early nineteenth century began with Milone, the father of Orlando, and carried on through the death of Rinaldo, a journey which ran to three volumes and three thousand pages. To see every Orlando play from beginning to end would take more than three years of theater evenings.

The Orlando marionettes, although known in northern France, Belgium, and elsewhere to a certain extent, found their warmest and most sympathetic acceptance in Sicily. Why here? It's easy to generalize; but it may be that in this prodigious epic Sicilians found reflections of their own bloodstained past, of their complicated intrigues and family feuds, of Saracen invasions, of violence and revenge.

In its slow progress from medieval France to Renaissance Italy, the story also has taken on many Sicilian colors and flavors. Rogero is now Ruggiero. Ganelon de Mayence is Gano di Maganza. Rinaldo is now prince of Montalbano, and in some ways even overshadows Orlando. He is the most colorful of the paladins, a ladies' man who will risk any danger for love. He now has seven hundred followers, once bandits but here a kind of Robin Hood fellowship whom Rinaldo calls "heroes of the countryside"—a kinship Sicilian audiences understand. Altogether the Orlando plays require some three hundred characters, not counting foot soldiers, witches, dragons, angels, devils, and women.

119

Belgium and Sicily still boast active Orlando
companies. Below: Brussels troupe of Armand Deschamps
performs in 11th-century church. Right: Outdoor show in Catania.

There is a fierce power and an air of excitement about the marionetti of Sicily. The paladins are four to five feet tall—nearly life-size—and with their armor weigh up to eighty pounds apiece. Size denotes rank. A captain is necessarily shorter than Prince Orlando or his cousin Oliver by half a head, and a foot soldier, the faceless ones of the armies of either side, may be fifteen inches shorter than a paladin, weighing in at a mere fourteen pounds. The Emperor Charlemagne, reputedly a seven-footer in life, is also a very large marionette. In fact, only a giant may top the knight.

The paladin figures are majestically designed, with broad shoulders, slim waists, and expanses of shining metal. The bodies are roughly shaped from one piece of wood. Slots are cut in the base of the torso to hinge the stiff wooden legs, excelsior and cloth are used as padding to fill out the chest, and a heavy iron sword is bolted into the marionette's right hand and is controlled by a thick iron rod attached at the guard. The operator works the sword rod with his right hand, while his left holds the hooked end of an even heavier rod extending down through the wooden head and neck where it again hooks through an iron loop in the body.

The armor is hammered out of brass plates, quite heavy in weight and handsomely embossed. It can stand up under a pounding, although usually there is one Orlando figure in shining armor, velvet cape, and beautiful plumes for the talking scenes and another (the stunt man) slightly battered figure for the fighting. Many a fine shield has been ruined in a week of combat and has had to be replaced. Nothing is wasted, however. The dented shield usually is passed down the line to a lesser knight or a foot soldier.

Over the years Orlando and his fellow knights have achieved enormous style. Their carriage is erect and movement is controlled only through the impetus of the iron rod, which lifts or twists the body at the neck. The swinging body motion also governs the stiff-legged stride which is so impressive. The paladin swings a leg backward to gain momentum and then, with a twist of the body, marches forward with a thump, ka-thump, ka-thump rhythm, each step resounding on the hollow wooden floor. An iron strip under the instep prevents the feet from breaking, as alternately they take the full weight of the walking figure. This stride is famous all over Sicily. Students stiffen up and fall into the Orlando walk just for fun when they meet in the street.

The very proud, regal style of the knights dictates an elaborate language of gesture to help convey their moods and feelings. The back of the hand to the cheek means weeping, the palm to the face means thought.

Palermo, Sicily, marionette theaters continue
to show adventures of Orlando and Angelica, as in
drawing above. Right: American Manteo
family offers audiences such startling visual
effects as this fiery explosion. Flamethrower is
the Christian magician Maligigi, his
intended victim the Saracen giant at right. To make
fire, powdered resin is thrown from
side and ignited with torch just as magician's
arm is swung at advancing foe.

122

Heraldry also identifies the knights. Ruggiero's shield bears an eagle argent on an azure ground. Rinaldo has a lion rampant. Olivero bears a sun and a motto: "Till he comes."

The first references to the Orlando story being played by marionettes appear in the sixteenth century. We do not know what the plays were like, although we do know that the type of marionette (with the heavy hooked rod through the head) had been in use since Roman times.

More evidence begins to show up in the seventeenth century. In an episode in Cervantes's *Don Quixote,* the Don is watching a marionette show wherein the Emperor Charlemagne berates one Don Gayferos, whose wife has been imprisoned by the Moors and who has done nothing to rescue her. Gayferos, angered by the scolding, demands to borrow the magic sword Durlindana from Don Rolando (Orlando). It is during the ensuing rescue attempt that Don Quixote draws his sword, rushes forward from the audience, and hacks the

Moors to pieces, demolishing the puppet show.

The same episode occurs again some eighty-nine years later in England in Tom Durfey's *Comical History of Don Quixote,* a bluff and bawdy play suited to the humors of Restoration England.

Don Gayferos is a purely Spanish creation, but it has always been standard procedure to introduce local characters wherever Orlando is played. Charlemagne's court is peopled with Sicilian heroes in Sicily, Frenchmen in France, and so on. In Liége, in Belgium, where at one time in the 1920s there were sixty-nine marionette companies playing the *Paladins of France,* it was entirely natural to have Tchanchet (the local Kasperle), a little old clown in an enormous stovepipe hat, appear in modern dress on the same stage with Orlando.

To the puppeteer "Orlando" is a way of life. The exciting mythology, the creation of the actors, and the nightly performing completely absorb the being of the player.

One such puppeteer was Agrippino Manteo, who was orphaned in 1887, at the age of four, in Catania, Sicily. Having no place to live, Agrippino and his sister began to sleep behind the stage of the puppet theater of Pepino Crimi. Pepino was already a second-generation puppeteer, one of eleven children of a former university professor who established a theater of the *palladini* in 1858.

When he became old enough, Agrippino earned his living in the Crimi theater. He was fascinated by the work and determined to have his own theater when he grew up.

He did. At twenty-one he emigrated with his new wife to Argentina, where he worked as a baker until he could build enough marionettes

Don Quixote and Sancho Panza watch
Orlando battle involving the magic sword Durlindana
in sketch by noted artist Gustave Dore.
Soon the impressionable Don will draw his own sword
and rescue puppet hero from Moors.

to open his theater. Four years later the Manteos, now increased by three children, added a restaurant to their theater. The family lived in one big room behind the stage. Mama Manteo cooked for the restaurant and sewed costumes for the marionettes.

World War I disrupted their lives. Agrippino returned to Europe to serve in the Italian army, and after the war decided to go to the United States, instead of returning to Argentina, where the original marionettes still were packed away. There were a few companies of Italian marionetti in New York in the early twenties, but Agrippino was the genius. He worked nights to build a troupe, with two men hammering brass into the intricate shapes of the armor, another two soldering the brass, and a fifth man making the clothes. He acquired sixty additional figures from an old player and in 1923 opened a theater on Catherine Street, on New York's Lower East Side.

His first show began with the Constantine cycle, which takes six months to play, and ends the first month with the old Roman emperor's conversion to Christianity. I was there to see it once. I recall Constantine clearly as he lay on a bed, his armor removed, and his pinkish cloth skin covered with red, yellow, and black spots of leprosy. No one, from the local shamans to the devil, was able to help him, but when Constantine finally allowed the Pope to come to his bedside and convert him, the cardboard spots dramatically fluttered into the sky, each one pulling the next along with it by a short length of black string.

After the Constantine plays came the paladin cycle, starting with the grandfather of Orlando and Rinaldo, carrying through the villainies of the wicked Gano di Maganza, and concluding with the Crusades. Altogether it was a tremendous tour de force, and at the core of it were Agrippino Manteo's dramatic inventiveness and irreplaceable scripts. I have seen these scripts, all in Papa's handwriting. They are written in a small mountain of copybooks, each containing a bare outline of the action, plus certain key lines and poems transcribed in full. They all bear the marks of battle. Here there is a thumb print red with the blood of a giant (beet juice in an eggshell that broke when the sword hit), there a tear occasioned when some unlucky foot soldier's head flew too far.

By 1928 the Manteo children had grown and Papa had a full troupe of puppeteers: Ida, Michael, Dom, Pino, and Johnny. Now he moved to his famous theater at 109 Mulberry Street. There was only one outsider, Mr. Aiello, who played piano in the pit during scene changes, or whenever Papa, sitting in the wings, gave him his cue by ringing a little bell.

The audience was mostly men and mostly from the neighborhood, as would have been true in the old country. Gradually, however, the artistry of the Manteos began to attract visitors from uptown, among them Tony Sarg.

These were busy years for the Manteos. They played a show every night. During the day they were in their attic workroom repairing wounded warriors, mending torn costumes, and polishing armor. Orlando never went on without a shine. (Imagine the cleanup job after a gallon of beet juice has poured down a tube and through the ears, eyes, nose, and corners of the mouth of a dying Orlando, who has just burst a blood vessel blowing his ivory horn.)

125

Over the years the Manteos accumulated hundreds of marionettes. Some were brought from other operators, most they made themselves. "My father was a fanatic for marionettes," recalls Michael Manteo. "Mr. Chufo, a sculptor and wood carver, made our heads. Papa made the rest. Papa would say: 'Mr. Chufo, next week Rinaldo comes out as a young boy. We need two heads—one for armor.' My father never says it's no good. When Mr. Chufo makes it, it's always right."

It was completely a family enterprise. Papa spoke for all the male characters, daughter Ida, for the women. The boys manipulated the knights from a plank bridge twenty-four feet long, two feet wide, and three and a half feet above the floor. The planks were two inches thick and made an excellent sounding board for the stamping feet of the operators. A back rail, against which they leaned for support, was made of six-by-six-inch lumber, rounded on top to cushion the body or the hand. On a pipe across the front of this rail, above the backdrop, hung all the marionettes in the scene, but not actually in the boys' hands.

High on the backwall behind the bridge, rolled up on racks, were half a hundred painted drops, which the boys could set by reaching over their heads and dropping them in. A permanent backdrop made of steel was used for all the fighting scenes. Anything lighter would have been chopped to ribbons during the carnage.

Scene changes were made quickly and smoothly —unless there was a three-foot pile of dead and decapitated knights that had to be unscrambled from the stage and reassembled before the show could go on. (Decapitation was achieved by a downthrust of the control rod and a quick turn to disengage the head hook from the loop in the body. Expertly timed with a sword stroke, the maneuver never failed to delight the audience.)

Orlando was an athletic event backstage. Mike remembers one show when the mighty Papa Manteo hit so hard that he knocked Mike's marionette out of his hand, and when the curtain went down Mike got a bawling out. Once was enough, however, and none of the muscular Manteos had to worry about holding on to a marionette. Sometimes when two warriors leap at each other the puppeteers employ springs in the ceiling to help lift the enormous weight of the figures, as adversary meets adversary with the crash of one hundred and fifty pounds of metal and wood.

In one struggle between two sorcerers who could change themselves into anything they wished, the Manteo boys were required to manipulate two fifteen-foot dragons, two lions, two serpents, two bears, two griffons, two tigers, and two eagles.

In another, a hundred characters appeared on stage—fifty Christians and fifty pagans, all principals. (Women, devils, and soldiers don't count.) "You have to remember a hundred names," Mike said. "The audience does. In the battle of fifty against fifty we had to remember who died. My brother would say, 'Hey, Mike, did this guy die last night?' 'Yep,' I'd say. 'Upstairs with him.' And Pino would say, 'This one?' And I'd answer, 'Nope, hang him over there. We need him tonight.'"

"We never rehearsed at any time," said Mike. "By looking at my father we got the inspiration. When the curtain was down my father would say, 'Who's holding Orlando?' 'Dom' was the answer. 'Who's got Rinaldo?' 'Mike.' 'All right,

Folk-art faces belong to Orlando marionettes of old Belgian troupe. These fine figures are now preserved in Munich City Museum. Both marionettes have bodies of painted wood, but one in foreground also wears metal armor.

then, when Orlando turns his back, then Gano pulls the dagger.' So it went. We lived. it. We wanted to see how it came out. We wanted to please Papa and the scene came out perfectly. Papa never complimented us—oh, maybe sometimes to other people. . . .

"How long would it take to teach a man what I know now?" says Mike. "Years. Years."

The Mulberry Street theater varied its performance only once a year, for the festival of Saint Gennaro. This celebrates the saint's intervention to halt the eruption of Mount Vesuvius. Naples celebrates the event every year, and every year up to 1935, it was dramatized by the marionetti in New York. The run of Orlando or Constantine was suspended about the second week of September and the theater was made over for the new spectacle.

Mulberry Street itself becomes a carnival at Saint Gennaro time. Cars are detoured about the several blocks where the festival is to take place, and the area is decorated with arches of bright lights. Bands play at the street intersections. Booths are set up along the sidewalks to sell candies, sausages, hats, games, and chances; all the regular stores stay open late, while the proprietors and their families seat themselves on chairs in front.

Halfway down the street is the Manteo theater. The performances last about twenty minutes and are almost continuous. Mr. Aiello plays the overture and the curtain rises on a peaceful countryside, with Vesuvius in the distance. A donkey cart crosses upstage, countryfolk enter and talk. These figures are somewhat smaller than the marionetti of the Orlando cycle and help to emphasize the fearsome spectacle of the mountain.

Now the lights flicker and there is a dull rumbling, like far-off thunder. The people glance apprehensively at the mountain and flee. The countryside grows dark. A smoky green light appears at the peak of Vesuvius and sparks and fire shoot into the sky. Lava erupts from the cone and begins to roll down the mountainside and over the grassy slopes. The bubbling, boiling lava advances, accompanied by the most ominous music from Mr. Aiello, until finally the lava fills the entire forestage down to the footlights.

Suddenly, in the ceiling of the theater an opening some four feet square appears, and through it descends a painted cloud, bringing a large, lavishly gowned figure of Saint Gennaro. He blesses the upturned faces in the audience below and then turns and dismisses his cloud. Now he addresses himself to Vesuvio. For a long time he exhorts the mountain and the lava. Gradually the bubbling and boiling cease. The grass slowly reappears, and once again the stony slope of the volcano is covered with a mantle of green, as the lava obligingly reverses its course, flows uphill, and is swallowed by Vesuvio.

Lights up. The cloud returns and the saint departs, ascending (through the opening in the ceiling) to his heavenly abode.

It was a remarkably effective performance. My recollection of it is as clear as though I'd seen it last night. The green fire in Vesuvio's top and the boiling lava, made by the turning of long scrolls placed in rising succession across the stage, are completely fantastic, but believable in the context of this piece of puppetry. Even today, when I have occasion to think of Saint Gennaro, it is the image of the marionette that occurs. He was completely the character, with no feeling of the actor

Papa Manteo rehearses his children in the family's theater on New York's Lower East Side. The theater was a major attraction for many years under Manteo's dedicated direction. The entire family participated.

to confuse the conception. There is something about having the symbols right there in front of you, in three dimensions, no matter how stylized, that is very much of the truth. There they are— clear, concise, to the point. In the Middle Ages this must have been a powerful way to keep the memory of the miracle alive in people's minds.

Agrippino Manteo has long since died. The days of the Mulberry Street theater are no more, although the younger generation of Manteos still keeps the shows alive with the two hundred fig- ures that remain. Only a short time ago I felt the old pleasure and excitement as Orlando was tricked, enchanted, and given a gorilla's head. I sat back, comfortable and confident. For, half an hour later, by the directions of an ink-stained copybook and the capacious memories of several lifetimes of experience, vengeance would come. Bradamante, blond and gentle, and speaking in Ida Manteo's flutey soprano, arrived bearing Or- lando's magic sword, Durlindana, and a furious battle against fire and witchcraft ensued.

ORIENTAL TRADITION

8

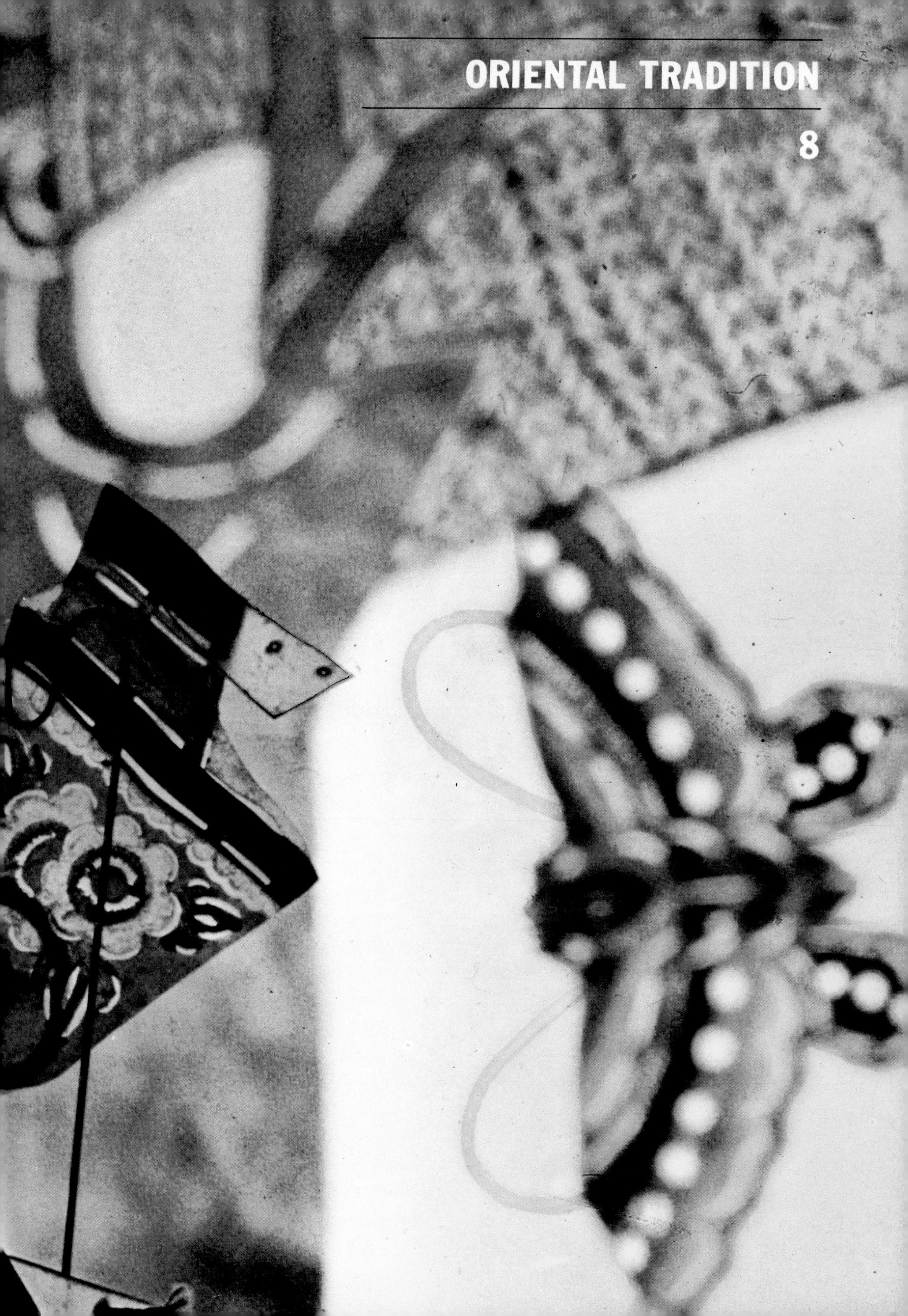

China undoubtedly had some cultural contacts beyond her borders in ancient times. In the Chou dynasty (c. 1000 B.C.), the Emperor Mu reportedly returned from a visit to Turkestan, in Central Asia, with the materials and artisans for making many new things, among them marionettes. But this may only be legend.

As for other forms of puppetry, the record is also obscure. China has them all: shadow figures, hand puppets, rod puppets. Shadows could certainly have come from the nomads of Central Asia, or perhaps from Indonesia, along with the rods. Or across the old silk route from India, along with Buddhism. But some of China's multifarious puppetry undoubtedly was generated on the spot, as it has so often happened elsewhere.

Japan's puppetry is thought to have come from Korea since her first puppeteers were considered to be outcastes, but it was not until the odd and peaceful period of isolation during the so-called Tokugawa shogunate in the seventeenth and eighteenth centuries that her unique and best-known style of puppetry—Bunraku—was evolved.

Opportunities to see puppetry in China are extremely limited these days because of the political restrictions on foreigners. Communist China uses its puppetry to spread government information among its unlettered masses.

Hand puppets in China have long been a one-man operation. The puppeteer stands inside a small booth with just enough room for himself. The level of the playboard is just above his head, and from its four sides a cloth hangs to the ground to hide him from the audience. At stage rear is the façade of a building with doors right and left through which characters can make entrances and exits; it is elaborately decorated with embroidered silk, lacquer, and tassels. Over all is an awning. The weight of the stage is supported by a single pole, leaned against a wall behind the operator.

The Chinese hand puppet is proportioned to fit the human hand closely. The operator's thumb and third finger fill the arms without artificial extensions. Heads are small. I have some clay ones (with real hair moustaches) measuring less than two inches high. There is sometimes a charming effect that happens when watching such a puppet, particularly if it is very small and requires the help of the audience's imagination to complete the picture.

The hand puppeteer plays all parts—his off-stage voice introducing, explaining, and conversing with each character—a voice of God, as it were. He provides whatever music may be needed, usually with a gong. Occasionally he uses the reed to produce a Punchlike squeak, although there are no Punches or Kasperles in Chinese puppet drama. Mostly, the plays are classics.

In one play an old shepherd tells of a fierce tiger that lives on the mountain. He boasts that he has no fear of the beast and that he will kill it. The tiger appears and puts his nose down on the playboard, at which point the shepherd says, "Oh, a pussy cat," and starts to play with it. (Mistaken identity is made for puppetry.) Now comes the other voice, that of the puppeteer, who warns: "Careful. Don't fool with the tiger. Don't be an idiot." But the old man continues to annoy the beast and then runs off. The super voice again cries, "Scared you, eh?" But the shepherd comes back with a spear and boldly pokes the tiger in the nose, saying he has killed it and that he will take its valuable skin. Suddenly the tiger springs up, swallows the old man whole, and goes to sleep. From off stage the shepherd's wife is heard calling her husband. She enters and stumbles against the tiger, but the "voice" warns her that the tiger has eaten her man. She seizes the spear and with a mighty lunge kills the tiger. She then reaches inside to drag out her husband, whom she berates for having been such a fool.

Finally, she makes him carry her home. Gongs. Many Chinese puppet plays have female heroes.

Judging from the photographs I have seen, the Chinese marionette is notable for the great number of strings—in some cases as many as forty—used to control it. An average one stands about twenty-four inches high and is sometimes equipped with a wide range of expressive motions. The mouth, the eyes, individual fingers, even the

eyebrows in some instances may be made to move.

The marionette performs in front of a simple backdrop without formal scenery. The operator stands at stage level, hidden by the drop and a low proscenium, and holds his controller forward, nearly as high as his head.

The repertoire is in the tradition of the classical live theater: stories of heroism, battles, betrayals, unrequited love, women wronged and saved — all the history and folklore that have enriched Chinese drama in the past. In addition, the stories have been changed to fit the needs of the new regime. There are works about traitors, foreign invaders, depraved and unjust emperors, greedy landowners, stupid officials, and other enemies of the common people.

The rod technique is reported to be in the ascendancy, inasmuch as it can be learned quickly. It has a long tradition in the theater, but has come into greater prominence through the influence of Russia. For some time, at any rate, the Chinese were adapting Russian rod techniques and creating figures in modern dress. They have even adapted Russian plays in which rod puppets play on the same stage with live actors.

The most highly stylized and, in my opinion, the most beautiful of all Chinese puppets are the shadow figures. There are two principal kinds: the Pekingese, or northern, shadow and the Cantonese, or southern, shadow. The Pekingese are smaller and more delicate. They are made of a fine leather taken from the belly of a donkey and painted in brilliant, translucent colors.

These bits of leather jewelry are about fourteen inches in height and are controlled by a stiff wire, which runs parallel to the front of the figure and then bends to fasten at the front of the neck. This

Chinese hand-puppet operator in "bag theater" (top) is seen in 18th-century painting. At left, a modern Chinese crowd observes puppet show on a similar stage. This type leans against a wall for support.

unique arrangement permits the figure to bow and walk, but does not interfere with the delicate tracery of the colored shadow. Since one body may be used with several different heads, the neck embodies a flat collar of leather which enables heads to be interchanged. Extra heads are slipped into slots in a muslin book for safekeeping. There is an old superstition that if the heads are not removed at night the puppets will come to life and make mischief. In other words, maybe the "shadows of ancestors" are welcome when we invoke them, but let's not have them running around loose at night.

The legs are jointed with a single knot at the hip, and one for each knee; walking is accomplished by a graceful swinging of the legs. The arms are hinged at shoulder, elbow, and wrist, and can be moved to right or left by additional rods.

Scenery is used at the top and borders of the shadow screen and may be quite elaborate, although all of it is constructed to fold up very small for easy transportation.

Shadow plays came into being between the seventh and ninth centuries A.D., and reached their highest point of development in the eleventh. A typical one of this period concerns the fantastic adventures of Lei Feng Ta, the White Serpent Lady. One episode is *The Theft of the Miraculous Grass*, which White Serpent must acquire in order to cure her lover. Another is *The Flooding of the Monastery of the Golden Mountain*, in which White Serpent does battle with the powers of heaven, who have taken her husband away.

A little playlet of folk origin is the fable of the crane and the tortoise. The boastful crane and the patient tortoise are unlikely antagonists, and

much of the humor lies in this fact. "How long can such by-play be made to last?" writes Sergei Obraztsov, the Russian puppet master, who has seen it. "Apparently for the whole of seven minutes, and for seven minutes the audience is in fits of laughter."

The Cantonese shadows are larger than the Pekingese and necessarily made of thicker leather. A red face indicates boldness, black means honesty. The control rod is like that of Karaghioz, with the supporting rod held at an angle, back toward the puppeteer.

Japan has had a tradition of hand, string, and rod puppetry from early feudal times, but the western world is most familiar with the Bunraku method, which is unlike that of any other country in the world. Its dramatic material has achieved a high degree of sophistication and so have its puppets, both in design and manipulation. The puppets are beautifully designed and costumed. Yet at the same time their method of operation is essentially primitive. I say this because the operator holds the figure just in front of his body, and, therefore, it is just a step away from the primitive mask. In modern Bunraku, the principal operator is aided by two hooded assistants, but because the knowledgeable audience is used to this convention the focus is on the characters. The technique, as in all puppetry, is taken for granted.

The Bunraku figures are large, from three and a half to four and a half feet tall, but are much lighter in weight than marionettes of a comparable size, since the principal puppeteer must hold the weight of the figure forward, in front of him. An opening in the back enables the puppeteer to hold a control stick with his left hand, which turns or nods the head, while with a series of levers he may move the mouth, eyes, and eyebrows in much the same way as a ventriloquist's dummy is operated. The puppet's right arm, moved by the operator's right hand, is often jointed and controlled by levers, so as to bend the puppet's thumb or fingers. Thus, it can make elaborate gestures and pick things up, or play a musical instrument. The voluminous sleeves of the puppet's kimono allow the puppeteer to slip his hand unobtrusively down behind the wooden hand to assist in handling a sword or a heavy prop. Indeed the flowing kimonos or elaborate armor are essential to the grand manner of Bunraku; the same movements in modern dress would be unthinkable.

The first of the principal puppeteer's two black-hooded assistants controls the left arm and hand and is known as a "left-hand man." The other, usually an apprentice, moves the legs. This trio of operators imparts a very special kind of motion to the principals in the Bunraku theater. It is as though the character dances through the motions of everyday life.

In addition to the major figures, there are a number of subordinate characters for the minor, and usually comic, roles of servants and peasants. These are more limited figures and can be handled by one man. Faces are likely to be extremely caricatured and without moving features. The left arm and both legs must shift for themselves.

Apprentice puppeteers begin their long training on figures like these, then graduate to the legs of a major figure. They achieve the rank of puppeteer when they are able to handle the left hand. Puppeteers are trained, incidentally, to operate either male or female figures, but not

Above: Chinese shadow figure of highly complicated cutout pattern. Opposite, upper right: A group of Peking shadow figures. Flags on backs denote high rank. Cutout wheel at waist of figures gives strength and transparency to them. The duck at right could perform effectively with movable neck and leg joints. The ox at far right has wagging tail operated by string attached to stick.

both. Once the choice is made, it is never changed.

Japanese puppeteers are expected only to become artists at moving the figures. The narration of the play is the responsibility of the so-called *joruri* reciter. He sits at stage left, on an elongated section of the apron, speaking, reading, singing, and occasionally superimposing one over the other. It is every bit as skillful as the action on stage. The reciter describes the settings and costumes, explains the motives and emotions of the characters as the play progresses, and reads the dialogue in a variety of subtle voices, changing his tone with the mood of play or character. A group of samisen musicians, sitting behind him on the apron, gives rhythm and pace to the play.

The Bunraku-za of Osaka, rebuilt in 1955, has a company of thirty-one puppeteers, thirty-eight *joruri*, and forty-seven samisen players. Its new theater has a thousand seats.

The repertoire of the Bunraku theater today consists of some twenty plays, most of them by Chikamatsu Monzaemon, the greatest dramatist in Japanese history. He lived from 1653 to 1725, and some one hundred and thirty of his plays survive. He wrote originally for human actors, but then switched to puppets, which he—and other Japanese dramatists—found infinitely superior. The stage manners of the puppets were restrained; they did not indulge in uncalled-for improvisations. They could be relied on for precise interpretations of the meticulous scripts.

Chikamatsu's plays are today the foundation stones of the Japanese national drama, much as Shakespeare's plays are basic to western drama.

Opposite: Sketch (bottom, left) shows Chinese marionette control. Japanese woodcut of 18th-century (bottom, right) depicts hand puppets, probably *Kitsune* (fox spirit). At left, Bunraku principal operator (unmasked) controls body, head, and right hand of puppet. Left-hand operator with black hood is visible below puppet's sword handle. Legs are controlled by apprentice who also wears hood. (He is hidden by others). Below is panoramic view of Bunraku theater. *Joruri* reciter and samisen player are traditionally at stage left.

Puppet theater in Japan began about the tenth century A.D., probably for religious purposes. Later it became the hobby of mounted hunters, when they were not active with their bows and arrows. Sixteenth-century records speak of puppetry being used in the spread of Buddhism.

By the late sixteenth-century, the art became secularized and puppetry became one of the diversions and accomplishments acquired by the courtesans of Kobe and Osaka for the amusement of their patrons. Early in the seventeenth century the first narration with samisen accompaniment in Osaka was *Joruri Junidan Zoshi*—"Concerning the Loves of the Princess Joruri." Later the combination of this style of theater with puppetry created the new dramatic form.

This was a brilliant period in Japanese history. It was, first of all, a time of prosperity, when tradesmen and merchants were acquiring not only wealth but status. As a consequence, the Bunraku plays concerning the life of the nobility were eagerly patronized by the lower-caste tradesmen. This was the only touch they could have with the culture of the court, which was beyond their reach socially. When political stability was achieved under the leadership of the Tokugawa shoguns, the arts—and particularly the puppet drama—reached great heights. For a period (1727-47), the art of the Kabuki theater waned and the puppets were supreme. Only by borrowing scripts, music, and style from the puppet theater was the Kabuki able to make a comeback at all. Anyone who has followed the Kabuki theater can recognize the nonpersonal, puppetlike quality of the performance.

Puppeteers carved their own figures in the early days, the heads generally from cherry wood.

But in the time of Chikamatsu, two excellent sculptors—Sasaya Hachibei and Sasaya Yoshibei—set a style which has been followed ever since. Most contemporary heads are imitations of those of the two Sasayas. Many fine heads were destroyed when the Osaka theater was bombed during the Second World War, and many of the best of the survivors are in museums or private collections today.

On the island of Awaji, just south of Osaka, there is a simpler type folk Bunraku practiced by the farming population. During their slack seasons, the months of January and May, a puppet fever seizes the inhabitants of this small island and almost everybody participates as puppeteer, stage manager, musician, or spectator. At one time as many as thirty-five companies assembled for the festivals, and even today they can muster seven or eight groups. The style is not as refined as in Osaka, but the performances are notable for their verve and enthusiasm.

Japan is a combination of the extremely modern, with the beauty and grace of the traditional. Along with the beautiful and traditional Bunraku, modern puppetry has developed well. About 1923 two new groups of marionette and hand puppets appeared, bringing to Japan the styles then popular in Germany. "PUK" theater, a descendant of one of these groups started by Toji Kawajiri, made remarkable progress and became the largest in a field of many. Despite suppression during the Second World War, when two of PUK's members died in prison, the theater has made a fresh start and now thrives under the direction of Taji Kawajiri, brother of its founder.

Japanese puppetry continues in a thoroughly modern, but entirely Japanese spirit.

Bunraku puppet head of *Bunshichi* expresses valor and masculinity. Modern heads are modeled from such classic ones as this. Note eyebrow articulation and movable eyes. Head is mounted on control handle which also supports body.

9
IMPACT OF GENIUS

Preceding pages: George Sand's son, Maurice, drew this
picture of his puppet theater. Here a fashionable crowd watches
a puppet performance in his studio at Passy, in Paris.

We have noted that in the courts of India, China, and the Ottoman empire, the most talented poets, playwrights, and designers concerned themselves with the art of the puppet. We have no such authority for Europe. In all probability it was the wandering showman and his family travelling from town to town who supplied most of the secular puppet entertainment. But as long as puppetry remained a folk art, it kept its vitality. The itinerant showman made his own puppets as best he could and his instinct for survival kept him playing the type of entertainment that pleased his audiences most. There were undoubtedly individual players of real genius at manipulation and improvisation but in a humble profession.

It was not until the sixteenth century that we hear of the specialist writing or composing for the puppet—and then infrequently.

While the ancesters of Punch, Kasparek, Polichinelle, and their rowdy tribe stood by the common people, there was the beginning of another class of puppets performing for the nobility and the very rich. In the seventeenth century in Europe, a fine artist—be he painter, musician, or dancer—had to have a patron or he starved. Maybe he had a patron and starved anyway. Any elaborate indoor theatrical production outside of the church was too expensive for most of the people. When opera began to take form in Italy, the idea was quickly taken up by the marionettes. The first marionette opera was written by a designer-poet-mathematician-producer by the name of Acciajuoli. He opened in Florence in 1670 and wound up his first tour twelve years later in Venice. However, he played in theaters, not in the streets and fairs. About the same time, the Italian composer, Jean Baptiste Lully, who had given the opera its form, was producing his own creations in Paris. He was so successful and powerful that he became virtual dictator of the musical theater in Paris. He allowed only three theaters to play, with no variations in style and no competition. That kind of monopoly was possible in those days. All one needed was a friendly king.

Molière, whose acting company preceded that of Lully at the Palais Royale was such a favorite with Louis XIV that he obtained an exclusive right for his players to use the spoken word. All the other acting companies were confined to pantomime. They had to resort to wearing huge coat pockets in which to carry scrolls with bits of dialogue lettered on them. Live children dressed like cupids and holding banners from trumpets were lowered on ropes to announce places and situations. The competing acting companies were in a bad way. But the maverick marionettes immediately began to move in with less trouble. They, of course, lifted all of the scores of the legitimate operas and the scripts of the melodramas. One needed a license to play, but who

knew about copyright! When a puppet troupe was put out of one theater, it would pop up somewhere else. After all, it didn't use much equipment.

The marionette opera became extremely popular. For a while Lully thought he was going to lose out to the puppets. The struggle with the legitimate theater went on for almost fifty years. Each side wanted to hobble the other. It wasn't until 1720 that a special parliament was called to rule on the matter. The legitimate theater wanted to put limits on the puppets—among other things to allow only the swazzle or "pratique," as they called it, to be used for the voices. Finally, the court ruled in favor of the marionettes, allowing six or seven to appear on the stage at one time and speak in regular voices. This so encouraged the puppeteers that one of them, Francisque, got together with three poets to parody the opera. The result was that they invented the Opera Comique. It seems only fair that in a short time the live opera stole the "comique" back from the puppets.

A bit later, the German composer Christoph Willibald Gluck was composing opera for marionettes to entertain his noble patrons, among them Marie Antoinette, Prince Esterhazy of Hungary engaged one Josef Haydn, an Austrian, in 1761 to be household composer at his estate. It was Haydn's duty to preside over his patron's live theater and puppet theater. One of Haydn's finest works, the opera *Philemon and Baucis*, was composed for the visit of the Empress Maria Theresa. It was a great success "due to the Prince's fine Italian singers and the able manipulation of the marionettes." Haydn also wrote *The Witches' Sabbath*, *Genefiefa*, *Dido*, and *Vendetta*, all marionette operas.

Mozart wrote no puppet operas, although

Left: Marionettes of Ivo Puhonny production of *King Violin* are reminiscent of types used in 18th-century opera, such as Venetian marionette above. Haydn and Glück composed music for puppet actors.

Venetian artist Guardi painted scene
above in 18th century. Here hand puppets have been
permitted to amuse nuns and visitors in convent.
Right: In 18th-century France, "comedians of wood" could
be found in ornate theaters like this one.

many of his works have had puppets superimposed. However, he was a great fan of Kasperle (originally created in 1781 by a big-nosed actor named Laroche). In Salzburg Mozart often went to masquerades dressed as the little puppet rebel, possibly as a sort of protest against the city which treated him so shabbily and which has now made an industry of his name.

The Italian, Carlo Gozzi, who wrote in the manner of the commedia dell' arte, wrote *The Love of Three Oranges* as a puppet play long before Sergei Prokofiev was commissioned by the Chicago Civic Opera to write a score for it in 1925.

In these days of large theaters and even larger civic auditoriums, it is perhaps difficult to realize that the privately owned showplace seated very few people. Often there were more actors and musicians than spectators. Even the public theaters for the rich and the intellectuals didn't need to be large. Such a place was that of the puppeteer Dominique Seraphin. His operation gives us some idea of eighteenth-century show business. This Frenchman, who, with his heirs, operated continuously for nearly one hundred years, was one of the liveliest and most influential puppeteers of his time. In February, 1747, Dominique Seraphin Francois was born "on the road" into a family of wandering players which trouped through Germany, Italy, and France. Seraphin was taught to play the fiddle, but at the age of twenty-three, he decided to go to Paris and open a theater of shadow puppets. Known in France as *Ombres Chinoises,* they were the French descendents of the Chinese shadow show brought halfway around the world by sailing ships at a time when the West was rediscovering the East. The *Ombres Chinoises* of the French were made of solid cardboard. Unlike their highly colored and pierced predecessors, they cast a black shadow. Some of them are so ingeniously articulated that they are a mechanic's delight.

Seraphin got his theater started in 1776, and in 1781 moved it to Versailles, where he was immediately successful playing to the nobles and notables. When he moved his theater back to Paris in 1784, a newspaperman wrote, "People come in crowds to see this kind of show. There is always a performance at six in the evening and on Sundays and holidays, two shows, the first at five and the second at seven. Those whom we call the 'little people,' the workingmen, don't often go to the Chinese Shadows; but in revenge, the good bourgeois are delighted. I came in and got a very good seat in a handsome well-lighted room. There is no orchestra, just a harpsichord well played in the intervals and during the scenes. It's a highly intelligent show; we laughed a lot and that's enough."

Les Comédiens de bois.

Six years later Seraphin sold out to someone who didn't have the spark, and was forced to take over again rather than see his theater die. Later he added marionettes for variety, and a little black dog who was trained to grab the devil in his teeth just as he was carrying Polichinelle off to hell. This was a great success and Seraphin put out a handbill with the following message:

"One moment! Stop and read me. A change of scene. New additions in pretty taste to embellish my OMBRES CHINOISES. I have marionettes, but marionettes that you will believe to be charming little children. You must see them as well as my little dog Gobemouche. Come see my shadows. A new show every day."

He died in 1800 leaving the theater to his nephew, and the succession of the family kept it busy until 1870. Maindron chides Seraphin for having given a political turn to his theater: "The memory of Seraphin, founder director of the Chinese Shadows, would have a happier aura if he had not so lightly forgotten all he owed to the French court who had been responsible for his fortune. Beginning in 1789, he allowed himself to be influenced by the ideas of the day and ordered his authors and helpers to propagate them. Introducing politics into this theater, he lauded the courage and loyalty of the women who went to Versailles to bring the royal family back to the Tuileries in 'The Patriotic Druggist.' He played 'Harlequin, Patriotic Pirate' (which the year before had been called 'Harlequin Pirate'); he played the 'Demonseigneurisation,' in 1793 'National Federation,' and in 1794 'Apple to the Fairest or Fall From the Throne'—a regrettable spot on the life of one so unique and so sincerely artistic."

Seraphin may have been on the side of beating a dead horse, but he was only following the traditional direction of Polichinelle. We imagine these pieces were amusing if they were anything like the other plays that were produced at his theater through the years.

Cassandre's Wig, written by a descendant, Mlle. Pauline Seraphin, is an engaging sample of what Parisians laughed at in 1846, while its founder's tradition was still going strong. The action suggests hand puppets. The script is repro-

duced in its entirety in Maindron's *Marionettes et Guignols.*

It was at this time that the celebrated authoress and playwright, George Sand, began an experiment in puppetry. Actually, it was her son, Maurice, who first became interested and began playing with homemade puppets over the back of a chair. This so intrigued his mother that she encouraged and created their first *Théâtre des Amis* in her home at Nohant, in Switzerland. She describes the making of one of their first puppets: "I remember making the monster, whose huge throat was to engulf Pierrot, from a pair of slippers lined in red and a sleeve of bluish silk. This monster, which we still have, and who has always been called the 'green' monster, has always been blue. None of his numerous audience has ever mentioned it."

It was within this simple atmosphere that the fertile imaginations of Maurice Sand and two associates began to create. One of them, Victor Borie, burned the theater down while staging a fire scene. The effect was a success, but they had to build a new theater. The new castellet was

Ombres Chinoises shadow figures reached high development in France. Upper left: Shadow performance of *Puss and Boots.* Middle: 18th-century Seraphin figures like these were simple at first, later gave way to more complicated mechanical types. Upper right: Backstage at the famous Caran d'Ache theater. Note musicians and light projector. Above. Zinc figure by Henri Riviere from *Chat Noire.*

twice as large as the original. There in Nohant, before the most distinguished people of France, the *Théâtre des Amis* continued to delight its audience for over thirty years with new plays and creations.

By 1872, they had produced one hundred and twenty different plays. The magnetism of the tiny theater, its creator, and her salon attracted such giants as the painter Eugene Delacroix and Georges Bizet, the composer. At one time, Chopin and Liszt played piano duets for the performances. George Sand herself costumed the growing cast.

In order to get more puppets on stage than four or six hands could hold, Maurice devised a piton, or spike, that hid in the wig at the back of the head so that he could hook the puppets onto chair backs and other furniture. This led to the molding of a paper upper body in order to make the chests hold their shape after the hand had been withdrawn. The entire cast was then re-vamped and George had to recostume all the puppets. At one time, the Nohant theater boasted a hundred and twenty-five characters: dukes, countesses, kings, and others all elaborately dressed by their playwright. Mme. Sand liked to use a glossy black round headed upholstery nail for the eye because it "seemed to reflect a light from deep inside" from all angles.

In 1859, Mme. Sand set down in *Homme de Neige* some of her thoughts about the nature of puppets: "Do you know what a puppet theater is? . . . It is a theater of two operators, thus four hands, that is to say four characters in a scene. This allows for quite a number of burattini.

"What's that—burattini?"

"It is the primitive, classic puppet and it is the best. It's not the marionette made of many parts,

hung from the ceiling by strings and which walks without grazing the ground, making a ridiculous and unnatural noise. The mechanical perfection of some marionettes permits the perfect imitation of human gestures. No doubt one could imitate nature more completely with the help of more mechanical perfections, but I ask myself what would be the artistic advantage of creating a theater of automata. The closer one imitates people, the more this theater of mechanical actors becomes a sad and frightening thing.

"Look here. What do you see? A rag and a block that scarcely seems to have a shape. But watch me slip my hand into this little leather sack. See my index finger slip into the hollowed head, my thumb and my middle finger fill up these sleeves and control these little wooden hands which seem short to you. They're not open or closed and that's intentional, so that you won't notice that they're not moving. This figure, barely roughed out and painted in flat drab colors, through its movement little by little begins to live. If I showed you a red-cheeked, var-nished German marionette, covered with spangles animated by springs, you could not forget that it is a puppet. Whereas my burattino, supple, obedient to all the motions of my fingers, goes, comes, turns its head, crosses its arms, raises them to the sky, moves them every way, bows, claps, knocks on the wall in happiness or despair. And you believe you see all these emotions reflected in his face, don't you? Where does this magic come from? How can a head so sketchily made, so homely to look at up close, suddenly with the play of light take on a reality of expression far beyond its real dimensions? Yes, I maintain that when you see the hand puppet on the hand of

Devil and Faust marionettes (opposite, left) were made in 1700's by Kopetzky, father of Czech puppetry. Florentine opera puppet of 18th century (opposite, right) is now preserved in puppet collection of Munich City Museum.

Nohant theater puppets were modeled by
Maurice Sand, costumed by his mother, George. Such
puppets performed in Mme. Sand's salons.

a true artist, in a well-designed theater in proper proportions to the characters, you completely forget that you are not the same size as these little beings. You even forget that the voice they speak with is not their own. This impossible marriage between a head as large as my fist and a voice as loud as my own exists by a sort of mysterious drunkenness, so that I may enchant you little by little and the magic is upon us. Do you know where the magic comes from? It happens because this burattino is not an automat, because he obeys my whim, my inspiration, my spirit and because all his movements are the result of

my ideas and the words I bestow, because he is really me—and not a puppet."

It is perhaps unfortunate that Mme. Sand had not become acquainted with good marionettes, rods, or shadows. Her genius might have flowed in those directions as well.

Franz Count Pocci, general manager for the court theaters of Munich, was the first to write a repertoire for the German puppet stage. He had his own private marionette theater on his estate, as many nobles did, but he was a great admirer of the wandering players, and particularly the fairground Kasperle, as the titles of some of his plays attest: *Kasperle Night Watchman, Kasperle Gets Rich*. Pocci was instrumental in launching Papa Schmid, the long time director of Munich's 29 Blumenstrasse, who put on his last production at the age of ninety.

Every once in a while, at different periods and in different parts of the world, there comes a time of happy balance between freedom, economic security, and spare time when the artists can get together to play. Such was the case in France in May, 1862, when a group of artists, writers, poets, musicians, and government notables got together to create the *Theatron Erotikon de la Rue de la Sante*. A few of the names will be remembered: Bizet, who often played the piano for the plays; Lemercier de Neuville and Duranty of the Tuileries, both hand-puppeteers and prominent writers of puppet plays; and Felicien Rops, the illustrator. The interesting thing about the Theatron Erotikon was the tremendous creative effort contributed by these enthusiasts to produce shows in an auditorium with a capacity of only twenty-one people. De Neuville had painted a gallery of spectators, caricatured friends, high on the back wall of the room. Into this tiny theater was poured a concentration of talented effort for upwards of a year, with de Neuville and Jean du Boys operating the shows. Amedee Roland and du Boys, the original instigators of the Erotikon are forgotten today, but the experiment presaged the increasing numbers of top playwrights, musicians, and painters who eventually would contribute to European puppet productions. Several books of the plays of this theater have been published, one illustrated by Rops, but Maindron says that there was nothing in the performances that would offend a "maiden."

The idea that practitioners from all the arts should get together to produce a puppet show for their own enjoyment was new and would be repeated in Munich, Berlin, Rome, and New York.

The fun that went into creating this tiny theater continued into the cafes and cabarets. One was especially successful: *Le Chat Noir*, whose shadow show was notable for its intellectual clientele and its artistic staff. The guiding spirit, Henri Riviere was a painter, illustrator, wood engraver, and lithographer, as well as a mechanic. He had eight or nine designers on his staff including the cartoonist and illustrator Caran d'Ache. From a modest beginning in the Chat Noir cabaret where he used a white napkin as his shadow screen, Riviere expanded the Chat to become a complete theater. His more than forty productions in ten years have been described as poetic masterpieces of color, grace, and emotion. His romantic figures were about eighteen inches high, carefully cut out of sheet zinc and sometimes having colored paper in the apertures. His sets were ingenious—sometimes projected by arc light in color and made with multilayered colored glass. He was able to get the effect of great depth with subtle gradations of shade.

Although the auditorium was small by modern standards, he had quite a staff. Besides his literary committee of nine, he had: a Greek Chorus, Regisseur, Secretary General, a librarian, orchestra conductor, choirmaster, tympanist, master mechanic, and ten "mechanics," whom I assume were puppeteers. Just handling one of his figures required an actor with precise mechanical skill.

The European cities had built sophisticated audiences. The time was ripe for puppetry to satisfy these audiences on a large scale.

153

During the latter part of the nineteenth century the principal effort of most European puppetry was to amaze and to astound. Plays were spectacular—literary quality and characterization were less important. The trick effect was everything. Clown figures flew apart and became six little clowns. Sea battles were fought by puppet navies, and burning ships sank amid rockets' red glare, Greek fire, and cannons' roar. In France, La Mère Gigogne delighted audiences by suddenly producing her innumerable marionette children—she was reported to have one hundred and seventy-seven—from the pockets of her skirt.

And as long as spectators gasped and shook their heads and said, "I don't see how in the world they do it," the puppeteers were content.

England led the western world in the size and mobility of her marionette troupes. (Even French companies found it advantageous to travel under English names.) British companies made regular European tours and some even circled the globe, in step with the expanding empire.

Many of them had begun as vaudeville troupes, featuring bell ringers, acrobats, clowns, or actors, first with puppetry as a side line, then switching to the more popular puppetry exclusively. Clunn-Lewis and Barnard were two of the famous British companies whose repertoire included plays, but whose stock in trade was the trick marionette and the vaudeville turn.

The troupes were entirely self-sufficient and self-contained, carrying their equipment in trains of up to a dozen wagons, with additional living vans for the puppeteers themselves. They carried pianos and organs to accompany the performances, and everybody doubled in brass during the parades before the show. Portable seating accommodated as many as a thousand spectators.

Companies such as these developed the mechanics, if not the art, of puppetry to a high degree. Their marionettes were large—three feet and more—and of a realism that was tempered only by the folk quality inherent in the work of the designers. They performed on spacious stages filled with elaborate scenery and carefully screened off from snoopers backstage. Puppeteers were extremely jealous of their technical proficiency and guarded the secrets of their puppets' construction and manipulation. The great Thomas Holden, probably the best-known English puppeteer of the time, hung a wall of canvas entirely around the backstage elements of his show to keep anybody, even the stagehands, from learning too much.

Holden came of a fairgrounds family. In the early 1870s he was stage manager of the Bullock troupe, which carried three hundred figures. It also boasted a proscenium fourteen feet wide, and eight feet high, with a depth of eight feet under a high bridge, and required ten operators.

Holden was famous on the continent, as well as in England, traveling as far as Russia and using a flamboyant publicity and poster campaign to attract audiences. He relied on, or pretended to rely on, the newest mechanical and electrical apparatus of the day, and claimed that his complicated machines and "secret" inventions raised his show far above the level of his competition. In a brochure, dated 1887, and printed in France, Holden comments on his operation. The smoke screen of complication that beclouds the description is undoubtedly an effort to confuse his competitors by saying much and revealing little.

Preceding pages (top to bottom, left to right): Garibaldi hand puppet by Karl Birkenmeier, traditional 19th-century French figure, Richard Teschner rod puppet "Woman with Death's Head"; "Schutzmann" hand puppet of Toni Schmid, "Cassim" marionette by Tony Sarg, two fantastic Teschner puppets; Paul Brann marionette, hand puppet by Agi Kissel; judge marionette of Papa Schmid; Mr. Pum by Hilmar Binter.

"My job behind the scenes is not as easy as it might be," he says. "In keeping all these little figures active I've moistened more than one shirt. Rushing from the hydraulic machine to the electric pile, the pneumatic apparatus to the magnetic, one often catches cold, especially in certain theaters where the air currents seem to have taken up their abode. It's not the pleasantest kind of work. Beside the weight to lift, and the strings to pull, I am sometimes standing, sometimes kneeling, most often lying flat, my face in a dangerous and uncomfortable position, sometimes hanging by one foot, or clutching with one arm to an iron bar, rushing from right to left, up and down, singing, talking, yelling according to the needs of the moment, hardly having time to breathe, changing my voice quality according to the characters and always sweating as though in a Russian bath. . . .

"But that's enough. I won't divulge another secret of my profession. I leave to the spectator the task of untangling the innumerable strings—and if he takes a fancy, to compete with me. I advise him to immediately arm himself with . . . a few hundred yards of canvas, a Singer Sewing Machine to sew it up, forty pounds of paints, brushes with trained men to use them, good blocks of wood to make into intelligent-looking puppets, five hundred old clock gears, a hundred watch springs, fifteen pounds of hair, one hundred fifty pairs of artificial eyes, two small engines, a furnace, iron wire, etc."

Etc., indeed. Thomas Holden, the most famous and successful puppeteer of his time, shows the chip on his shoulder. If he really went through all those gyrations to get his show on, he was overextending himself. It is true that physically a puppeteer works extremely hard. He does sing and shout and perspire. But it can be very exhilarating to put on a good show, and can generate a lot of good-natured euphoria backstage. Also, Holden gives the impression that he worked alone, which was not the case. When he formed his own company, it was a big one, like Bullock's.

However put-on he felt himself to be, Holden did have a fine array of come-apart, turnabout figures. Strings from above, below, and from the sides would operate "a clown who gets into bed, snuggles down and goes to sleep with all the movements of a flesh and blood human being."

Other standard acts of the time were the lady who turned into a balloon; the coach that turned upside down, became a balloon, and flew off; and the ostrich that ran on stage, squatted, laid an egg, whereupon the egg hatched a huge snake that scared mama ostrich. (I have seen this one myself in vaudeville. It can be very funny.)

European troupes also visited the United States from time to time. Madame Jewell, a relative of Holden's, played the American vaudeville circuit for a good many years with a show that featured a live monkey weight lifter, as well as marionettes. The Schichtl company, from Germany, was popular in the States, as were many other European touring troupes.

A few Americans began to gain international importance. Walter Deaves probably covered more ground than any puppeteer of his time. He traveled with his father's company as far as Mexico just after the American Civil War, and as a child of three appeared on stage as a policeman who arrested some of the marionettes.

Eventually he took over the company and thereafter traveled widely. One world tour lasted

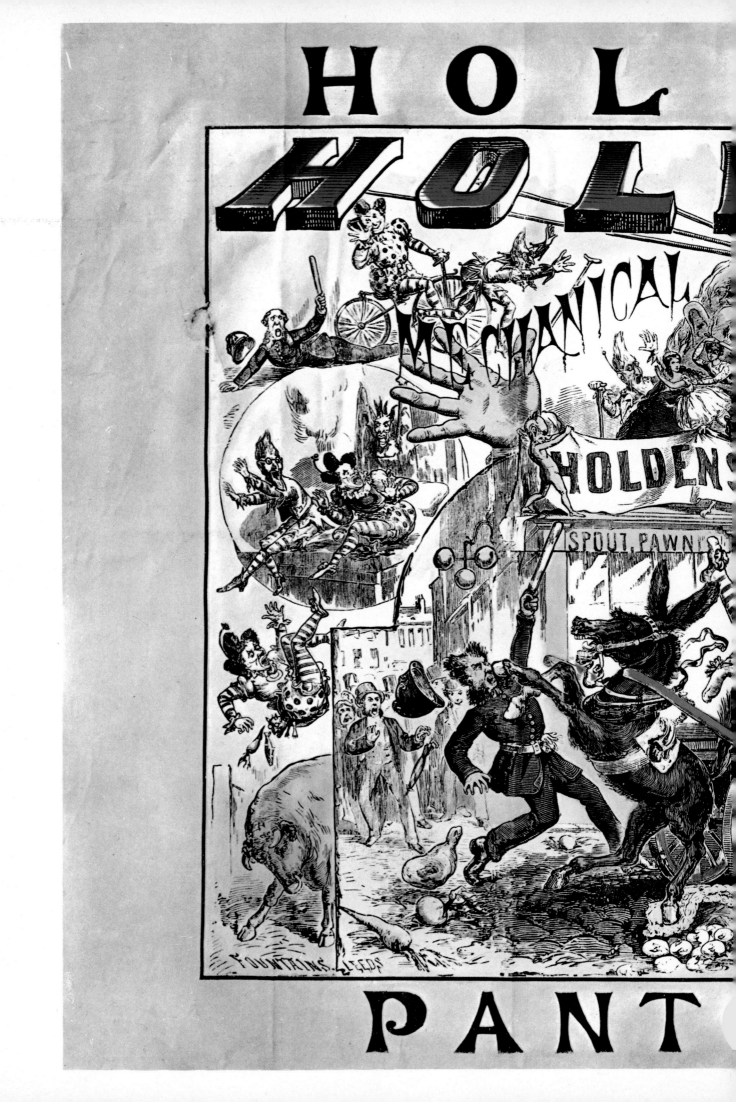

nette stage was flanked by balcony boxes or tables peopled with puppet spectators. Below and in front of the little stage was a puppet orchestra. This array, requiring several cloth drops, would fill the entire vaudeville stage, and the effect was spectacular.

Deaves's show was too early for me, but I saw one like it some years later. This was Mantell's Mannequins, an American show which came to the Midwest when I was a boy. "Mantell's Marionette Hippodrome," one early poster read. "Fairyland Transformation — Big Scenic Novelty — Seventeen Gorgeous Drop Curtains—Forty-five Elegant Talking-Acting Figures in a Comical Pantomime."

It was everything they said it was. The Mantells were Len and Esther Ayres (now retired on the West Coast) and one additional puppeteer. They had cut the hour-long show advertised in their posters to a twelve-minute vaudeville act, and offered fast-paced music, dancing, and trick marionettes. The puppet orchestra was conducted by a very active leader who swiveled, waved his baton, and bowed, and who was operated from off stage, at the side. The other instrumentalists all were worked by one wire. Two theater boxes flanking the puppet proscenium contained other puppet spectators, clapping and gawking as each act appeared. One of the characters would stretch his neck way out whenever the shimmy dancer came on stage, although not far enough to avoid being beaten over the head with his wife's handbag.

Everything had been boiled down to solid sight gags and laughs, and as soon as the laugh was over the puppets were whisked off and a new act brought on. I remember eight Russian dancers

more than seven years and played not only the major cities of the continents, but such unlikely island dates as New Guinea, Borneo, Java, Sumatra, the Seychelles, Zanzibar, and Samoa. His wife and two children and two additional operators accompanied him.

When vaudeville began to come into its own in the United States in the late 1880s, Deaves developed a show-within-a-show format that set the style for puppet vaudeville players everywhere. A central proscenium with a raised mario-

which were on stage all of fifteen seconds, just time for the big hand. The Mantell's piano player was the most hilarious I have ever seen, and I have seen many excellent ones. His head was a mop of active white hair, and he attacked the piano as though it were an adversary, ending up by diving at the keyboard from a distance and finally dancing on the keys.

The Mantells used the two-bar control with very loose-jointed active figures. Their performances had received a high polish, and they were bill toppers in the United States and abroad—which, on one tour, included India, Japan, Australia, and the Philippines.

These traveling troupes and their puppets that were rooted in the folk-art tradition were soon to give way to more intellectual and sophisticated expressions. Yet interestingly enough, for all their limitations, they seem to have left enduring marks wherever they touched down in their travels about the world, and an old trick or two turns up in many a modern puppet concert. Only a few years ago, in a little town near the southern tip of India, I saw an archaic survival of this nostalgic kind of vaudeville. It was a strange, hybrid marionette show attached to a vagabond Indian circus. In addition to the ever-present two-string Indian snake charmer and his huge cobra, it included a juggler and a ballroom dancing couple borrowed —or left over—from the European marionette tradition.

Of course, puppetry was not all in the hands of the tricksters. Other artists had continued to work, and by the time the twentieth century arrived, a new Surge was on and the general public was becoming aware that the puppet was capable of creating something deeper than sur-

prise and laughter. In addition a new kind of puppet would soon appear—the rod puppet.

In 1911, an event occurred that had a profound effect on a large segment of popular puppetry. Richard Teschner of Vienna and his new wife traveled to Holland on their honeymoon, and there he encountered and became intrigued with the high artistic quality of the Javanese *wayang* figures and their simple, effective means of operation. Teschner was already an artist of high repute and an accomplished puppeteer. He was in the first rank of European stage designers and

Salici troupe acrobat (opposite) performed in European vaudeville circuit and later in America. Mantell's Mannequins were operated by two-bar control illustrated above. Simple seven- or nine-string type allowed for broad action and quick packing on frequent road trips.

had founded his own marionette company in Prague in 1906. His figures were conventional, but his theater evidently caused a stir. He was invited to open a permanent marionette theater in Berlin and urged by the established puppeteer Brann to come join him in Munich.

Teschner decided to go his own way, however—and that way led right to the Javanese rod puppets. He visited museums in The Hague and Amsterdam to study their collections of *wayang* figures brought by the Dutch from their eastern colonies, and bought others for himself which he took back to his studio in Vienna.

At first Teschner began to create puppets in the Javanese style, but with European refinements. The fusion of the Javanese style and system with Germanic technical artistry produced startling results. His figures were fourteen to eighteen inches high. Instead of the central rod of the Javanese figures, Teschner used a strong, light tube fitted with flanges which could be slipped into a slotted playboard at the edge of his proscenium to hold the standing figures upright. Metal belaying plates between the padded slots held the strong, thin black rods that operated the hands when not in use. Each head was mounted on a double pivot inside and could be inclined sideways or nodded up and down by sutures which entered the tube at the neck and left it below the flanges, each one belayed by a clove hitch through a small bead. The thumb and forefinger could thus handle all head motion.

Teschner even arranged for his figures to bend at the waist by installing a coil spring in the middle of the tube. This allowed the figure to bow whenever an internal rod was lowered below the spring.

His theater, which he called his *Figuren Spiegel,* and which is now preserved in the Austrian National Library Theater Collection, has a circular proscenium a little over fifty inches in diameter surrounded by golden signs of the zodiac in relief—and covered by a slightly convex glass like a watch crystal. There is just room for three operators to work seated behind this ingenious and beautiful stage.

When it is considered that Teschner's performances always were given in his studio and never to audiences of more than seventy people, the intimate character of his little theater does not seem to have been a mistake. Probably the whole concept would have suffered if he had worked in larger dimensions.

He labored long and experimented endlessly to perfect his figures and the mechanisms by which they operated, to invent new scientific effects, and to conceive appropriate stories for the weird characters that peopled his imagination.

He projected scenic images from the rear through a transparent backdrop, sometimes putting smoke and chemical activity into the beam of light. Clouds moved across his horizons, fire leapt into the sky.

Nothing was too much trouble. A moving mouth would have been superfluous in his two-and-a-half-inch heads, but to increase their dramatic effect he made a few. One was a gorilla of what appears to be wood, whose upper and lower lips retracted, baring the fangs. Often to achieve a desired delicacy of detail he worked with dental drills under a lens, a fantastic artist-jeweler. Infinite patience, and money from his wife's family, allowed Teschner to try anything that he wished.

Russian Lady Macbeth rod puppet
by Nina Effimova (top, left). Teschner watersprite
(top, right) has lap and cord joints.
Bottom: Tatterman Peer Gynt set by Von Duren.

Richard Teschner, seen above in his study, created elaborate rod-puppet theater in Vienna. Left: Company prepares puppets backstage. Note belaying plates to hold rods. Opposite, top: "Dragonkiller" puppets show flanged rods fitting into slotted playboard. Right: Circular face of *Figurenspiegel* stage had magical appearance, was surrounded by signs of the Zodiac.

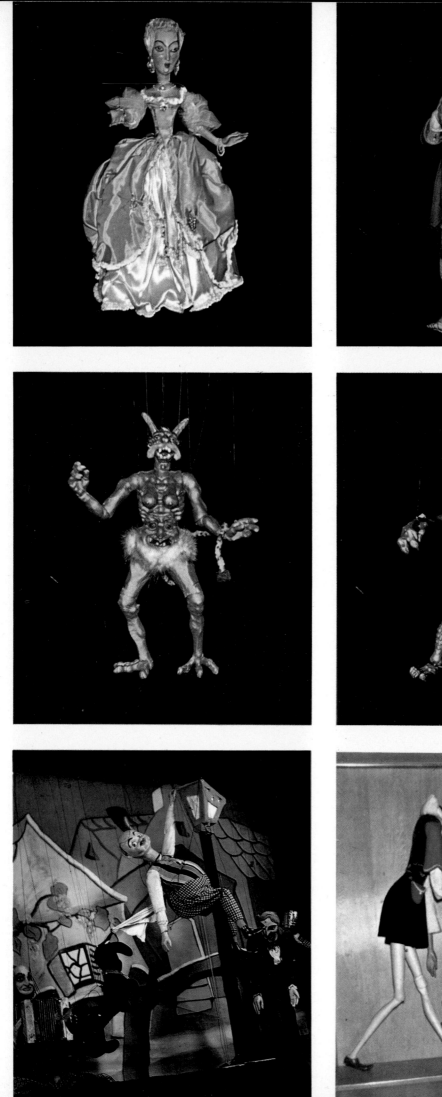

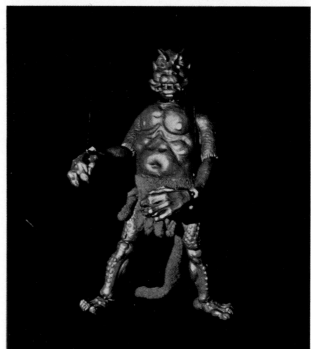

At first his plays were pantomimes on Oriental themes, with musical accompaniment, but later his imagination flowed in all directions. He soon abandoned the Javanese shapes to create his own, but always used the rod control. Some of his subjects border on the macabre. One character is a woman whose chalk-white face suddenly can become a skull; one play, *The Orchid*, of Chinese origin, concerns a flower that consumes all who come near it until overcome by the spirit of good.

Around 1933 he created the *Farbenklavier*, or color piano. The pianist was a clown. Above the back of the instrument was a square frame on which dissolving colors and shapes were projected as the puppet played. This was probably the first fusion of music and abstract moving color. Teschner also played the mandolin and was partial to a music box, for which he perforated his own metal discs.

In combination, his effects often were of unearthly beauty. Light, sound, and pantomimic action combined into the truly international language of puppetry. Scenes dissolved smoothly from one to another. Unnecessary detail was eliminated.

Although he influenced and was influenced by the theatrical giants of the day, he worked very much by himself, and was surprisingly secretive for one so far in advance of his field. Most of the backstage photographs of his theater were taken only during the final years of his professional life. One American puppeteer who visited Teschner in 1931 told me that the master had given him a puppet only on condition that he swear not to divulge the manner of its operation.

Until the Second World War, Teschner's shows were by invitation, and it was not until after the war that he was obliged to charge admission. He died in 1948.

At present the great number of his figures are preserved in the Austrian National Library under the expert care of Dr. Franz Hadamowsky, who has written a fine monograph on Teschner's contributions to puppetry. The Munich Stadtmuseum also has some of his figures. Everything is well cared for and in good working condition, which is something unusual when we consider collections of old puppets.

Teschner's rod puppets were highly respected in the European puppet world, but did not immediately bring about many changes in those places where the string tradition was firmly entrenched. While some experimenting was done in Paris, it was in Russia that rods really took hold. The existing tradition was not strongly established, there were few marionette performers, and for a time the revolution cleared the way for new thinking in the theater, as well as in other areas of life.

In Moscow in 1917-18, Nina Effimova, a well-known painter, and her equally well-known sculptor husband, Ivan Effimov, began to produce puppet shows. Their first ones employed hand puppets, but soon they were captivated by the "Javanese" style puppets that Teschner had brought to Europe's attention, and the Effimovs undertook their own experiments with them.

Initial efforts were aimed at an intellectual audience, but later on the couple began to create for children and effectively laid the groundwork for the educational puppet techniques so firmly rooted in the Soviet curriculum today. Beginning with the Effimovs, the Russians have achieved the current apex of technical mastery in this field.

Paul Brann marionettes in Munich Puppet Collection (top, left and right) include Faustian devil portrayals of Lloyd George (middle, left) and Clemenceau (middle, right) made during World War I. Bottom, left: Piccoli Theater marionettes of Vittorio Podrecca toured the world. Bottom, right: Vojtech Sucharda created marionettes like these for Library Theater of Prague in 1928.

The rod idea made little headway in western Europe. Teschner's exciting pioneer efforts were well known and respected, but perhaps because a Surge was under way with the emergence of successful established marionette theaters, headed by serious artists, the tide was too strong.

Paul Brann was one of these artists, a trained theater man who understood and loved puppetry. The son of a Silesian farmer, Brann had attended the University of Berlin and studied stage direction with the great Max Reinhardt. He ran a permanent marionette theater in Munich from 1906 until the early 1930s, bringing the best available artists to the service of his craft. He produced serious plays and operas, both especially written for the puppet theater. Tours took his companies to sixteen countries including Java. Among the contributors to his Theater of Munich Artists were sculptor Olaf Gulbransen, playwrights Arthur Schnitzler and Hans Thoma, and designer Lucien Bernhard. Munich at the time was a ferment of artistic and cultural activity. Paul Klee and Wassily Kandinsky, among Brann's many artist-patrons, considered puppetry as an independent art.

Because he was of Jewish ancestry, Brann had to leave Munich when Hitler came to power. He moved to England, where his theater was extremely popular, and lived there until his death in 1955 at the age of eighty-two. In 1962, some two hundred of his marionettes were brought back to Munich and placed in the remarkable Stadtmuseum, which contains the largest and best-cared-for collection of puppets in the world.

Perhaps the most articulate of the new puppeteers was Ivo Puhonny, a professional since 1900, whose marionette theater eventually found a home at the Casino in Baden-Baden, Germany. An illustrator and cofounder of *Graphis,* the international magazine of advertising art, Puhonny was closely associated with the best artistic influences of his time. He had studied in Java, China, and Japan before opening his own theater; he designed his own figures and directed his performances. He was an artist who understood the uses of marionettes. Here are some Puhonny observations:

"To make marionettes, to build them a theater, to organize their performances is a delightful exercise in the arts." He thought that to really understand the possibilities of puppetry one must "make his puppets himself, and paint the scenery . . . ," but added that "the dilettante in the marionette theater possessing great enthusiasm, but only superficial talents, who has neither rich treasures of practical experience nor expert hands to offer, will never sense the great joy of the creative artist, nor will he add anything to the art or appreciation of puppetry. The thoughtless plunging into an unperfected art lowers the general standards of the marionette show. The public does not charge the clumsiness and inadequacy they see to the worker, but imagines it to be an intrinsic part of a puppet performance, and sees therein only a pleasing pastime . . . charming but after all only a form of child's play to be observed with indulgent eyes."

As an example of the contrast between the master and the hack, he described a visit to an old professional theater where he "beheld a whole puppet outfit hung up, rank and file, at rest. Most of the puppets were of unquestionable antiquity and were probably the work of a former puppet showman. Their wooden faces ogled me with

Czech puppeteer Josef Skupa created popular marionette
characters Hurvinek and Spejbl (above, left). Note distinctive
control (top, left) used by Czech Puppet Theater.
Marionette of Ivo Puhonny (above, right) was member of his
theater at Casino in Baden Baden, Germany, in 1930's.

such animation as to make a living chorus of an operetta seem sweetly insipid by comparison.

"Then, proudly, the owner of the theater showed me his newest figures. He had had them made by a professional carver, and they shone with an indescribable boredom. They were merely figures, no longer born of the spirit and experience of the puppet player, but the offspring of his instinct for enterprise."

Like Brann and Puhonny, the great Czech puppeteer Josef Skupa stayed loyal to the string marionette, in a country where there were over three thousand, two hundred amateur companies. Skupa and the other outstanding puppeteers of the time did not copy each other so much as they drew strength from the common fund of inspiration that was building up in Europe.

Skupa in particular was developing a tradition of his own around the father-and-son puppet team of Spejbl and Hurvinek. Skupa, a native of Pilsen and a former professor of Latin, created Spejbl in 1920. At first Spejbl was simply a member of the marionette cast at the Pilsen vacation center, but his voice, gestures, and vocabulary marked him as someone special, and before long he was spectacularly popular. Spejbl, who wears a full-dress suit and wooden shoes, is a brash pretender to knowledge and culture.

The sculptor, Karel Nosek, gained a measure of immortality by carving Spejbl, and six years later the figure of Hurvinek, Spejbl's bright son, who constantly but pleasantly exposes the errors

of his half-educated, know-it-all father, was added to the troupe. The antics of the two helped to build Josef Skupa's five-hundred-seat theater in Prague and to make it a permanent part of the city's dramatic life in spite of war, revolution, and occupation.

It is perhaps difficult to imagine from photographs and written descriptions just how charming these two characters were, but their effect was as positive and direct as that of Punch or Popeye. Their very simplicity and surrealistic quality made them believable in outrageous situations. Skupa operated Spejbl and spoke for both characters; his wife handled Hurvinek. Friends of mine who saw the show as children still get a happy look about the eyes at the mention of

these two memorable characters.

During the occupation of Czechoslovakia by the Nazis, the Czech puppeteers organized daring, illegal performances, sometimes in homes, sometimes in basements. These shows came to be known as "Daisies," and they were bright beacons of information and inspiration for the beleaguered Czechs. The noted Czech playwright Karel Capek, who wrote *R.U.R.* and *The Insects,* composed anti-Fascist prose pieces for the puppet players. And Dr. Jan Malik, now a leader in the Czech National Puppet Theater, designed figures and sets for Daisy productions.

Skupa also joined this intellectual resistance. Malik's biography of him says: "The puppet theater of Professor Skupa made itself famous

Legendary Papa Schmid (left) poses with Kasperle. Middle: Ivo Puhonny seated in studio surrounded by some of his many marionettes. Right: The marionettes of Vittorio Podrecca's Piccoli Theater were often modelled after popular human performers of the day—here the Marx Brothers.

EX·LIBRIS

Dr. Jindřich Veselý

for the wartime tours it arranged with programs for adults, the allegorical points of which, while imperceptible to the censor, were received by the public with bated breath and hidden emotions."

Even in the concentration camp at Ravensburg, in southern Germany, Czech women prisoners put together a puppet show out of scraps of material to keep up their morale.

The field of puppetry was, in fact, a kind of ideological battleground, the Czechs by their surreptitious shows feeding the patriotism and national solidarity of their countrymen, the Nazis, relentlessly suppressing them whenever and wherever they could. Even as Skupa was playing his underground performances in Prague, Nazi propaganda agencies were spreading the word that he was touring Germany in Hitler's behalf.

Eventually all Czech puppetry was suppressed. More than a hundred skilled puppeteers and writers died under torture or in concentration camps. Skupa was imprisoned in a Dresden jail in 1944, but made an almost miraculous escape during a fire.

At the war's end the Czech puppet theater pulled itself together again. Malik and Skupa were among the guiding spirits who survived to help re-establish it. Professor Skupa has since died, but his theater continues under the direction of Dr. Ota Popp and a company of over forty performers and artisans.

Another outstanding Czech is Vojtech Sucharda, who headed the Library Theater, established in 1928 with financing from the Municipal Savings Bank of Prague. It is a marvel of ingenuity. Besides having the most modern lighting equipment, it has electrically operated bridges which can be raised or lowered, or moved forward or backward, to suit the needs of the performance. Sucharda's figures are beautifully designed and sculpturally imaginative. It was Sucharda, incidentally, who redesigned the moving figures for the clock in the Prague Rathaus tower after they were destroyed in the war.

Italy's contribution to the Surge was Vittorio Podrecca, another complete puppeteer who understood his medium from the ground up. His *Teatro dei Piccoli,* although it still clung to the old-fashioned curtain backstage to hide its secrets, artistically was in the forefront of the international marionette movement. Podrecca used to greet his audiences in sixteen languages, and with a perfect right, because his troupe had played around the world and had created puppets, playlets, and acts based on the peoples and locales it had visited. During the second of four visits to the United States, the repertoire included English acrobats, Cuban rumba dancers, Argentine gau-

Book plate (above) belonged to first president of UNIMA, portrays Kasparek triumphant over Devil and Death. Josef Skupa (opposite, top left) posed with his Spejbl and Hurvinek. During war Czech puppetry was forbidden by Nazis, thus prompting cartoon (top, right) of Spejbl and Hurvinek in concentration camp. Skupa built special Prague theater (bottom) for puppets in 1920's.

chos, Peruvian folk dancers, Spanish bullfighters, innumerable Italian clown numbers and animal inventions, a fantastic African acrobat, and spoofs of Josephine Baker and the Marx Brothers.

Podrecca's marionettes were mostly mild caricatures of people, but they were satirical in nature. They made fun of the ballet, the police, the operatic tenor. The pianist was a burlesque of Vladimir de Pachmann, the Russian concert artist. Podrecca's bright and successful ideas were pilfered and adapted by many other puppet companies.

Anything that could be observed, of course, was fair game. Backstage was another matter. When Podrecca played in Atlantic City, one of America's prominent marionette producers went backstage fascinated to find out how the Josephine Baker marionette was put together. The producer was stopped at Podrecca's canvas barrier, but only temporarily. Later that night she returned to the theater and sneaked under the canvas. The place was totally dark, but she made

her way on her knees along the lines of hanging marionettes, feeling them one by one. She found Josephine. In time Podrecca acknowledged that the canvas was ridiculous and took it down.

The important thing about Podrecca was that like Brann, Puhonny, and Skupa, he had inspired and encouraged the best talents of his country to contribute to his theater.

Here, then, were four new spirits in puppetry arising in countries where the string tradition remained strong. When the century had come to the quarter mark, the fusion of the fine artist and the popular professional puppeteer was well under way. In Baden-Baden in 1927, the first idea of an international marionette organization was born. The idea that a group of marionette masters might have something to share with, rather than to conceal from, each other was revolutionary.

Ivo Puhonny's theater was the site of the first meeting for international co-operation and friendship in a profession descended from the magic

UNIMA symbol (above) was designed by Ivo Puhonny, appeared on cover of organization's magazine. Otto Morach's production of *Master Peter's Puppet Show* from *Don Quixote* featured music by Manuel de Falla, script by Garcia Lorca and sets by Adolph Appia. Play was shown in Zurich in 1926.

and secrecy of the witch doctor. The organization which resulted was called UNIMA (Union Internationale des Marionettes). It was formally established in Prague the following year. Eventually, as it grew in strength and influence, it came to include the leading puppet theaters and puppeteers in the world. Dr. Malik became its first secretary in 1930, Jindrich Vesely, also a Czech, its president, at the third congress, held in Liége, Belgium, in September. Among those present were Puhonny, Tsumo Miyajima of Japan, Warsaage of Belgium, two companies from England, Guignol from Paris, the Mourguets' Guignol from Lyon, Geza Blattner from Paris, Harro Siegel, then of Berlin, and Professor Skupa; in all, a distinguished gathering.

It was the hope of the congress to hold its next meeting in Chicago at the 1933 World's Fair, but the meeting never came about. The early Thirties were a time of uncertainty and unrest

throughout the world, and black days were ahead for almost everyone, including many of the puppet companies that had so long been a familiar and welcome sight in Europe. In Hitler's Germany in October, 1933, the inheritors of Papa Schmid's theater were forced by the Nazi government to close, and from then on licenses were revoked and puppeteers imprisoned. In addition thirty-nine wandering companies had been wiped out. But UNIMA would rise again after World War II and achieve a membership of more than two thousand, despite the border restrictions.

Tony Sarg made it to Chicago in 1933, though. Here was the strongest expression of the Surge in America, the man who perhaps more than anyone familiarized and endeared puppetry to the United States. He had been born in Guatemala in 1880, the son of a German consul. He was sent to military school in Fribourg, Germany, and was also taught to play the violin and cello,

as were his brother and sister. Tony's great natural talent, however, was drawing. He just drew, and this is probably the reason he developed his completely individual style. He was influenced to a certain degree by the work of the great Munich draftsman Heinrich Kley, and by the Czech folk painters, but essentially everything he did was pure Sarg. Eventually he became one of the highest paid illustrators of his time.

Tony began his work as an illustrator in England, where he lived in the building that had inspired Charles Dickens's *The Old Curiosity Shop.* Tony rented the second story, lived in the smaller of two rooms, and fitted out the larger as "Little Nell's Bedroom." He charged sixpence admission and paid his rent five times over.

It was in London, too, that he started his famous collection of old toys, which ultimately led to his interest in marionettes. He saw the Holden

company many times, as well, and became fired with the idea of creating marionettes. Holden's canvas wall kept him from learning anything backstage, and he sensibly decided that he could learn all he needed to know from out front.

Actually, there isn't much anyone can hide from an intelligent and curious puppeteer in the audience. The play and the action all are visible. The design is apparent. A few mechanical devices are perhaps hidden from view—but a good mechanic can figure out his own procedures for getting the effect.

Anyhow, as Shakespeare once said, "The play's the thing." The whole period of the Surge was an effort to demonstrate that dramatic impact through story and character is just as important as theatrical effects. In any event, Sarg found Holden's shows ingenious, but lacking in artistry.

Sarg came to New York in 1915 and rented a

Tony Sarg poses (left) with an armful of his marionettes from play, *Ali Baba.* At right is self-portrait by Sarg. A talented illustrator, Sarg designed costumes, props, sets, posters, and playbills for his troupe. Puppets themselves were made by puppeteers following his designs.

studio at the top of the Flatiron Building, at Twenty-third Street. There, with illustrators Frank Godwin and Charles E. "Mat" Searle, he began to produce marionette shows for friends. Their first production was *A Night in Delhi,* a purely western notion of Indian dancing, music, and fun. Inevitably it included a wriggling cobra and an Oriental hootchy-kootchy. I never saw this one, but I knew all the principals. It must have been lively. Tony exuded energy and it showed in everything he did.

His first professional break came as a result of World War I. The Broadway producer Winthrop Ames had intended to bring a European marionette show to New York. He wanted Brann or the Papa Schmidt theater, but he was thwarted by the outbreak of hostilities between Germany and the United States. So he approached Tony.

The show that developed included *The Green Suit,* Count Pocci's *Three Wishes,* and *The Stolen Jewel.* Tony made three-foot marionette figures, each one of which required an operator and an actor to speak its lines. The show was an artistic success, but not a financial one.

For his next production, Thackeray's humorous fairy tale, *The Rose and the Ring,* Tony reduced his figures to eighteen inches, and finally settled on two feet as an ideal height for an audience the size of his. He also reverted to the standard practice of having the puppeteers speak their characters' lines.

Tony learned a lot about drama and figure construction from Ellen Van Volkenburgh, who had started a puppet theater in Chicago, and from Helen Haiman Joseph, who had done the same in Cleveland and who eventually wrote an excellent history of marionettes. Tony also pioneered and experimented on his own a good deal, and

177

Mat Searle (far left) for many years managed Sarg's company. Sarg's largest
creations were Macy parade balloons after original designs (left and below, left).
Below: Elsie Dvorak was only live actor in Sarg's *Alice in Wonderland*.

through his many years of trouping back and
forth across the country, Americans began to gain
an appreciation of serious marionette plays.

I first heard of Tony when he brought *Rip Van
Winkle* to Mason City, Iowa, in 1921. This was
his first big show, the start of nearly two decades
of road tours. I saw the *Rip* show in the high-
school auditorium and decided that night that this
was the life for me.

It was a spectacular and lively show that rolled
on for two hours. It had fourteen scenes and was
based, of course, on Washington Irving's classic
story. There was singing, dancing, bowling in the
mountains, and a wild, nightmare fantasy full of
invented creatures who appeared when Rip got
drunk on schnapps.

The operation was handled by five puppeteers,
headed by Mat Searle, a floorman, and a pianist.
After four months on the road, the performance
was highly polished and went off expertly. When

the company came out dressed in smocks and
berets to take a bow, it seemed an enviable group
to aspire to, indeed.

A few years later I did join the Sarg company.
It was a period of great fun and excitement for
me. Tony by 1927 was America's most prolific
puppeteer, designer of children's barber shops
and restaurants, bon vivant, and lavish party-
giver. He was endlessly inventive, one of his
triumphs being the gas-filled, animated monsters
now known across the land as the Macy Parade
balloons. They are descendants of the pageantry
figures of medieval Europe and big brothers of
the modern giant Indian and Indonesian religious
figures. To me they are simply upside-down marionettes, manipulated by strings from below rather
than above.

The fact that the balloons had to be carefully
shepherded under New York City's elevated train
structures (long since removed) meant that Tony

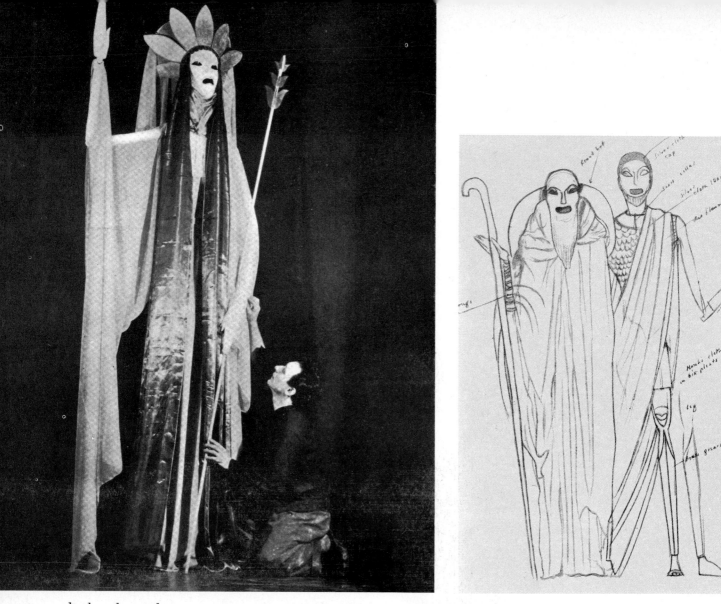

had to design his monsters in several units, all of a certain minimum width. (We pulled them under the El on their sides.) As a consequence, they were long and active.

The grandest one I remember was a dragon, one hundred and twenty-five feet long, which was composed of a head and body section and twenty-one graduated spheres for a tail. He undulated between ten and fifty feet above the ground with a ponderous, majestic humor, under the control of fifty handlers and a sort of "dragon director" I had trained, using a numbers system I had worked out while a cheerleader at college. The balloons were made of rubberized silk and filled with helium.

Possibly Tony's biggest show, however, was the one he put on at the Chicago Fair in 1933. It was seen by more than three million people. Industry was just beginning to use puppetry for advertising and public relations.

In 1934 the city of New York, then led by its vigorous mayor, Fiorello LaGuardia, undertook a number of work projects to help combat the persistent unemployment of the Depression years. One of these projects was a marionette company. Two years later, President Franklin Roosevelt thought it might be a good idea to organize fifty marionette companies to tour the United States and explain the processes of democracy and the philosophy of the New Deal.

**Giant marionettes of Remo Bufano (above)
were a feature of Robert Edmond Jones staging for
Stravinsky's version of** *Oedipus Rex.*
**Puppets are still preserved in Brander Matthews
Theater Collection of Columbia University.**

Tony was the logical spearhead of such an effort, and he went to Washington where presidential assistant Harry Hopkins outlined the plan. It was to begin with the New York group, headed by another puppeteer of great skill and integrity, Remo Bufano. Sadly, the project became bogged in a morass of partisan politics and never got off the ground.

It was a lost opportunity, and about as close as we have ever come, I guess, to having Federal support for puppetry. Not that I think government-sponsored puppetry would have been much better here than it has been anywhere else. But in a country whose tradition of puppetry has not been strong, it certainly would have been an interesting boost.

Remo Bufano never operated on such a large scale as Tony, but he was on the whole somewhat more experimental. Like Tony he was an indefatigable worker who labored mightily to achieve an effect. We used to say Tony's chief building material was adhesive tape, because it was fast. But Bufano also worked fast, so fast, in fact, that his puppets often were finished in his mind and put aside before they were ever quite completed in a tangible sense. Nonetheless, Bufano was extremely inventive.

Bufano's parents had come from Italy, and he had been born on New York's East Side. He was a little fellow, but outgoing and popular, and determined to become an actor.

His first show was a hand-puppet burlesque on the old *Orlando Furioso* epic. The puppets were small enough to be used with a squeaker—in particular, a delightfully silly dragon for which Bufano used a kazoo with great effect.

Remo's smallness perhaps led him to aspire to largeness. Certainly many of his figures were of enormous size. He built a thirty-five-foot clown which was the dominant figure of a scene in Billy Rose's memorable *Jumbo,* but is perhaps best remembered for the giant marionettes he prepared for the Robert Edmund Jones production of *Oedipus Rex.* He also made replicas of Tenniel's Walrus and Carpenter for Eva LeGallienne's *Alice in Wonderland* that were larger than life-size.

The Surge is perhaps an arbitrary designation. Certainly the men who energized it were still operating and, indeed, at the height of their powers, when the next wave of creativity in the puppet theater developed after World War I. Yet for all the years they coexisted, they went their own ways. Possibly one man's lifetime was just enough to perfect his style and bring it to a peak. Or maybe the success of his own idea precluded further experiment. The men who caused the Surge had broken with their past and developed their individual styles before or during the war. The Modern Trend sprang from a still more adventurous creative generation—as did the art and literature of the times.

Yet the debt to the men of that big push is great and must be acknowledged. It is impossible to say what puppetry might have been if there had not been this bridge from the traditionalism of the wandering showmen and the vaudeville tricks of Holden to the radicalism of Bauhaus puppetry. Yet it can be said in truth that the path of the postwar generation was somewhat easier because of the advances made during the Surge. For here was laid down a new premise—that the best puppetry derived from the highest artistic and creative effort.

181

MODERN MAGIC

11

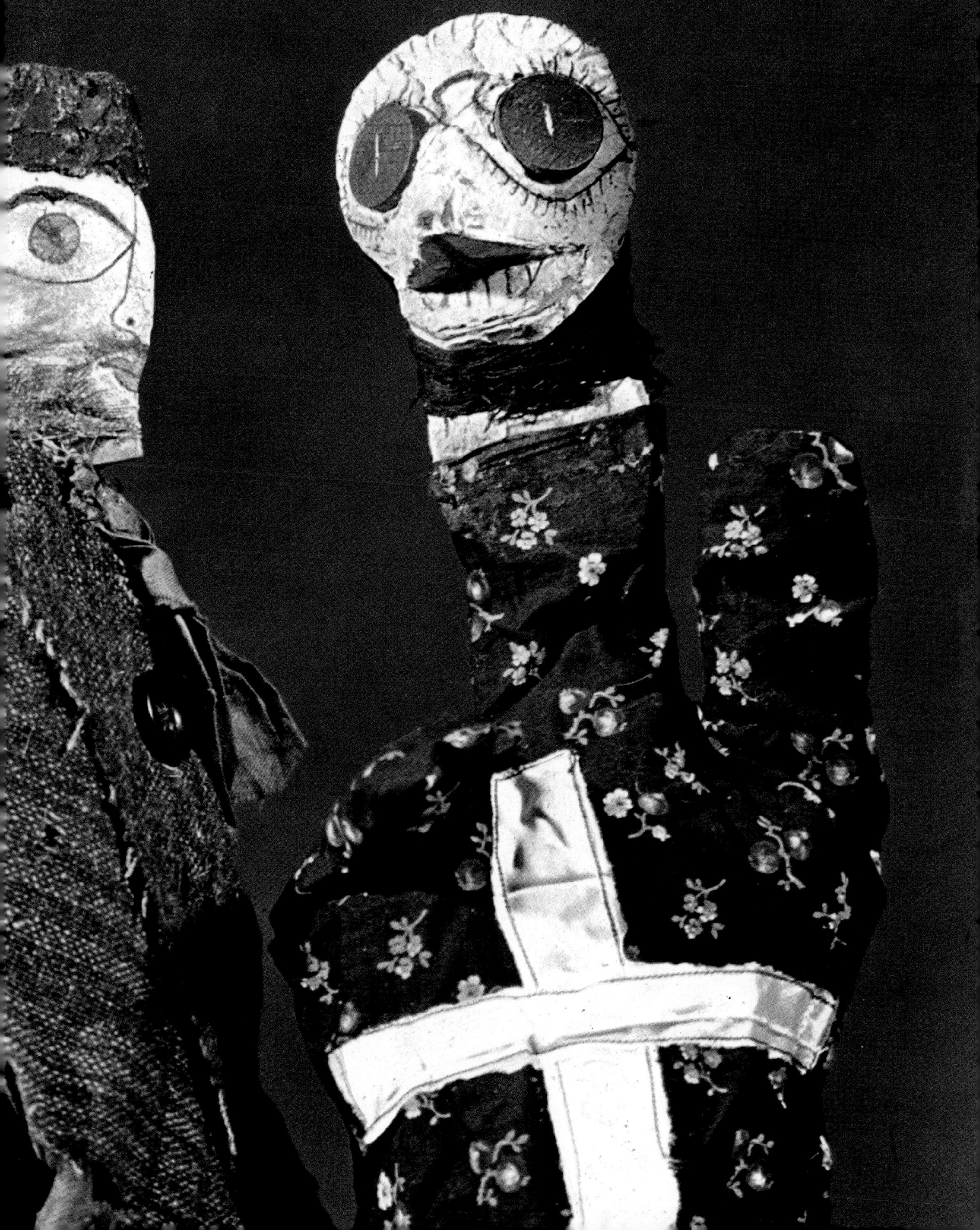

Overlapping the Surge of popular puppetry, and coexisting with it, were a number of new, experimental trends. They were not necessarily recognized as such while they were happening, yet in retrospect it can be seen that the directions puppetry was to take were being established by the struggling moderns. Some designers went back to sources of the ancient wisdom that existed at the birth of puppetry, while others sought inspiration in the iconoclastic attitudes toward art and design which were arising in Europe just before World War I and asserted themselves ever more strongly immediately thereafter. They were expressed in new forms and materials, in abstractions, images, and symbols. The enthusiasm of the Surge had provided artistic puppetry for the broadest audience, enlisting the finest talent to create plays, sets, music, and puppets. But the dramatis personae still looked like people, animals, and devils. Caricatures they were, to be sure, and extremely good ones, but they had not yet become abstractions or symbols. The successful showmen, like Brann, Teschner, Sarg, and Podrecca, each had developed a style of his own and was not affected by the artistic rumblings then going on in Europe. True, the dominance of the mechanical-marvel style of puppetry was almost over, but it remained for the struggling younger experimenters, who were caught up in the revolution in art and design, to pioneer the advanced and exciting puppetry that prevails in the world today.

The live theater was undergoing profound changes in staging and lighting. Everywhere painters and sculptors were looking for new sources of inspiration and invention. Picasso went back to primitive roots and based some of his work on African sculpture. Alexander Archipenko was one of the first to portray the human body in terms of architecture. While "modern art" and "modern theater" were hatching, new concepts of puppetry appeared. It was not that puppetry developed apart from the other arts, but that the theatrical and graphic artists were beginning to exchange ideas.

Probably the most energetic and influential center of the new creativity was the Bauhaus, the famous German school of design at Weimar, but there were other and earlier expressions of it elsewhere.

Among the first was Alfred Jarry's delightfully outrageous play, *Ubu Roi,* which made its debut as a marionette play in Rennes, southwest of Paris, in 1888. As a student, Jarry was a brilliant nonconformist who caricatured one of his teachers as King Ubu. Later, in 1896, when the play was performed in Paris by masked humans, it was both violently cheered and violently booed. Nevertheless, it made Jarry famous at twenty-three. He lived the rest of his short life as an eccentric, somewhat in the character of the King he had created, and many of his future writings made use of parts of the play.

Although considerably ahead of the postwar experimental period, Jarry had an enormous influence on later styles of playwriting and on the concepts of puppets themselves. His play, an irreverent slap at bourgeois morality and stupidity, has been called the first surrealist play. The noted actor and dramatist Sascha Guitry considered it "one of the most powerful burlesques of all time."

It is ridiculous to attempt this play with "unadulterated" human beings. Only when the costumes endow the actors with a near-puppet quality, does the play come off as well as it does with a manufactured cast.

The possibilities of the puppet actor and his certain clear advantages over human beings intrigued many artists and intellectuals of the new twentieth century. Among them was Gordon Craig, the English stage designer and producer who was perhaps puppetry's most articulate advocate and who, for a short time around 1918, published a little magazine called "The Marionette" in Florence. Here is an excerpt from one of Craig's statements on this theme:

"What are marionettes? Men without egoism.

"What are men? Egoists. . . .

"I compare marionettes with men purposely, not with actors, for actors are comparable only with themselves.

"Being egoists, men do well to interpret what they know best . . . that is, themselves. Not being egoists, marionettes are with us to interpret other things.

"If there is a solemn thing at all in Life, only a marionette can interpret it on the stage. People have said that Truth is the one solemn thing—well, then that is what marionettes can show."

Alexandra Exter, a highly skillful Russian painter and stage designer who had worked among the "fauves" in Paris, returned to Russia and began experimenting with new marionette forms in 1917. Her marionettes, though not completely abstract, show a strong influence of cubism, and included oil cloth, copper screen, wood turnings, silk celluloid, and the like in their makeup. Though a pioneer in her day, I have found no trace of her influence in present-day Russian puppetry.

A year earlier, in Zurich, the Dada movement had sprung into being. Its founders were artists and writers who seemed bent on the destruction of conventional art, but who succeeded in sharpening the techniques of painting and creating new and concise uses of the language they tore apart. Dadaism spread to France and Germany, where, by 1919 and the war's end, the bitter and satirical George Grosz was a prime mover. In the devastation of the postwar Germany, he and his fellow artists, John Heartfield and Oscar Kokoschka, produced some satirical Dada marionette performances at the *Cabaret Schall und Rauch* in the basement of the Max Reinhardt theater. They were quickly closed for disrespect of political authority.

Among the Dadaists, Otto Griebel was the most active in puppetry. In Dresden he produced a Dada version of *Lohengrin* with Otto Kunze, the puppeteer-musicologist-historian, and Max Linnebach, an innovator whose name is connected with many modern lighting techniques. They also produced a burlesque version of *Faust*. This, of course, had to happen. Faust, never sacred to Kasper, became the victim of the puppeteers.

In 1924, Griebel and Kunze had carried their Dada puppetry to the freer atmosphere of Switzerland and continued experimenting. One of their favorite excercises, typically Dada, was extemporizing an entire play. Adolph Appia, the father of much of our modern concept of stage lighting and design, was already collaborating with Otto Morach, the Swiss puppeteer, when they arrived and had staged a well-documented production of *Master Peter's Puppet Show* the year before. The

Klee painting entitled "The Puppet Theater"
is now in collection of Bern, Switzerland, Art Museum.
Childlike style of painting is typical of Klee.

operetta was based on a poem of Garcia Lorca and music of Manuel DeFalla which had originally been commissioned by the eccentric Princess de Polignac in Paris. The photographs show an aliveness in the design of the characters, and a simplicity and freedom of plastic form lacking in the more nearly human caricatures of contemporary productions. It was a start, although a second look at these figures leads me to believe that some of them moved stiffly. The articulation hadn't caught up with the new shapes. But later craftsmen and gadgeteers would know how to ease up such actions and make them move.

In 1919, Walter Gropius, the architect, founded a school which was to have a profound effect on most of the design of the twentieth century. The Bauhaus was founded on the principles that function was to be the criterion of design, that art and architecture could be fused, that in the machine age craftsmen must run the machines, and that students should create, not copy what someone else had created.

If dumping the old classic styles was revolutionary, so was the idea that a student and not just the teacher was full of invention. The idea was to meet much artistic and political opposition. Finally the creative sparks had to fly in all directions, but not before they had changed the approach to design—including puppetry—in the entire Western world.

Gropius gathered the Swiss, Paul Klee, and the Russian, Wassily Kandinsky, from the Schwabing district of Munich where they had been students. Xanti Schawinsky came from Switzerland and Oscar Schlemmer from Stuttgart to work in the drama department of the school. I mention these four principally because of their influence on puppetry. It was Schlemmer and Schawinsky who created ballets with symbolic scenery, music composed for conventional instruments plus tin pans and dynamite caps, and costumes that transformed dancers into demipuppets with huge shapes built over them and the human inside merely supplying the movement. Other puppets were purely mechanical in their components. Schawinsky choreographed puppet-like figures of paper, wood, and metal to show how different materials and colors behave in motion to music.

Klee himself made fifty hand puppets for his son, Felix, who entertained with them at the Bauhaus. Kandinsky contributed ideas for the performances and was always in the audience. He and Klee had been great fans of the Paul Brann Theater, which had brought their attention to puppetry and caused them to write about it as an independent art. Twenty of Klee's original figures were destroyed when the Americans bombed Dessau, the second home of the Bauhaus, in World War II, but the remainder are in the museum at Bern.

When Hitler came to power in 1933, he suppressed this inquiring art of the Bauhaus, as Stalin did later to the very important beginnings of new stage design in Russia.

In the spring of 1925, Alexander Tairov's experimental Kamerny theater was touring Europe. While in Dresden, the brilliant star of the company, the young Vladimir Sokolov, a fine actor, dancer, and acrobat, fell from a trapeze and broke his ankle. When the company moved on, Sokolov and his wife were obliged to remain in Dresden, where they stayed for two years. The accident led to a meeting with Heinrich Apel, a descendant of a long line of Dresden puppeteers, and the fusion of Sokolov's revolutionary theatrical ideas with Apel's traditional puppetry produced interesting results. According to Kunze, who saw it, their first production was a hilarious blending of their two backgrounds in a dramatization of *The Viu, the Last Witch of Russia* by Gogol.

The work with Apel's theater led Sokolov, who joined Reinhardt, to experiments with the impact of puppetry and philosophy on the fusion of music and puppet action as a new art form. The latter part of his life was spent in the American theater and films.

France also was caught up in getting away from the conventional theater. It was a time when the artists were free to try anything and they did. It was a climate of questions and the artists questioned everything. Gaston Baty, the well-known Parisian scenic designer and producer, for a while

leaned toward puppets as a complete substitute for actors. He toned down this thinking somewhat later, but never lost his fascination for puppetry and produced a good many shows in his own "guignol" theater in Paris.

Geza Blattner, a Hungarian painter, had come to Paris in 1918. He and some other artists had worked in Budapest to produce puppet shows and for a while he had worked with the Hincz family, mainstays of puppetry in Budapest for many years. But it was in Paris with its theatrical excitement that he decided to make puppetry his life work. By 1925 he had opened his Arc en Ciel theater with a triple-purpose proscenium. It was rigged so that he could play marionettes, hand puppets, and his own personal version of the rod figures. He called this type the "key" puppet, because although it was supported by a rig he wore around his waist and neck, the figure

was made to articulate by pressing on a series of wooden keys fastened near the bottom of the control rod. Some of his hand puppets' heads are simple, delightful, almost geometric shapes, with which he broke away completely from realism, and I imagine his was by far the most revolutionary performance at the Liége UNIMA conference in 1930.

Another Frenchman, the architect Maurice Temporal, was busy with puppets in Paris at that time, and although he worked only as an amateur he inspired and taught a whole generation of future puppeteers. Among them was his son, Jean Loup Temporal, who now creates charming plays and puppet shows for children. This is not the tradition in which he was raised, however. Men like his father and Blattner played for a sophisticated adult audience. Jean Loup once told me that when he was a boy if anyone had told him that puppet shows were for children he wouldn't have believed them.

I'm sorry now that I never witnessed one of these shows. I was in Paris in the summer of 1927, playing my accordion in cafes at night and sketching in the afternoons, but I probably would have turned up my nose at Blattner. As an American, I was used to a much more conservative kind of show.

It was not until after World War II that America began to get a taste of the modern brand of puppetry—and it came as a pleasant jolt. Yves Joly of France had come to play in the United States and our new television spread his shows across the whole country. If anyone can be said to have stripped puppetry to its skeleton and started afresh, it is Joly, who threw away the puppet and allowed his hands to assume the

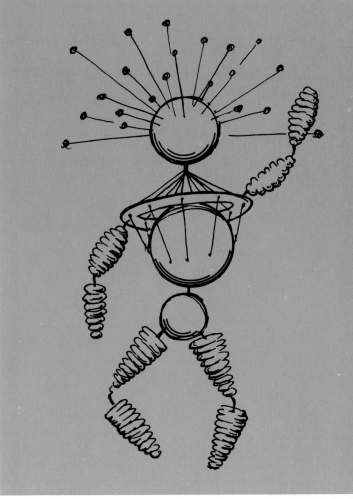

189

Opposite, left: "Ubu Roi" drawing by author Jarry has been model for puppets. Next left: Animal-trainer puppet by Xanti Schawinsky had man inside (note leg). Dada production of *Lohengrin* (above) was originated by Kunze and Griebel in Dresden. Below: Bauhaus figure by Hilde Rantsch.

attitudes of the most sophisticated drama. Working with pantomime and music, his company of hands created ballet, satire, and melodrama. Occasionally a glove has been used to represent costume, or a small hat or other prop to symbolize authority, caste, or status. Here is an anatomized concept of puppetry: creating meaning in the imagination of an audience by getting under the skin of the motion. Joly's imagination has led him to experiment with paper shapes and other materials, and his work has cleared the way for the next inventive wave.

Probably the most influential and creative force in modern, mid-century puppetry, has been Georges Lafaye. Beginning with conventional rod puppets as did Joly, Lafaye created figures that seem to float in light. He was one of the first to use human hands with a puppet head and body. His pioneering efforts are numerous. In a pantomime to music, a giant devours its young. A highly erotic "Striptease" is achieved by human hands and a giant balloon.

Lafaye now works with four or five others costumed in black, holding his creations into a curtain of light that comes from deep troughs positioned across the top and bottom of his stage. The method might be considered an extension of the old Black Art technique used by magicians, but Lafaye's dramatic ideas and artistry have carried it far beyond this. His best known number is *John and Marsha,* in which an old-fashioned top hat (John) and a feather boa (Marsha) perform an amorous pas-de-deux in the air surrounded only by one's imagination, and pantomimed to a record in which John and Marsha repeat each other's name in endless variety. This number has become internationally famous and

has been paid the ultimate tribute of being lifted outright by other puppeteers. The influence of Lafaye has been enormous.

The Black Theater of Prague was started by a puppeteer who had worked with Malik and who had seen Lafaye in Paris. The Black Theater itself, although not presuming to be so, is an exciting form of puppetry since it uses man-operated moving symbols along with live actors. A sewing machine raises its head to greet a human tailor, a camera's bellows arches forward on its own to look down young lady's cleavage and out of its lens comes a live hand to chuck her under the chin, a flock of birds forms itself into antlers upon

Principal André Tahon puppet in group picture opposite is Papotin, the black-robed fellow below Harlequin. Mouse characters are a Tahon trademark. Above: Rod-puppet bride by French puppet playwright, Jean Loup Temporal.

the head of a cuckolded man—all these are puppets, some seen in fluorescent and some in incan-
descent light.

Lafaye's first American tour started me using
strobe effects again in the undersea scene in *Davy
Jones' Locker*. I have also produced a number
for the Chrysler Corporation at the New York
World's Fair in which the glowing skeleton of a
life-sized automobile assembles itself in the air.

One of the most potent theaters to burst upon
the puppet world recently is that of Michael
Meschke of Stockholm. I say "burst" because
since his career was launched in 1958, he has
come forth with many highly sensitive productions using more than a dozen styles of puppetry.
Starting in a country without any strong puppet
tradition to follow, he has likewise had nothing
to hold him back, and each of his concepts has
been performed in a style best suited to it. In
his most recent production, Jarry's *Ubu Roi*, Ubu
and his wife are played by humans inside mask-
ing costumes. The rest of the cast are flat cutouts
of different sizes, some held by actors, some used
as rod puppets, some on wheels.

Other productions, such as his *Tales of Hoffmann,* and *Himel Spelet,* a Christmas play for

**Black-light artistry of Georges Lafaye
includes John and Marsha (above), hilarious and
world-famous ballet by top hat and
feather boa, and more representational number
involving La Marguerite and admirers.**

string marionettes, are each distinctively styled, but poetic and sensitive. His varieties and pantomimes employ other styles.

Meschke's stage is flexible, so that he may broaden or narrow his picture or use any method of puppetry. And although his acting company is limited compared to a supported theater, his choice of subject is broader. His repertoire includes Pinter, Shakespeare, Shaw, Dürrenmatt, Aristophanes, Chekov, and O'Casey. Stravinsky has made a special arrangement of *Histoire du soldat* for him. Visiting troupes have come from Liége, Paris, Rome, Java, and Warsaw to perform their plays in his theater.

A young Frenchman who has developed a unique style of design is André Tahon. Starting as a boy in the company of the elder Temporal, Tahon started working as a single in European clubs and cabarets about 1953, and acquired a company of four members who work with hand and rod puppets. He has won first prize for sculptural design from UNIMA in Bucharest. Tahon's most famous number is that of the snail and the caterpillar, wherein the *escargot* and the *chenille* exchange habitats. He does this with gusto and vocal acrobatics. Since coming to America he has appeared on many of the major television shows and at Disneyland.

Germany has had one of the longest and most solid traditions of puppetry in Europe. In spite of war and upheaval there are more than a hundred companies, both amateur and professional, operating in all of Germany today. Munich again has its permanent theater at 29 Blumenstrasse playing opera in the evening and folktales for children in the afternoons. As in the prewar period, children have to line up early to get a seat before the adults. Doris Boer-Puhonny, daughter of the famous Ivo Puhonny, plays her marionettes in Hamburg.

One of the most active companies today is that of Albrecht Roser of Stuttgart, whose travels have carried him around the world. Roser has tried everything from full-length plays to the cabaret turn in full view, and his puppetry has consequently acquired a high polish. His engaging clown Gustav is well known throughout Europe.

Stuttgart is also the home of Fritz Herbert Bross, whose wood sculpture is most effective, and of Anni Weigand, whose tube puppets have won international prizes, although her operation is strictly amateur.

Harro Siegel, one of the early members of UNIMA, is noted for the quality of his sculpture. It has a classic feeling, yet it is entirely his own and entirely marionette. He places a sensitive emphasis on his design and manipulation of hands. His production of *Faust* has toured extensively.

The list would be incomplete without mention of the huge, mellow-voiced Carl Schroeder of Radebeul, whose hand puppets have made him famous and whose style is distinctive. His own large hands give him a sensitive control over a larger-than-usual puppet. In contrast, his puppets' hands are quite delicate. Schroeder is now at the head of *Dresden Trikfilm* making live motion pictures of hand puppets.

A modern player in the Bauhaus concept of freedom is Fred Schneckenburger of Zurich. Schneckenburger has employed unusual materials and shapes to create weird, horrendous, exciting, and funny puppets which he operates to special music and tapes in his cabaret. The effort of such a pioneer is to be applauded. In his visual result Schneckenburger is a total nonconformist. He creates his own idiom. He does not borrow from the cinema, the live theater or from current puppetry, but builds with new bricks his own burlesque of contemporary life.

England's Waldo Lanchester of Stratford-on-Avon, a deft operator for whom G. B. Shaw wrote the marionette play, *Shakes vs. Shaw,* is credited with having started the revival of British puppetry in the 1930's after the reign of the big, Holden-type companies. Outside of the ever-present Punch men, a dozen or so professional string, rod, and hand-puppet companies are operating in England.

An outstanding English production has been a musical version of Kingsley's *The Water Babies* by the Hogarth company of Jan Bussell and Ann Hogarth, which is done on a large scale with three-foot marionettes and a large high-bridge stage. I did not see this show, but one of my company did and was completely charmed by the imaginative design and especially the "heart" that went into the acting.

The Hogarth company also produced a spectacular rod-puppet performance on the theme of the Greek legend *Europa,* using forty student puppeteers. The set occupied an entire theater proscenium with a full cyclorama and three ascending levels for the puppeteers to operate from. The scenery changed before the eyes of the audience, mountains heaving up as Cadmus descended to the oracle, and rolling away to reveal the sea, docks and harbors sliding in, forests growing, and the city of Thebes rising from the ground.

English puppeteers like those in the United States, must vary their efforts to make a living. As with other performing artists, they play for television, in the music hall, in commercial films, for children and adults.

On the other side of the fence, there are countries where the continued existence of puppetry is guaranteed. In spite of two violent wars and extreme changes in governments, Europe has remained a fertile place for puppetry's growth. It has always had some kind of centrally supported theater, a hangover from the court-sponsored art of the monarchies. With this background it is not surprising that the Communist countries have close to two hundred government-supported puppet companies.

194

Examples of modern European trends in puppetry: (1) Albrecht Roser marionette, Stuttgart. (2) Pierrot marionette by Fritz Herbert Bross. (3) Fred Schneckenburger rod puppet. (4) Marionettes from Hogarth production of Kingsley's *Water Babies,* London, 1963. (5) Michael Meschke production of *Ubu Roi* follows Franciszka Themerson drawings for Jarry book. (6) Meschke's *Tales of Hoffmann.*

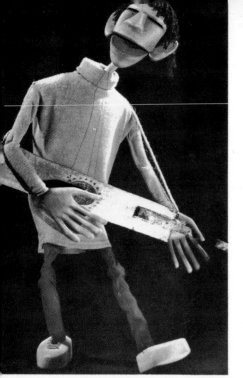

1

2 3

4

5

6

Top, left: "Archangel" by Adam Kilian, Poland. Top, right: "Princess," also by Kilian. Above: Hungarian puppet by Vera Brody of Central Puppet Theater, Budapest. Middle, right: Rod figure from Obraztsov *I GoGo*. Right: Russian poster for *Divine Comedy*. Opposite: Obraztsov concert singer by Vera Terekhova.

Since the war the governments of Eastern Europe have recognized the educational and attitude-forming power of the performing arts. For this reason, their theater has a different purpose from that in the West. When we consider that in the Communist countries all the performing arts, including puppetry, are part of the educational system, the spread of information is important. The repertoire (i.e. curriculum) of one company is often very similar to that of its national central theater. The puppeteer and the ballet dancer belong to the same "union" as the

librarian. (The union is not like those in the West. It may suggest, but not bargain for its membership.) Since these companies are answerable to the state, there is a politician at the top of each. It is most fortunate when the politician is also a theater person.

What a difference from the competition of Broadway! In the first place, the physical plants, the theaters, rehearsal halls, studios, and so forth, are government owned and controlled. In the second place, the performing artist, sculptor, or playwright is on salary the year around, even while he is learning. This condition translates itself in Poland into over twenty-four nationally supported puppet theaters and more than fifteen hundred professionals connected with them. This does not mean that the most talented or hardest working do not receive greater rewards, such as housing or better vacations. They do. It does mean that a performer is gainfully employed most of the time and that his calling is highly respected. This is doubly rewarding if it is the calling of his choice.

It also results in large padded staffs such as may be found in any bureaucratic operation. In Tony Sarg's day fifteen to twenty people—and only half that number on the road—produced and operated three and one-half hours of production which toured the United States for eight months. My own touring company for live shows has seldom been larger. On the other hand, a company of fifty people or more is not unusual in the Communist countries.

In return for this government support the performing arts must give something. In general, they must provide theatrical productions in line with the government policy, or find suitable illus-

trations of it in local cultural material such as folk tales, myths, and stories of national heroes of the past. The importance of this was impressed upon us during our own company's tour of six Russian cities when we were constantly asked: "What is your message? What are you trying to tell us?" It was hard for them to believe we were only there to entertain.

Until recently the Communist countries have had most latitude in folklore and anti-Western, anticapitalist themes—satirizing Hollywood, the Dollar, and Wall Street. Occasionally a critical look at Russian things is permitted, such as *The Little Golden Calf*, a mild satire on Russian social chiselers.

One very popular play in the Communist countries is *The Divine Comedy*, a spoof of Genesis by the Russian playwright Isidor Stock. God and the archangels are portrayed by masked human actors, while Adam, Eve, the cherubim, the seraphim, and the animals are puppets. Here is the old religious puppet play turned around. The

Christian world might question the divinity of the play, but it certainly is a comedy. The Lord, egged on by one of the angels, creates light and darkness, the firmament and stars, then the earth, and the animals. He and the angels then put together a man and a woman, although only after many amusing mistakes by the angels who put four legs on one and four arms on the other. The woman turns out to be a hellcat and Adam asks to be returned to dust. The Lord decides to make a woman out of a part of Adam to be sure they are compatible. He returns the woman to the clay she was made of and puts Adam on the operating table. The angels hand scapels and instruments, while the Lord pulls Eve out of Adam's ribs. She is sweet and compliant, but this time Adam is gun-shy and is finally won over only when she starts to wait on him.

In the end, after the fall, when God forgives the sinners, they decide to stay on Earth with all its hardships rather than return to their former safe, celibate heaven.

Left: Concert-singer rod puppet by Obraztsov needs two operators, one for arms, other for head and body. *Divine Comedy* has been parodied by Russian and Czech puppet companies: Above, left: Adam and Eve in Moscow production. Above, right: Lord and archangels (played by human actors) in Prague production.

The Communist educational system divides audiences into three age groups: very little children; somewhat older, grade-school children; and adults. The child does not see entertainment beyond his level until he is considered ready for it. Often puppet shows are the first indoctrination a child experiences.

In children's plays, besides local national folklore, many titles are borrowed from the West such as: *Puss-in-Boots, Dr. Doolittle, The Wizard of Oz* (the villain, appropriately, is the Wicked Witch of the West). Kipling is prominent, as is Hans Christian Andersen.

Obviously, the scope of this activity has passed well beyond the province of the "loner." The days of the all-around individual operator in Eastern Europe seem to be on the way out, unless he happens to be in charge of a theater's production. There have been some rather disastrous results artistically when a politician has been in charge of theatrical production, despite the obvious advantages of money and manpower. This is by no means a situation confined solely to the Communist countries, although it can happen there more often.

Of all the countries in Eastern Europe, Poland has the most puppet theaters per capita and the most experimentation. Poland has managed to keep the flow of its puppet evolution healthy by diversity. The central management, it seems, has encouraged this experimentation and there is a rich backlog of talented designers and playwrights working in new, wildly imaginative ways. There is some, though not much, string marionette activity, and a great deal of rod and hand puppetry. Both varieties play to a great extent in combination with human actors. The Groteska theaters

in Lodz and Warsaw utilize the huge human head (i.e. mask) over the head of a live actor, giving a symbolic, puppetlike quality to him.

In the last few years such plays as *Guignol in Trouble* and *Captive in Tiutiurlistan* have had a good deal of international European exposure. The *Captive,* according to Henryk Jurkowski, the coordinator of Polish puppetry, is "a play about friendship and peace and the need of sacrificing oneself for the sake of others." *The Woodman and the Wayside Flower* is a play about the beauty and the love of one's country. But then Jurkowski says about two other popular plays that "children want and need entertainment with a simple story and without complicated educational problems." In other words, sometimes kids want pure entertainment without the lesson.

Among Poland's top designers working for puppetry is Adam Kilian. The son of a puppeteer, Kilian was raised in the tradition and has applied his considerable talents to both puppetry and to the legitimate theater. He has initiated many new styles and adopted old ones. He has gone back to old national folklore for inspiration. In one production, *The Wedding,* he has created huge puppets out of basket work in the manner of an old Polish folk art and mixed these monsters in the same play with human actors.

In addition to the searching going on there is still time for the medieval Szopka performance at Christmas time, when beautiful old pieces, and even some newly built cathedrals, are brought out for the religious puppetry.

The Poles have travelled extensively over Europe with the great plastic art of their creation. I quote a wistful commentary from one of their leaders: "Polish puppets have a tendency to be

200

beautiful, sculptural and poetic without much dramatic conflict." If this be true, I am confident the drama is not far off, since the Poles are trying everything.

The modern Russian puppet theater claims to have started during the First World War, and to have found its use in education soon thereafter. Today's Russian puppetry appears to have felt the impact of Sergei Obraztsov. His is another example of a theater dominated by the complete puppeteer. Originally trained as an artist and opera singer, Obraztsov was able to create his one-man hand-puppet show and to play it to live audiences long enough to develop into a thorough showman and perceptive director.

Obraztsov still performs some of his early hand-puppet satires to the accompaniment of his own singing. From his performances today we can see why the government picked him to head up the Moscow Central Theater in 1930. In the beginning its output was entirely for a children's audience, although by now more than half of its shows are for adults. The first production was entitled *Jim and Dollar* (in English, not Russian), and was the story of a little American Negro boy who had lost his job and wanted to come to the Soviet Union with his little dog, Dollar. He finds a jazz band that is going to Europe but is told that he must play an instrument if he is to go along. He finally pulls down a drain pipe to play on and is admitted to the band. "From here on begins the propaganda," I was told.

Sergei Obraztsov heads up an organization of around two hundred and twenty people, including two playing companies, and the carpenters, designers, actors, sculptors, painters, musicians,

playwrights, statisticians, and secretaries necessary to keep them in operation. By Western standards a staff this size would be considered wasteful or financially impossible, but in Russia it is considered important to keep this much manpower engaged in "education." Despite this specialization the result is smoothly produced shows, because the boss is a complete puppeteer who understands what it's all about. The Central Theater has a great deal of influence on the operation of the more than eighty other state-supported Soviet puppet theaters.

One of the great differences I observed between Eastern and Western types of operation was that a row of chairs was set in a semicircle behind the stage for the eighteen puppeteers to sit on when they were not playing. A performer would get up to do his specialty and then sit down again. In my company we ten must all be busy all of the time. However, I noticed that about eight of the Russians did most of the work.

Many of the Russian puppet theaters still have original members of thirty years' standing as their principal actors, and they are extremely good, although I was asked how we were able to get good young people for our company. The Russian system of training actors makes the recruiting of young puppeteers somewhat difficult, inasmuch as all young theatrical aspirants are trained at an academy and from there they go to the stage, ballet, puppets, or films. As a consequence not many young ones have had a chance to get the "bug" as do young people in the West, who often start their own companies at the age of twelve.

The Moscow Central Theater has developed a considerable repertoire of adult plays. Eugene Speransky, one of the theater's original group and the author of a new book on playwriting for puppets, has done two plays shown regularly in the Moscow repertoire. *The Flutter of Her Eyelashes* is a satire on Hollywood.

Speransky's latest play, *I GoGo*, is a considerable breakthrough in concept and design for the Russian puppet theater. With the coming of *I GoGo*, the design of Russian puppetry is probably freer than anything it has done up to now. A delightfully outrageous mermaid, a demi-demon whose supple body appeared in many metamorphoses, was more powerful in design, action and voice by her very contrast with the humans who appeared on stage from time to time. The author has used a number of exciting techniques and some excellent puppet gambits.

I GoGo attacks the forces of evil. The action takes place in a science-fiction laboratory with a raised platform across an entire theater stage on either side of which are benches overflowing with electronic apparatus. In the center, raised a little higher still, is a huge (eleven-by-seven-foot) television screen which is actually the main rod-puppet opening within the live setting, the bottom edge being about man-height from the stage floor.

This set provides many other opportunities for hand and rod puppets to appear, the most dramatic being the first appearance of the forces of evil, when an entire cast of devils suddenly materializes in space out of the darkness to a burst of music. Effects were numerous. At one time a head repeated itself one by one into the distance. On another occasion, a huge head appeared; it was about four feet high, made of the flexible material, supported on a board, and operated by the hands of the puppeteers inside of it. At some points I felt that the *I GoGo* story was the victim of its many new techniques.

I GoGo has been a breakthrough not only in subject matter, but in techniques for the Obraztsov company. The designer, Boris Tuzlukov, has used sculptured polyethylene foam in many ways. Large chunks have been sculptured with scissors into hands, faces, and bodies and covered with knitted cloth to prevent breakage. Flat slabs of foam have been used for costume construction and it is particularly well suited to the rod-puppet technique because the operator, being close, can exert force against its springiness.

If Sergei Obraztsov's early operation was somewhat limited by Stalinism in its choice of subject and freedom of design (*The Unusual Concert* was was once banned because it had "no positive hero"), it certainly has made up for it in mechanical techniques and in discipline of performance. I have never seen rod puppets anywhere with such sure and careful workmanship which offered such technical accuracy and subtlety of control.

The educational position of the Russian puppet theater allows for no secrecy in the old traditional sense. When we played in Moscow our backstage was constantly host to the Obraztsov company, and we were made equally at home behind the scenes at their performances and in their workshop. I was often embarrassed when they placed me in a chair almost on stage during a performance. We got to be very good friends with the Moscow group. They were curious about our performances and there was nothing they would not show us about their own.

One of the oldest permanent companies in the Soviet Union is that of Eugene Demeni who has carried on a string-marionette operation for thirty-

five years despite the general tendency in the Soviet Union to employ the less difficult rod and hand puppets.

Probably more foreigners are aware of Obraztsov's *Unusual Concert* than any of the other works. It has been his window to the West and it plays more to out of towners and visitors from abroad than to Muscovites, since it depends more on pantomime and music than the rest of his productions. One of his companies usually plays this show two or three times a week in Moscow— and has for eighteen years. In his own words, Sergei describes it as a satire on "bad" performers: "bad" singing, a "bad" Italian basso, a "bad" gypsy chorus. Actually, it points up the funny things about the European music-hall fare of twenty years ago and has acquired an extremely high polish during its long run. Obraztsov had a good many figures rebuilt for his American tour in the fall of 1963, when he and his twenty-five operators played a highly successful run in New York's Broadway Theater. This was a part of the first international intercultural exchange wherein one puppet show from abroad was "traded" for one of our own.

The puppet theater in Tiflis, in Georgia, is almost as old as the Moscow group, having been formed three years later. We received an enthusiastic welcome from the Georgian puppet group, although officially we had not been told about them and had to discover them for ourselves, since no Georgian puppeteers had been permitted backstage at our performances. (With the exception of the friendly Moscow company, the Russians were generally reluctant to allow people to come backstage to see us and our operation.)

The Georgians have a permanent theater in Tiflis with about two hundred fifty seats and we were shown a rehearsal of a Georgian folktale and some wild Georgian dancing.

After World War II when Czechoslovakia, with its long tradition of string-operated marionettes, began working with rod puppets, it went its own individual way and with very good reason. Puppetry is very much in the blood of the Czech people. There are still over twelve hundred amateur puppet theaters in the country today and they have been working in their own way for a long time. In addition, there are sixteen professional companies, the largest of these being the Central Theater in Prague, with a company of sixty to seventy people. Its stage for rod puppets is also completely Czech, employing a pit in the main stage floor with raising and lowering ramps at the bottom for the operators to stand on, and to hold set pieces.

The man who designed this ingenious stage and who has had much to do with its productions is Jan Malik, one of the original founders of UNIMA and still its general secretary. Malik understands every phase of puppetry and has labored diligently for his craft despite the interruptions of war and occupation. Before the war Malik designed, built, and produced shows using marionettes of simple elementary shapes which broke completely with the old tradition. He has also written a number of plays. One famous all over Europe is *Micek Flicek,* the story of a wandering bouncing ball.

As a participant in the performances, Dr. Malik plays the part of the Lord in the Czech version of *Divine Comedy.* Dr. Malik is such a creative force in puppetry that I felt a little resentful when, on the occasion of our first meeting, I found him

205

Modern puppets come in variety of forms. (1) Faust and Mephisto marionettes of Harro Siegel, Germany. (2) Kasperle hand puppet by Fritz Herbert Bross, Germany. (3) Two puppets from *The Fan,* Spieldose, Munich. (4) Tube puppets in Anni Weigand Stuttgart Youth House production of *A Ship Will Arrive.* (5) Scene from *Sinbad,* Baisil Milovsoroff, Vermont. (6) Shadow puppet by Americans Tony Urbano and Jerry Jensik. (7) Albrecht Roser's "Gustav," Germany.

1

2

3

4

5

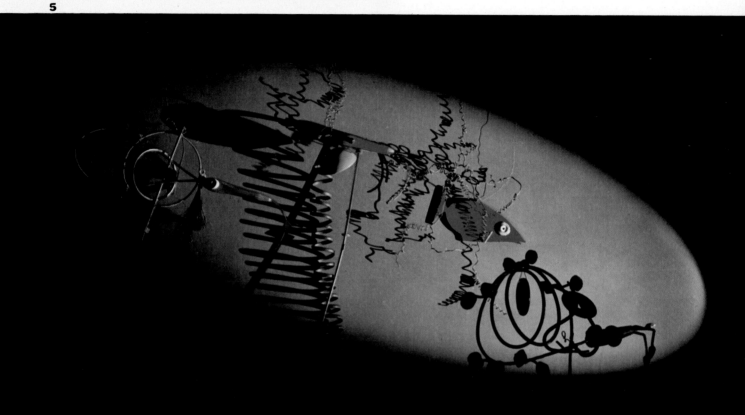

6

7

1

2

3

4

5

6

7

8

snowed under with official business.

Skupa's well-equipped theater of Hurvinek and Spejbl continues playing to young and old with its prewar popularity, though with a larger office force since the government has taken over.

The Czechs print many colorfully illustrated books on puppet plays, which are used by the children's amateur companies.

The Czechs also have developed the art of animated puppet motion pictures to a high degree. Karel Zeman is one of the most adept, and Jiri Trncka, who once worked under Malik with marionettes, will be well remembered in America for his film of *The Chinese Nightingale*.

Modern Hungary has a central theater with many moving branches. Under the direction of Dr. Deszo Szilagyi, the Budapest Central Theater has a program of adult productions during most of the year and in the summertime light, fast-travelling troupes of eight to ten operators entertaining inexpensively indoors and outdoors with such pieces as Hungarian versions of *Pinocchio*, as well as old Hungarian folktales. Despite recent warnings at UNIMA about "children must not see the wolf bite," at a Hungarian verson of the *Three Little Pigs* I saw the wolf skinned and roasted while he complained loudly and the children were delighted.

Vera Brody, designer and scenic artist, has contributed greatly to the style of present-day Hungarian puppetry. One notable production of *Aladdin* by the Budapest Theater is quite stylized in design and has met with much critical praise in the Western European countries.

Romania has had a close neighbor in the Turkish and Greek Karaghioz, and her own great early period of puppetry was while she was under Ottoman rule at the end of the eighteenth and beginning of the nineteenth century, when as in Czechoslovakia, no other national theater was in existence. Romania's best playwrights then wrote for the puppet theater.

Unfortunately, in the second half of the nineteenth century, there were some repressive laws against the Romanian cultural arts and the puppets were suppressed along with them. It was not until the early 1920's that puppetry began to rise again, under the influence of Podrecca and Skupa. Professor Teodor Nastase, managing director of the Romanian National Opera, was one of the fine producers of puppetry of this period.

Today Romania has twenty professional "state" theaters, stemming in 1949 from the pioneer Tandarica under the direction of Margarita Niculescu and still going strong.

The theaters absorb the talents of some six hundred performers and have played in recent years to audiences totaling one hundred and fifty thousand persons. Bucharest has been host to three international puppetry conferences.

In our times, change comes faster than ever.

If nineteenth-century puppetry wandered far from its origins, the Surge, by cementing the artist to folk puppetry, began to bring back the true meanings. But the artist probed deeper and felt that there was much more to the craft than a comment on the live theater.

Today's creative puppeteer wants to get back to the symbolic uses that first brought puppetry to life. But, just as he is beginning to arrive at some of the old truths, he is confronted with the inescapable fact of television, which can energize the live quality of his output immensely, or if he is not careful, mechanize it into dull stupidity.

209

Eastern European puppetry of today includes: (1) Czech Jan Malik's play, *Immortal Laugh.* (2) Czech Jiri Trncka's Don Quixote marionette. (3) Basketry figures by Polish Adam Kilian. (4) Polish *Miniatura* production. (5) Romanian Tandarica theater figure by Getlu Naum. (6) Romanian Tandarica theater puppets by Ioana Constantinescu. (7) Hungarian play, *Traveler Without Money.* (8) Hungarian folk figures by Vera Brody.

Putting on a puppet show is unlike any other kind of show business. The most exciting difference is the great latitude puppeteers have in design. Our actors are made to suit the style of the play they appear in and the audience they play for.

First, consider the audience, which governs the action, shape, and size of the puppets—in that order of importance. The limits are flexible: Puppets can be big, small, rough, smooth, simple, or extreme. That is part of their fascination. In choosing the qualities his puppet characters are to have, the puppeteer must ask himself: How big will the audience be? One? Two? Two hundred? A thousand? And what kind of an audience will it be? Sophisticated? Unused to puppets? Or a different language group? All these factors will affect the design.

I design for the middle range of the audience. For a very large audience of thousands, the action is conceived in big sweeps and the characters molded in simple planes, with large features that will catch light. Sometimes they can be larger than life size. Such figures would never do in a night club, where the audience is literally on top of you. I remember one forty-foot dragon we played before a Radio City Music Hall audience of six thousand. Three of us got onto a U-shaped bridge at stage level and were hoisted twenty-five feet into the flies in order to coil and arch our dragon around a live dancer five feet tall. In another show in memory of Anna Pavlova, a pair of ballet slippers bourréed across the big stage in a spotlight in front of the corps de ballet. I was forty-feet up, working from a light bridge. These are unusual cases, but they illustrate the extremes of size that puppetry can accommodate.

Where the live ballet performer has had to devise extreme make-up to simplify and accentuate his face, the puppet playing to a large audience can be modeled in sweeps and planes that can be easily understood at a distance. Even in a puppet head half the size of a human one, the eyes and nose and mouth can be larger than their live counterparts and, hence, more visible.

Sometimes the nebulous modeling of the features of a tiny puppet can cause it to live in the mind of the audience by suggestion. There is the greatest latitude of choice, depending on the subject. For instance, I doubt if the divine quality found in great sculpture can be approached or equaled in a flat drawing. There is a quality of life in such sculpture, even without motion, and this also can be present in puppetry. An "animated" cartoon must keep up a certain speed of motion or it loses life and becomes just a drawing. A puppet may move extremely slowly, or even stop, without losing its living "thereness."

More important to putting on a show, but less spectacular than size and design is the concept of an idea. There is no subject that puppetry can't tackle but we must always make the strongest use of puppets. We must stay in the areas where live shows can't possibly compete. An example would be our underwater fable, *Davy Jones' Locker*. Or if we lift a piece of dramatic material designed for humans we can improve it for our own use. Cora and I once rearranged *Carmen,* using the Bizet music and theme, but doing everything from the point of view of the bull. In the live opera he is offstage. Not in ours. He is very much in evidence throughout the play.

An idea may come about in many ways. *Davy Jones' Locker* is a show that started with two iso-

lated thoughts which occurred some twenty-five years ago. One thought was about a sea monster who had shrunk from a colossal size because nobody believed in him. The other was about a pirate captain who was so mean that it hurt his face to smile. Over the years, details about pirates and underwater things began to fill in, and by the time we needed a play, I had a rough outline to give to a team of writers. By that time, too, there were pages with doodles and sketches of characters, sets, and possible action. Both puppets and backgrounds must be designed together, based on what is going to happen. Sometimes, for instance, no scenery at all may be preferable to a busy, complicated background. A dreamy, poetic theme, such as *Tales of Hoffmann* will be different from a loud, satirical piece, and mine will not be like someone else's. We attempt to find a simple and effective style that best tells the story to our audience. Surely no two stories have the same requirements, and a glance at the illustrations in this book indicate the hundreds of different problems and solutions that may arise.

There are many ways an idea can be generated. Sometimes a sound starts you off. A record of a prominent sister team suggested the three calves we used at the Chicago World's Fair, and later a more raucous trio of sisters led us to make the three kittens that brought us into the Ruban Bleu night club and the Ziegfeld Follies. A distinctive walk may suggest a framework around which to build a character. Or sometime the device of giving human characteristics to an animal face can make a more satisfactory puppet than just a caricature.

Caricature in drawing can be quite extreme and wonderful, but in three dimensions it's more difficult to be extreme. One of the first things I remember wanting to try with puppets was "cartooning" in three dimensions and in motion. I was much impressed by the simplicity and effectiveness of comic strips and decided to try to translate them into puppetry. I found, however, that there is a great deal more to making a cartoon in three dimensions than in two. In the round you have to satisfy the eye from every angle, and sometimes, especially in a friendly caricature, the tendency is to keep close to the original, which leaves us an inadequate human copy. Sometimes a random pattern in a rug, or the shadows in a stretch of gravel, will suggest a much wilder caricature than any amount of effort will produce. One time, I had a strange piece of luck

1

2 3 4

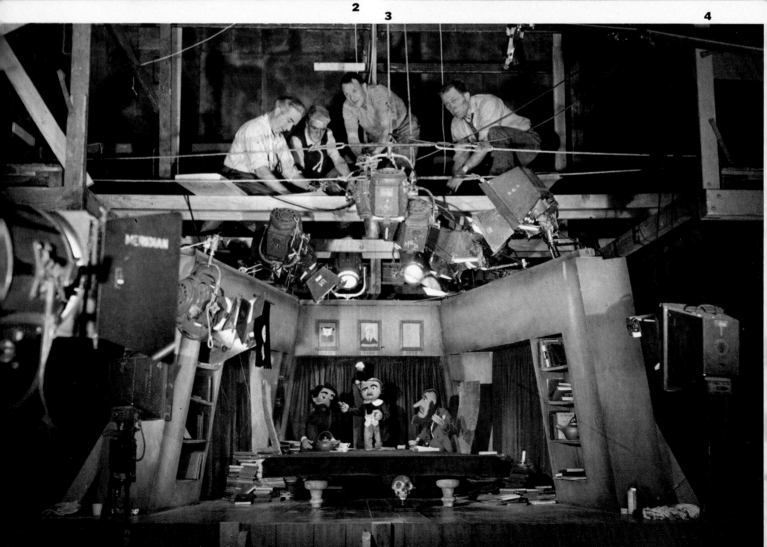

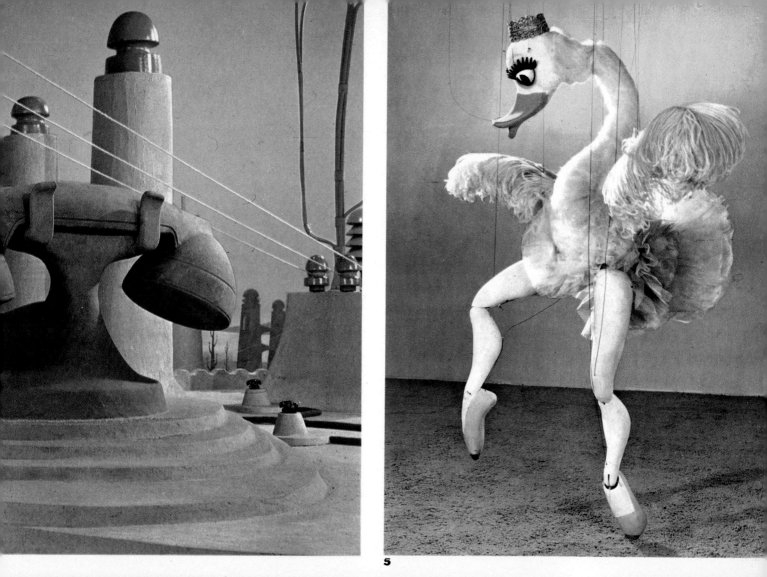

Scenes and characters from various Bil Baird enterprises: **(1)** *The Wee Cooper O'Fife*, a film short. **(2)** Rod puppets from outdoor show in India. **(3)** On Hollywood set of *The Strange Case of the Cosmic Rays*, an educational feature. **(4)** 9,000 prints were made of *Adventure in Telezonia* for telephone company. **(5)** Mme. Swanova. **(6)** Motor Blockettes from Chrysler World's Fair show.

when coming out of anesthesia. The hospital room was pleasant, with a wall that had been stippled with crumpled paper, and ruffled curtains. It wasn't really unusual, but for me, still groggy from anesthesia, these patterns began to live. I began to see a whole ballet playing itself out on the walls and curtains. First there appeared a troupe of little Dutch dwarfs as in Rip Van Winkle, then a whole ballet performing Mussolini's invasion of Ethiopia. I called for Cora to bring me pencil and paper, and imagined I was getting everything down: Ethiopian soldiers advancing, a rock with a profile resembling Haile Selassie, the earth opening up and swallowing the invaders. When I awoke next day there wasn't much of a story, but I had drawn one design that has influenced the shape and operation of all my dancers ever since. A few years later, when I had to enter the hospital again, I took along pads of paper and colored pencils—the works.

But nothing happened. They gave me a different anesthetic, I guess. In any event, I don't recommend dipping into artificial stimulants to get inspiration. The ordinary ones are a lot safer.

We must think of music in the same way we think of puppetry. It should also be a simplification. The sound of a full orchestra has a tendency to overwhelm the puppet show. Stravinsky's *Histoire du Soldat,* which was written for seven instruments and with puppets in mind, sounds just right. The voices of the individual instruments are like characters themselves. They are part of the puppetry.

Another aspect of playing to an audience is to determine its degree of sophistication. In America, by and large, the performing arts play to a primitive audience. I am making no complaint; that's just the way it is. A sophisticated audience is developing, but only in some of the large cities.

One of our night-club numbers involves a "stripper" who first takes off her skirt, then her bra, and finally her head. This act was a complete success in New York's posh Persian Room, but not on the one occasion we were booked into a real burlesque theater. When Bubbles lifted her head aloft there was embarrassed silence. The audience thought we'd broken the puppet. Another time, in a vaudeville house, our smooth, effortless operation got only a patter of applause. Cora suggested making everything look difficult. We strained and grimaced and the audience came through. It is a much happier situation when the audience accepts the method and concentrates on the play, but wherever puppets are still considered a novelty, we must adjust to the circumstances.

We are sometimes asked how we hide the strings or rods. This question usually comes from someone who has seen very little puppetry, because the answer is: We don't and it isn't necessary. Strings and rods are a part of our technique as much as a cut to a close-up is in motion pictures. The result is that the audience accepts strings or rods without question. There are parts of the world, however, where the sudden arrival of a big head close-up on the screen is cause for amazed laughter—because the audience is unused to film technique.

When the Russian rod puppets played on American television, there were a few people who tried to adjust their TV sets, thinking that the feet were being cut off because the picture was slipping, when actually, of course, there were

Baird company's traveling setup in temple square of Bhadgaon, Nepal. Top, left to right: Erecting stage, Bil shows rod puppet to Tibetan visitors, a fascinated Nepalese audience. Bottom: What it was looking at—Cora Baird operating dancing Groovy Gus. Pictures by Augustus Theodore.

no feet to be seen.

There are places where our audiences believed the puppets to be alive. In Nepal, after an outdoor show in the temple square of Bhdgaon, we were unable to pack up our stage because everybody thought packing was part of the show and pressed backstage to watch. Then Frank Sullivan and I each put on a hand puppet and walked back through the crowd pulling the people along. They followed closely, but wouldn't touch my puppet, Cheeky, when he held out a hand. Then Cheeky reached down and stole a hat. The owner reached back for it and felt the puppet's nose. He spoke a couple of words in Nepali and the crowd nearly tore the puppet from me in an effort to feel him. I suddenly realized that they'd thought all along that he was alive. Another time, in Afghanistan, I went into a shop to have a fur cap made. The owner spoke no English, but said he could speak German. I was about to answer, but a thought occurred to me and I

reached into my bag and came out with Cheeky. I had the puppet speak German and act as interpreter between the hatmaker and English-speaking me. They made all the arrangements and the Afghan never looked at me once.

With the foregoing in mind it is easier to understand how in the past a sophisticated priest class could use puppetry for the indoctrination of a primitive audience.

Another striking difference from the live theater is puppetry's compactness. When I design a show, the logistics are always in the back of my head. When we travel, everything has to fit into a truck of a certain size and there is just so much material we can carry. In the United States our limit has been just a little over two tons and on our foreign tours about double that because of extra electrical equipment and extra stages. This is reason enough for simple and compressible sets and properties.

In addition, however, my company has eight

Baird figures (left to right): Marionette stripper
Bubbles LaRue, a creation of 1942; Ollie Oilcan, head-puppet
performer at New York World's Fair; Crutchface, a marionette in
science-fiction act; President Franklin Roosevelt, a
rod puppet appearing in Broadway musical, *Flahooley.*

bodies moving backstage among the playing areas to handle the hundred or more puppets and all the props, scenery, and lights that a two-hour show requires. The disposition of these bodies is as important as the show on the stages. There is only a certain amount of room on the bridges, or in the hand-puppet areas, and we have to routine the shows carefully so that no two people hit the same space at the same time. A fall can be painful. Even the view from backstage of a hand-puppet area can look like the Laocoön group in the Vatican museum. Sometimes, for a very heavy scene, the man at the switchboard will hurriedly climb one of the bridges for a minute or two to bring on a marionette and then climb down for a light cue. The hand which holds a puppet one instant may hold a microphone the next, and seconds later a bass-drum stick. The action of the show must be planned accordingly.

In my company it is not enough to be just an actor, singer, designer, or builder. Often it is an extra ability that makes the valuable puppeteer. Certainly if you know how to build your puppet you can operate him better, and vice versa.

All of my puppeteers can operate hand or rod puppets or string marionettes as the occasion demands. Our carpenter and electrician spend part of their time manipulating puppets from the bridge or behind the playboard. And the combined musical talents of the troupe give us the capability of playing some fifteen or twenty instruments better than passably. If our singing voices are not of concert quality, the puppets' faces usually provide an adequate distraction.

There is one other skill our company boasts, one which makes an unique and vital contribution to puppetry. This is the art of the wood carver. In the United States the skillful carver is a rarity. I have been fortunate enough to inherit carvers from abroad: two Germans, one Czech, one Hungarian, and a Japanese. Incidentally, I highly recommend the craft as a balm for the mind and

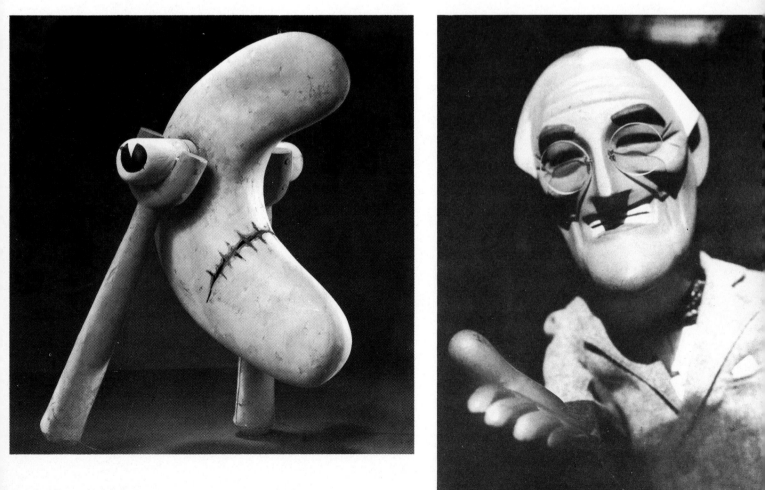

a discipline for the hands. I have never known a nervous carver.

We also have a puppeteer from the Budapest Hincz-Haisfi company, whose family tradition started in 1711 in south Germany.

In the United States the industrial uses of puppetry have been growing since the early Thirties. During the 1964-65 seasons at the New York World's Fair we had our biggest problem in logistics. In our industrial show for the Chrysler Corporation we were required to give continuous showings for twelve hours a day. Four stages on a revolving, seventy-foot drum played different segments of the show to four surrounding auditoriums, each seating six hundred people. Each segment lasted eight minutes and then the drum made a quarter turn to continue the operation. In all, this meant eighty-eight shows a day!

Four crews of twelve puppeteers, plus technical personnel, alternated throughout the day. The initial problem was to keep from becoming a slave to the machine and to make it work for us. Five million people in a season indicate that we came out on top of the monster.

There are certain universal qualities about marionettes that seem to have bubbled to the top of the repertoire of most experienced international troupes. I am not referring to anything highly artistic or to any outstanding play, but to the basic library of pantomime actions and funny sounds that performers have always used to satirize the fallible world of people. The dancing skeleton may be the most universal cliché. That concept must go back to cave-man days. Then there are the puppet acrobats doing tricks just a bit more outrageous than those of their more limited human counterparts. And the sapient ani-

Simple but ingenious artistry of marionette construction is seen in unadorned dancing figure. Below: Hand-puppet Cheeky in Moscow. Opposite: Marionette Scheherazade dances in musical, *Flahooley*. All figures by Baird.

mal—dog, donkey, or invented beast. There are all kinds of instrumentalists. About twenty-five years ago I vowed I'd never do a piano number. There had been so many hilarious ones: Podrecca, Salici, Skupa, Obraztsov, Sarg — and I've already spoken of Mantell's mop-haired virtuoso whose piano was his antagonist. Nevertheless, I've broken my vow a good many times.

The opera singer whose chest heaves and whose neck stretches for the high notes is another old one, but ever popular. The addition of an incongruous voice, such as Obraztsov's female gypsy who sings bass, brings a big laugh. The fast reciprocal motion—hula, shimmy, or cooch—is funny puppetry. As a freshman in college I threw together a snake charmer (with a dried-lemon head and a wooden nose) and a snake which danced and finally killed his boss. I didn't know it, but the number was already about a thousand years old. When I saw it in Rajasthan, the only difference was that the snake was bigger and the musician was standing up. And this is all strictly puppet repertoire. Try it with people and it either falls flat—or the attrition is too costly! The medi-

eval puppeteer-monks knew this when they had a skeleton cut off Herod's head, spear him on a pitchfork, and carry him into the flaming jaws of hell.

In the refinement of these classic bits of action, it's almost as though natural selection has been at work, and in some cases I'm sure it was. In the days of vaudeville, when an act running twelve minutes or so played twenty-one or more times a week, the best parts came to the top. The things that were accidentally funny got polished and the slow spots were weeded out without much thinking about it.

I have spoken about how much time and care goes into producing a show. Sometimes a show must be finished in a very short time, but with the proper ingredients it may come out right side up. Once, when I was much younger—and that's one important ingredient, right there—Alexander King, the raconteur, writer, and illustrator, came to me and said, "Bil, I've just turned down a great opportunity for us, but there isn't enough time to do it." I opened my mouth. He continued, "I just told Mrs. Luce (Clare Boothe Luce, later Ambassador to Italy) that I've written a play and she begged me to get you to do it for her party at the Waldorf. I told her we hadn't time."

It turned out there was a week to go. "Ridiculous," I said, as he had primed me to. "We can get—" and I named eight or nine of our talented theater friends I figured we could get to help.

Alex went home that night and wrote the play from scratch. It was a satire on elections, starting with Lincoln and Jefferson in Heaven listening to the radio and hearing their names being bandied about by a politician. They finally came down to Earth to haunt him out of office with the

Above: Nimble and expressive hands of the noted French puppeteer, Yves Joly, perform an intriguing finger ballet. Opposite: Backstage view during rehearsal of marionette show in Bairds' New York studio.

Ghost of his Public Record. I had to build the Presidents, the politician, and the ghost, plus a lot of babies to be kissed and tossed back at their mothers. The mothers, a line of bathing beauties, and a zebra for the party symbol, I had on hand. Everybody got the fever and we labored happily night and day. Nat Karson, then scenic designer for Radio City Music Hall, painted three sets. We recorded music and made sound effects. The new marionettes went on stage with paint still wet. Alex King prepared the program but listed the author of the play as Kiraly Sandor—Alexander King in Hungarian. He wasn't sure we wouldn't flop.

The play was a success and Alex was out front bowing as soon as the applause started. He beat me by three seconds, but I had to get down from the bridge.

It is possibly a comfortable thought to read that artists such as Craig, Shaw, and Anatole France have concluded that puppets are superior beings who will always outplay human actors. I am not denying the power or veracity of their words. But it must be remembered that the puppet, however sur-real or super-real, is the extension of some mere human being. He is the result of the concept, the animation, and the design of some one of us fallible creatures. We make either good puppets or bad ones, and although the puppets do succeed to some extent in filtering out the egos of their creators, some of our foibles seem to come through.

TODAY & TOMORROW

13

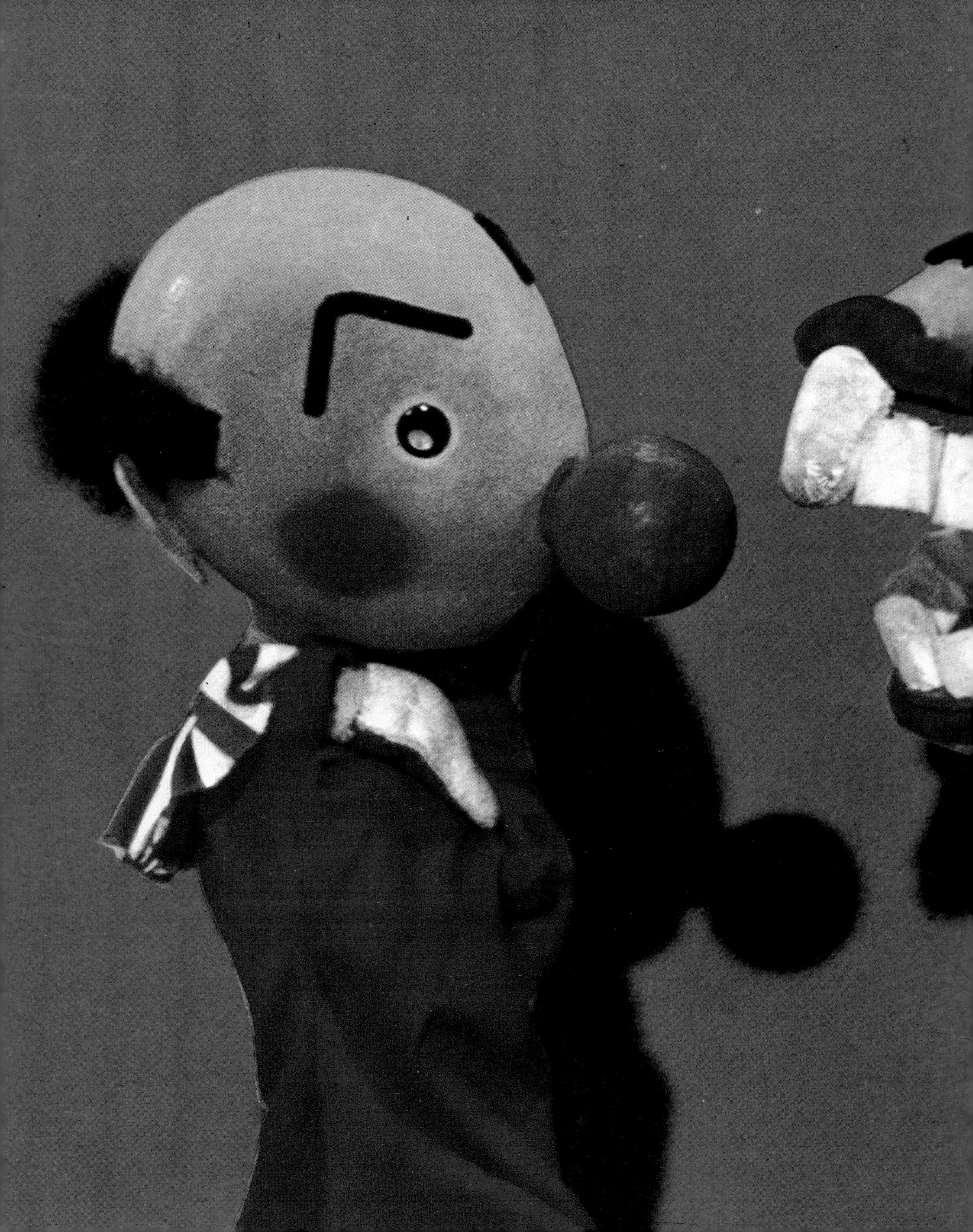

P uppetry in America has been different from puppetry in Europe for two important reasons: first, there has been no long single tradition of American puppetry; and second, the impact of the machine, notably television, on American entertainment.

America has had the good fortune to inherit its people from all over the world, and to have absorbed the puppet heritage of many of them into its culture. It is true that the Indians of the Northwest Coast and New Mexico had traditions of puppetry when the Europeans first came, but the newcomers didn't discover it right away. Besides they were interested in what they understood. The first known European puppeteer to land in the New World was among the personal servants of Hernando Cortez during his conquest of Mexico in the sixteenth century. The entourage included an acrobat and five musicians, and a puppeteer—additional evidence of the type of entertainment traveling with the armies.

Later arrivals had a more permanent effect. In colonial America what was probably a marionette show in the English style was first performed in 1738 on the site of New York's Fraunces Tavern. Definite evidence places another such show in Philadelphia in 1742. When the ill-fated Maximilian came from Austria to become emperor of Mexico, he brought Guignol with him and planted the seeds of hand puppetry in that country. In the nineteenth century when the Greeks began to arrive, they brought Karaghioz, and his shows played for a time to Greek-American audiences in New York, Chicago, and Cleveland. Orlando had his Italian-American audience on New York's Mulberry Street, and others in Philadelphia, Buffalo, and Cleveland. In San Fran-

cisco, shadows played to newcomers from China. But rich and numerous as were these influences pouring into our country, they didn't immediately begin to catch the attention of the general public. Some shows played only to audiences of their own national origin, and then began to disappear as the second generation threw off its ties with the past and busied itself with becoming Americans. It is true that the Italian tradition was strong enough to hold on, but I have hunted in vain for a Karaghiozis company reported to be playing in the neighborhood of New York's Pennsylvania Station.

Finally, it is the puppetry from Western Europe, first England and Germany, and later Italy and France, that have had the greatest effect on our own puppetry during the last hundred years.

In earlier chapters, I have spoken of most of the American companies as *touring* marionette shows. This generally has been the case, and most of their own modern habits were inherited from the school of the highly mechanized Holden

---

Preceding pages: Burr Tillstrom's Kukla and Ollie of
record-breaking television show. Above: Earliest-known American
puppet picture was drawn by Alexander Anderson, probably
about 1800, for puppet and variety show performing in New York.
Right: Punch and Judy at Rockaway Beach, N.Y., in 1870's.

Marionettes and from the German and English vaudeville troupes that traveled around the United States, culminating in the more serious efforts of Sarg in the Twenties and Thirties. Even Remo Bufano, who did some work with hand puppets as well as strings, and played mostly in the New York area, never had his own theater. Everybody was on the move. We were starting to build the American audience from scratch.

In the early part of the twentieth century, some of the newer influences from Europe were rubbing off on American puppetry. The emphasis was on plays. Nobody thought of building a big variety show. We can get a pretty good idea of the character of American puppetry in those days by reviewing a few notes on several significant companies.

Certainly no story of puppetry in America would be complete without mention of the Yiddish puppet theater of Maude and Cutler in New York. Although their operation was not nearly so extensive as Sarg's or Bufano's, and despite the fact that Maude and Cutler played in a foreign tongue, their appeal was international and their great good humor and excellent manipulation attracted a broad audience. Zuny Maude emigrated from Russia in 1906 at the age of fourteen. Early in life he became a wood sculptor and then a political cartoonist for one of the Jewish newspapers. Later he began to make hand puppets

and opened a small theater on Second Avenue. He took Yossel Cutler, a younger newcomer from Russia, as a partner. And for a time, the painter Jack Tworkov, later the head of the art department at Yale, worked with them.

The combination of Maude and Cutler made a happy contrast. Maude, the more serious of the pair, had a deep booming voice, and the jocular Cutler a high, incisive one. They both wrote material for their shows, most of which were humorous and satirical. I first saw them in 1931 in a hall on Fourteenth Street. They were playing everything from a spoof of *The Dybbuk* to *The Three Bears*. The latter sounded very funny even to those who didn't understand Yiddish, because, of course, the story was a familiar one and we all knew what they were saying in the strange-sounding language. Another satirical bit had cast Gabriel as janitor of the Pearly Gates. He conversed with the Lord whose voice came from behind a billowing white cloud in the background. When the young Obraztsov came to America in 1925, as an actor with the Moscow Art Theater, he visited Maude and Cutler and

Above: Troll king from Tatterman production of *Peer Gynt*. Sketch shows character as designed by Terence von Duren, picture the puppet carved by Roy Patton. Opposite: Marionette dancers of notable producer Sue Hastings.

was fascinated by their work.

Tony Sarg's popularity inspired others to work with marionettes. He ran a school for a year or so, beginning in 1924, and his first pupil, Sue Hastings, founded a thriving if hectic touring company that played in the eastern United States in theaters, schools, department stores, and fairs. Her companies were the training ground for a score of fine operators. During the time when the principal attitude in America was that puppets were for kids, Sue's marionettes took part in four Broadway musicals and made a tour of English music halls.

At the same time the Tatterman Company, headed by William Duncan and Edward Mabley, although inheriting the children's audience, made successful steps toward picking up an adult following. Their most significant show was a full-length production of *Peer Gynt* in 1936. The Tattermans gathered together an impressive array of sculptors, designers, and acting puppeteers for this show. This was the first time that such high-level talent had been aimed at an adult puppet audience in the United States. Nevertheless, the Tattermans had to tour the country and play in colleges and concert halls to find an American audience that was ready for serious puppetry.

The late Twenties was a period of innocence and prosperity, and about a dozen companies were touring the States and Canada. A great number of young, enthusiastic, artistic people were getting into puppetry as a career, and just when it looked as though a new wave of inventiveness was about to arrive, the Crash and the Depression were upon us and broke up many of our large marionette companies. As individual survivors and smaller groups started to pick up the pieces,

something revolutionary happened. Single operators began working in full view of the audience. Veteran puppeteers wouldn't have been caught like that, without a drape to hide behind, but the young ones didn't know any better, and that is often the genesis of progress. I remember my own aloof disdain of the new trend, and also how soon I adopted it. These were uncertain times in an overly crowded industry. Only the small unit could survive.

Frank Paris, who has his new studio in New York, was the first to operate his show in full view, wearing dark clothes and working his short-strung marionettes in a spotlight. Four or five big marionettes and a coat rack to hang them from was all the equipment he needed, but I remember how he thrilled the audiences at the Radio City Music Hall, especially with a lively Carmen Miranda, and his skaters, which he operated in swirling

circles around him.

A bit later, Paul Walton and Mickey O'Rourke opened in New York's posh Rainbow Room. They still play the American club circuit and Broadway musicals with a small folding stage which raises their marionettes about eighteen inches above the dance floor and provides a background up to the waist of the operators. They will be remembered for the hand puppets in the film of *Lili*.

Almost all American puppetry of this period had been content to follow pretty much in the pattern Sarg had set. There were a few individual artists, such as Bufano, whose styles could be recognized, but most of the puppets were mild caricatures or embellishments of people. A group of Sarg alumni got together to produce something special that might give puppetry a new look. The

result was the Gawpy Ballet, all birds and animals, beautifully designed by the sculptor Robert Hestwood, and with captivating music by his brother, Harold. I was one of the partners. We tried to crash Broadway in 1929 and ran just two nights. There wasn't an audience for an adult puppet show in New York, and if there was, we had no idea how to find it and entice it into a theater.

Another company, the Yale Puppeteers, tried to establish itself on Broadway with no more success than we had, but then moved West and became one of the few American companies to play in its own permanent theater. (I believe they were the first ones to use the word "puppeteer.") This group of three young men, just out of college, toured the United States in a small truck in the late Twenties, and finally opened the Turnabout Theater in Hollywood. The theater continued in operation until 1960. "Turnabout" meant that the one hundred and seventy-five streetcar seats faced a marionette stage for the first half of the performance and then at intermission were flipped over to face another stage at the opposite end of the theater where live actors played. This intriguing setup attracted crowds of tourists and Angelinos for about twenty-five years. Turnabout was an entirely adult effort, with most of its clever satirical plays and music written by the group's Forman Brown. Harry Burnett, another partner, worked both ends of the theater, playing with other actors on the live stage, as well as operating the marionettes.

Martin and Olga Stevens of Indiana toured the story of Joan of Arc and the Passion play with beautiful small marionettes, and gave a serious, powerfully dramatic feeling to some of the first religious puppetry in the United States.

In 1937 Rufus and Margo Rose, a husband and wife company, both of whom formerly were with Sarg on the road and at the Chicago Fair in 1933, built and operated the first full-length industrial motion picture using marionettes exclusively, another facet of American puppetry that was to grow.

There were still a lot of small marionette units playing the night clubs and vaudeville in 1937, and this was mostly true through World War II, when six or seven live acts and a motion picture were common in the big presentation houses. A few energetic puppeteers took small portable stages around the world to entertain the troops, following up close to the battle lines. But when peace came, the big theaters that had thrived on a wartime prosperity began to falter, and vaudeville, as such, died.

There was one American who felt and understood more about puppetry than most of us—and was very articulate about it. This was Basil Milovsoroff of Vermont, who emigrated to the United States from Siberia. Starting with beautiful, but conventional figures, Basil had become aware of the symbolic uses of puppetry, the things that the cave priest instinctively knew. He discovered meaning in natural forms. He could find a gnome in a gnarled branch of a tree; a leaf or a rock might suggest the simplest statement he could make in designing a being. He has worked almost alone in America in the visual shorthand that puppetry can be. Things might have been different if more of us had listened to him.

If anything like a style had developed in American puppetry it was by pure chance. Things had been moving too fast, and all of us had been jumping from clubs to fairs to vaudeville—each of which required a different approach—just to

make a living. There hadn't been much time to sit and think about what we were doing or why. We looked at the other shows and maybe lifted an idea here and there, but mostly we just worked long hours, had fun, and did what came naturally.

Then came the machine and changed all that. Television was the machine's name, and it came with a bang. In a theater we could play to a few hundred people, in the biggest ones to five or six thousand at a time. Within a few years, we were playing to millions, and sometimes tens of millions. And the changes that television brought were staggering. The medium grew quickly and changed quickly. It looked like an exciting new kind of theater, and a lot of us thought we'd better jump on. The problem has been something like that of a broncho ride—how to hold on.

Opposite: Frank Paris and his marionette dancer (Carmen Miranda) performing on stage of New York's huge Radio City Music Hall. Above: Movie *Lili* starred hand puppets of Walton and O'Rourke, along with Leslie Caron and Mel Ferrer.

Television has been neither better nor worse for puppetry than for any other performing art. It has made profound changes in puppetry's style and method of work for the new medium, but in basic principles none at all. The same things are funny, the same things are ridiculous. Television, besides increasing the audience, has speeded up our preparation, shortened the playing time, and changed our focus, as it has for the other per-

forming arts. And it has fostered mediocrity. But I believe the increase in the size of the audience may finally have a good effect.

The beginning of television was a period of real excitement and hope. The radio networks, which had attracted huge, loyal audiences with such performers as Fred Allen, W. C. Fields, Edgar Bergen, and the popular dance bands, all got into television at once and found they had a

Baisil Milovsoroff has fashioned puppets from natural forms such as tree branches (top). Tatar (right) is earlier figure. Tillstrom's Madame Oglepuss and Colonel Cracky (above, left) are TV favorites. Kukla and Ollie perform with Fran Allison in version of *St. George and the Dragon*.

great deal of time to fill with more than words and music. Hollywood, in those days a competitor, said, "No, you can't have our films," and for a few years television tried everything else. The networks' early attitude was, "Let's see what happens. We don't know what to do, but go play. Fill time."

One of the more fortunate things that happened was the show "Kukla, Fran, and Ollie," built on the firm foundation of Punch, but with a major difference. This show is the creation of Burr Tillstrom, one of the great loners, who had the good fortune to offer his talents during these experimental times. Here was a new experience in the theater. In films, an actor plays to an unseen audience months after he has performed for the camera. In live television, the performer plays to an unseen audience of the moment. In the case of Tillstrom the audience reacted immediately by mail. It was a love affair between the players and the audience from the beginning. Kukla, a diminutive character with the voice of a child and the wisdom of the ages, wears the costume of a Pagliacci. Fran is Fran Allison of the live world, who stands in front of the booth and believes. She is the modern equivalent of the Punch show's "bottler," who sings and helps to bridge the space between Kukla's fantasy world and the one we live in. Ollie—Oliver J. Dragon— if related at all to the crocodile of the Punch show, is of distant kinship, with a vegetarian disposition, but all the satire and a lot of delicate humor. These are the principals. The rest of the cast includes, among others, Beulah Witch, lonely, yet adjusting to the times with her jet broom; Fletcher Rabbit, a single-minded square; Madame Oglepuss, the society matron; and Cecil Bill, the stagehand who speaks in a two-syllable language that everybody understands. All of them are facets of Tillstrom's imagination and partners in a daily coffee klatch of gentle satire. The Kuklapolitans, as they are called, play right in your lap, but the closeness hurts them not at all. Their sculpture is so distinctive and they are so far from trying to look like "little people" that the viewer accepts them as Burr made them. They have attracted the widest strata of audience, from the most sophisticated adults to children. Prominent actors, who would think twice before going out of their way to praise another performer, are avid fans.

"Kukla, Fran, and Ollie" is instant theater triggered by the events of the day and the whim of its creator. The songs are rehearsed, but almost everything else happens on the spot. Sometimes they may decide to do Shakespeare, but more often it is something of the moment. Fran is so tuned to the Kuklapolitans that she can alter her course in midstream if Burr decides to change the subject. Much of the show's material comes from the audience. They send clothes, suggestions, false teeth for Ollie, hats. On one record day there arrived eleven thousand pieces of mail. Any news item or special national day (Beulah Witch was Miss Garlic Pickle of 1954) may be the source

of an idea. The audience always feels itself to be a part of the production. The knowledge that the show is going into homes has had a tendency to gentle the action. (Kukla once blew his nose on the curtain and the next day half a dozen handkerchiefs arrived in the mail. He never used the curtain again.)

The show has taken many forms, the most successful being fifteen minutes, five times a week. The support of millions of viewers gave the creator a confident approach that has kept the Kuklapolitans running steadily for more than a decade. This is a phenomenon in American television, where "overexposure" is often a fatal disease, and a tribute to Burr and his puppetry.

Burr Tillstrom played some Punch and Judy when he first started in puppetry in 1937, and later was charmed and excited by the work of the Englishman, Walter Wilkinson, whose hand puppets he saw at a convention of the Puppeteers of America in St. Louis. Kukla got his start playing at parties in Chicago and was named by Tamara Toumanova, the ballerina. It just happened to fit. Now on video tape, the Kuklapolitans travel the English-speaking world.

Tillstrom and video met without an unhappy ripple. It was a complete success from all angles. My own company's first experience with continuous television made some profound changes in our working patterns, excited us, and almost killed us in the process. We had been making films, which required the puppets to move their mouths, eyes, sometimes even their fingers. There were three-dimensional sets, changes of heads and hands, meticulous paint jobs—in short, a mass of detail. It had been taking about four months to produce twenty minutes of finished footage.

Our first television show, a tongue-in-cheek western, called for five fifteen-minute sequences a week. The network's thinking at that time was, "Puppets are small, they should be cheap. We'll use them to fill time." It took us painful months to adjust, and although we made simplified sets and stages, there was still too much to do in the time we had. Special puppet heads for close-ups had to go. Complicated lighting was out. We had to design all-purpose puppets for close-up viewing —clean, simple, and a bit farther out. Television puts the audience only a few feet from the show. If the puppet looks "almost human," the viewer will be painfully aware of the "almost" and will not believe what he sees. On the other hand, a character with a lot of style may come thoroughly alive. We had some of the basic cast before the television season began—a cowboy, his girl, a talking horse, an orphan boy, and two gangsters. But immediately we began to add more characters. The ones that caught on stayed in the show, the unpopular ones lost their jobs.

The strain of building and writing was terrific. Physically, the work was about as hard as anything we'd ever done. But the rush of ideas was stimulating. Besides new puppets and props, there were scripts to supervise, songs to write, wild experiments, and endless rehearsals. Yul Brynner, our first director, tried having all the puppeteers wear earphones so that he could speak to us individually on the bridge. We tried it once. After five minutes our cables were so intricately braided that we had to stop and untangle. Each of the five of us operated several characters, so we just couldn't learn all the lines. This necessitated my working out a pair of rolling scripts that ran just below the camera level at the foot of two of our

Opposite: Slugger Ryan, honkey-tonk piano player (top), got his start at New York's Radio City Music Hall, later was M.C. of first Baird TV show. Below: Heathcliff, the horse, watches Cora Baird operate early "Scriptanola."

stages. This type of machine is standard in all television studios today, but we had it going a year before anybody else.

By today's standards, our first few weeks' results would have been considered a flop, and we would have been out, but then we were filling time. By the end of a year were were running smoothly and enjoying it. In spite of the exhaustion, I am grateful for the experience because it taught us what we could do without. We eased up on the production and the puppets, but worked harder on the story. We ended the year having used a hundred and twenty-five characters, mostly new. Our hero, Snarky Parker, went back to the night clubs and to films, but most of the others went on to new shows on television.

Television has shaken the entire entertainment world in America, but it is a multiplier, not an art. It can proliferate the tawdry as well as the beautiful. If we remember that it is a medium for selling soap and soup instead of theater (five times as much is spent per minute on commercials as on the shows), then perhaps puppetry can learn to use TV to advantage. My company has done its share of selling soap, soup, beer, and underwear, and I have no quarrel with that. Commercials can be good puppetry and help pay for a ballet or two on the "outside."

It's just that I believe any really artistic experimentation and any positive advances in puppetry are going to be made in the club or theater before a live audience.

Nevertheless, there are aspects of the big multiplier that are exciting. On occasion television does bring together the best creative minds of the theater to put together a puppet show. I am thinking particularly of our own *Peter and the Wolf*,

Scenes from the Baird production of *Art Carney Meets Peter and the Wolf*, presented on television with special lyrics by Ogden Nash. (1) One of seven stages built for show has openings in tree and hillock for hand puppets. (2) Peter leaves home at start of journey. (3) Art Carney with Wolf and his lawyer, the Weasel. (4) View of bridge area above scene in picture No. 1. Note how bridge is supported on treetops, as shown in sketch on page 238. (5) Baird with second of several wolf heads and bodies created for various changes of mood.

(6) Five puppeteers manipulate hunters and Wolf from bridge as television technician looks on. This was an extraordinarily large set, measuring 65 feet wide, 40 feet deep. (7) Another view of set, as audience saw it, shows hunters returning through woods with captured Wolf. (8) Carney and squirrel hand puppet operated from inside tree. (9) Little Red Riding Hood visits Wolf in Grandma's clothes. This was one of several wolf stories interpolated in *Peter* show. (10) Puppeteers Cora Baird and Frank Sullivan working both sides of the bridge over set in picture No. 1.

with the actor, Art Carney. In this case, the creators of the show even had ample time to think. It was a story about "wolfness," the character of the wolf in mythology, and included Prokofiev's original music and story of Peter, plus themes from his other works. Ogden Nash and Sheldon Harnick wrote the lyrics for the songs. The dramatization, the orchestra, and the singing were all handled by top-caliber theater people. (I am proud, too, of the quality of my own staff.) And the entire production was in the sensitive hands of Burt Shevelove, who is as experienced with puppets as with actors. Art Carney was the only live actor playing with half a hundred puppets.

One important thing that happened was that when it was over, thirty-three million people had seen a puppet show with the best production we could give it. (It played twice again in the years that followed.) In America, where puppetry is still generally considered a novelty, this kind of "multiplication" helps us to gain acceptance as a grown-up performing art.

Sketch above shows treetop marionette
bridges devised by Bairds to obtain depth of operation
for TV performances. Opposite:
Death as a matador, a conception of the
Mexican puppeteer, Roberto Lago.

Peter and the Wolf required two and a half months of preparation, and the early rehearsals were all held in our own studio, where we could change and develop our cast as we went along. Before we were through, we found it necessary to produce seven different aspects of the wolf. There are physical differences in a TV production that just can't happen in the puppet theater. Our seven special stages eventually occupied one entire broadcasting studio. The orchestra was in another. I modeled miniature sets in clay so that the scenic people could build the final ones to fit puppets and puppeteers under, over, and inside them. We used every device we knew to tell the story.

One stage containing the woods where the hunters and the wolf and Peter appear was sixty-five feet wide and forty feet deep. Tree trunks supported our marionette bridges, with intermittent gaps between the walkways so that we could move a character forward from a distance among the trees or fly a bird about. A camera boom, minus the camera, and plus a puppeteer, allowed us to walk a character about a large set with a live actor. Usually television is not so generous as this.

In looking over the last eighteen years' backlog of puppets, I can immediately spot the ones made when we were up to our necks in some television series. For us that means something new every week. The figures are often rough and unfinished compared to those we make for films. I found one unfortunate walk-on with just half his face painted, the side that showed on camera. He behaved beautifully, but he couldn't turn around.

When it comes to bit parts on television, the live actor may have the advantage over the puppet. With a little make-up, you can use the actors again. With the puppet it may require a chisel.

Working in films is another world, and the art of puppetry has a much better chance of growing to greater stature in the medium. Just as a comparison: A three-minute number for television may get three hours of rehearsal, while a three-minute segment of a feature film may be given three weeks.

Television has even had an effect on our "live" puppet shows. The live audience, used to television, expects to see activity all the time, and the curtain cannot be closed for long stretches to change scenery. Since 1955, we have been using a traveling stage about thirty-six feet wide, with three openings: one large marionette stage occupies the center and two smaller stages flank it for hand and rod puppets, or whatever we need. We also come out in front of the stage and work with the puppets in full view. This enables us to keep the action going. When the curtain closes in the middle, something else starts immediately at one of the side stages.

We used this same touring setup in Russia, India, Nepal, and Afghanistan, although we added an outdoor setup to play in villages for the Asian tour.

Television has employed a goodly number of puppet acts on the big variety shows. Vaudeville is no more, but the players adjust. André Tahon has been quite active in the United States, and so have Lafaye and Joly, from France. Topo Gigio, the "Italian Mouse," who was originally a stop-animation film figure, has become a television celebrity, transformed by a four-man team using the Japanese Bunraku method and black light. Señor Wences, originally from Spain, skips

from night club to television and continues to amaze with his strange and wonderful Johnny, whose "Easy for you" has become an American byword.

Jim Henson, a regular on television, has created a troupe of strange characters, The Muppets. They lend their unearthly faces in a contrast to earthly voices on records. The contrast is humor Henson has peopled his television with creatures never seen before from his own imagination. And this weird population is a very happy contrast to just people. The airways are so full of the latter.

And Shari Lewis, a girl of many talents, talks and sings to two of her other selves at a time, both on her own program and as a guest artist on the big musical shows.

One effect of television on these players, besides taking them to millions of viewers, is to shorten their performances. (The nervous television industry keeps up a fast change of pace for fear that the viewer will switch to one of the other channels.) I guess this speed-up is more

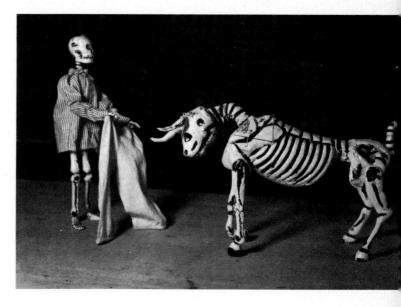

apparent to the Europeans. Both Wences, who used to play forty minutes in Spain, and Lafaye have expressed amazement at America's being supremely pleased with only ten minutes of their talents at a time.

Although in Communist countries puppetry is under the department of education, the emphasis of their shows is principally on attitude building. In America, on the other hand, a few definite steps have now been taken toward serious education. Prominent educators have masterminded a series of fifteen-minute films to teach French, which has been running for several years in the schools and on educational television. Our puppets are involved in most of the films, talking with the teacher, and reinforcing and repeating. It works. Tests have shown that the puppet sequences commanded the highest concentration of the classes.

Westinghouse also has used marionettes in its nine half-hour films on the different branches of mathematics. Marionettes work with visual symbols to illustrate points and reinforce memory. The series was produced very cheaply, and I am sure it could be polished to advantage, but the information supplied by the eminent Dr. Howard Fehr of Columbia Teachers College is solid, and the visual method is effective.

Television or no, the use of puppetry as an aid to the teacher is an established fact, and was pioneered to a large extent, in Mexico. More than any other puppeteer, Roberto Lago of Mexico City may be credited with giving Guignol a truly Mexican character. His play *Ya Viene Gorgognio Esparza* deals with those mystic forces of life and death that typify the fusion of Aztec and Spaniard. Death represented by a crowned skeleton, the witch, the cowboy, and the articulate horse, all figure in the story. After having established a permanent theater in the 1930's, Lago was recognized by the government and he went on to inspire and establish more than a dozen other groups. These companies, in turn, have worked with literally hundreds of teachers who use puppet techniques to improve literacy and public health, and spread civic historical information. He is responsible for the founding of a national puppet company in Venezuela and has toured in the United States. He has written that "the puppet's only real limitation is the *imitation* of the flesh-and-blood actor."

India's Literacy House, under the guidance of Mrs. Welthy Fisher, is training flying squads of puppets to go into the villages to help with specific problems. While my company was in Lucknow, we held a ten-day seminar and worked with writers, puppeteers, and musicians, gathered from all over India, to prepare plays on such subjects as smallpox inoculation vs. the witch doctor, family planning, honesty in business, watch out for the moneylender, don't wear all your wealth on your arms, and child marriage. In ten days the teachers at the seminar produced five plays with the puppets made at Literacy House. Mustaq Ahmad, in charge of the project, is a complete puppeteer and knows how valuable this form of teaching can be.

Dharpana School in Gujerat, under the direction of the well-known dancer, Mrinalini Sarabhai, is engaged in another such educational project, with puppets directly produced by India's representative to UNIMA, Meher Contractor. I believe that when India's basic contribution to puppetry is better understood, both Europe and

America will find more methods to borrow from the East to improve their own techniques, especially in simplicity of operation and special voices and music.

Samar Chatterjee teaches thousands with puppetry at the Children's Little Theater in Calcutta, where local youngsters come for classes in dance, song, and puppets.

These schools send their producers and artists to Prague, Moscow, and Bucharest to be educated in European puppetry because the courses are available. It is unfortunate that the United States does not offer a similar opportunity to teachers who would like to come here to study and to take back a bit of America to their countries. We have many applications, but no modus operandi.

The Egyptian government at one time approached the U. S. State Department for assistance in setting up a puppet theater in Cairo. We evidently had nothing for them, for eventually Romania sent two people from the Bucharest puppet theater. Russia, I am told, has a puppeteer in residence in Cairo.

There is no doubt that television is here to stay. We might as well make the best use of it we can. It works as a means of communicating and disseminating information. On the other hand, its ability to create first-rate art consistently remains in doubt. In many instances the puppeteer has a chance to do his show only once, and when it is over, he often wishes it had been better. There is little opportunity to profit from audience reaction and usually little time to think. As a result, a lot of puppetry, along with the rest of the video output, has been thoughtless junk. I believe that television must be used in combination with the other outlets for puppetry if we are to advance ourselves at all and get any perspective.

Certainly there are a lot of directions we can take to improve our puppetry and create a large and more understanding audience. They all are a part of the same process. The initial steps are easy in America. A one- or two-man organization with some talent has fairly easy access to tools and an abundance of materials. I know of a good many young puppeteers who started out with their ambitions and whatever extra stuff they found lying around the house.

The next problem is more serious. There are a lot of talented young puppeteers with no place to go. By this I mean there are few opportunities to apprentice and few places to gain experience working with and for others. It may be wonderful to learn everything by yourself—to work it out by trial and error—but it takes a lot of time. For even when a puppeteer becomes an experienced professional, there is still much to discover.

The paradox is that while there are these artificial and arbitrary hurdles for young people seek-

ing to make puppetry a career, puppetry itself in America is an almost uncharted field with many directions waiting to be explored. It is still growing up. There is no vocabulary, no jargon connected with it. And there is little money compared to the work that goes into it. I remember my father despaired of my ever making a living in the profession and a good bit of the time he was right. But that's not the fault of puppetry.

True we do not have government subsidy as many of the European companies do, but neither do other performing arts. A subsidy might keep a company above water until it caught hold and acquired a permanent audience, but I have seen enough good puppetry earn and hold its audience to know that subsidies are unnecessary where puppetry has a reasonable chance to operate.

I think the heart of the matter is quality. We are not going to grow up as a performing art and demand attention until we understand more about what we are doing and produce better shows. There is no censorship to inhibit us; we can explore virtually any idea we have a mind to. We can say almost anything we want to, but we don't say it.

We have people with a deep understanding of the nature of puppetry, like Milovsoroff, Kunze, and Schawinsky, but we don't listen to them. We appreciate the art of the folk puppeteer, but great as it is, it is limited. There are directions that hopefully we may follow. The composer, the playwright, director, and designer contribute just as much to an entertaining and artistic puppet show as they do to live theater. We must attract them to puppetry, let them stretch their talents, and share the enjoyment with us of inventing for our free-wheeling medium.

We must work with the ballet, using our moving, invented symbols (and I don't mean little people) as counterpoint to the ballet's superb human bodies and disciplined motions. Music and puppetry are highly compatible and much has been done to fuse our movement with orchestral sound. But with better understanding of what a puppet does best, composers can write more imaginative ballet for us. It could be highly abstract, it could be very funny, or sexy (as Lafaye has demonstrated), or brutal, but entertaining in a new way. It must not be a sentimental throwback, but a reflection of our own times.

Marionette opera has been popular on the continent, but has never made much headway in the United States. The puppet has usually burlesqued the familiar, and the European audience knew what was being kidded, but America does not have much familiar, indigenous opera. We must invent a new way to use the music with our

Above: Shari Lewis's Lamb Chop (left) and Hush Puppy are popular television characters. Outstanding TV players are the Muppets of Jim Henson. At right are his Wontkins and Will.

characters. Certainly it would be futile to try to copy the European opera we import, although something like Gilbert and Sullivan sung by animals might succeed. Or perhaps some American composer will write a satiric puppet opera to be performed by radioactive isotopes and the medium will be on its way again.

The only permanent puppet opera in America in recent years has played at the Kungsholm Restaurant in Chicago, where patrons may dine and then hear the world's finest recordings and look at a miniature stage, where tiny (fourteen- to fifteen-inch) figures, beautifully costumed and lighted, are pushed around in slots in the floor to indicate the positions of the characters as the show progresses. Articulation is at a minimum and their size so reduced as to leave a lot to the imagination. It works.

If puppets cannot add something to their performance that is superior to the way humans do it, then they should stick to their many other lasts. Certainly a svelte puppet Brünnhilde is superior in shape to a chubby one, and armor looks better on a muscular pair of calves than those of a skinny tenor, but there is something about the personality of an opera singer that helps to put across his music and draw the crowds. And personality is the one thing that the puppet does beautifully without.

In the live theater a critic can look at a show

and analyze it with a background of years of experience, from a standpoint of well-developed aesthetic criteria and a generally accepted and understood vocabulary. Even the most casual observers, although not able to analyze what they see in terms of structure, know that if they see a bad show, at least they might have expected something better.

These first principles unfortunately do not yet apply in puppetry. This is not the fault of the critics, or even the audience. Only a handful of people have ever had an opportunity to see as many as half a dozen full-length puppet plays. We are only beginning to supply critics with enough understanding of our craft for them to know what we are about—why, for instance, we cast a lion in a certain part instead of a man, or what is going on when a cocktail glass gets drunk and turns into a wolf with olives for eyes. Very

seldom have I read an evaluation of the sculpture of the figures in a puppet play, or an appreciation of the degree of caricature we employ. Yet we design our actors. There is no reason why such elements should not be explored and discussed along with the style of our motions or the degree of outrageousness of a concept.

We need more understanding of ourselves. Just as a painter studies other paintings, we need to know what has been done before in all areas of puppetry. Much of puppetry's past already has disappeared. Before more time is lost, we should establish libraries of plays. We need museums to preserve and display puppets of the past for study. Even if the creators are gone, we puppeteers can still hold on to our actors from the past. Otherwise, how can we continue and preserve the knowedge of such a complicated art?

Not too long ago a company of the once superb

Opposite: In educational films created by Bil Baird are Patapouf (left), teacher of first-year French, and legionaire who demonstrates difficulties of multiplication in ancient Rome. Top: Baird's "Banana Boat" number with famous singing frogs and sea-serpent interloper. Above: Indian shadows by Meher Contractor at Dharpana school, Ahmedabad. Left: Gorgognio Esparza and his horse, notable *charro* characters created in Mexico by Roberto Lago.

Piccoli marionettes came to rest in a Philadelphia warehouse. This was the end of the line after an unsteady tour of South and Central America, a halt in Mexico, a revival in Los Angeles, and a last jiggling gasp on television. Much of the old equipment is unchanged, but the ideas that brought it to life have been forgotten.

In 1960, a tangled pile of Salici marionettes was delivered to me by the trucking firm that had been storing them. "What'll I do with them, Bil?" said the truckman. "I don't want to throw them out." Yet they had been abandoned by the sons and daughters of Salici after the inspiration, the mainspring, the heart of the show had died. The younger Salicis had taken only a few sure-fire acts out of the lot—the pianist and the man who lit a cigarette and smoked—and returned to Europe to play in Italy and on the English beaches.

But how many ingenious joints, actions, inventions, funny motions, and astounding contrasts still were to be found buried in that snarl of strings for the person who had the knowledge to understand? How many stories of backstage repair with coat hangers or adhesive tape, or of emergency work on an arm or leg, hurriedly wired to prevent tangling? How many things simplified on the spot? Of course, an old troupe of puppets shouldn't be kept going indefinitely. Everything has to change and keep building. But the shame is that the reasons that made these shows great entertainment in the first place have been lost. I know of only two existing scripts of Tony Sarg's fifteen or more. Bufano has left even fewer.

How can we pass along some of the inspiration, original thinking, and invention that goes into making this thing work? Who has been able to inspire, to leave something behind that will grow?

Or who has left followers who know what to do, but not why? Will the best companies leave a school, or just a pile of puppets? How could Mantell, the pure American folk artist, pass on the results of his many years in vaudeville and on the road all over the world? What he learned through trial and error, and the polish he finally achieved, is not preserved here or in the playbills he left behind.

Even if museums and libraries give us a continuity with the past, however, we still need theaters in which to experiment. I don't know how this will come about, but the live theater has found its answer and so must we.

We must be in a position to invite foreign companies to play in the United States to an understanding audience. My own company has been fortunate enough to get a glimpse of puppetry in the rest of the world through our travels for the State Department, but only a fraction of the foreign shows ever comes here.

More of us might profit by the opportunity to know what the rest of the world is doing. Not just the professionals, but all of the inquiring ones. There is something very satisfying about building one's own small world and stocking it with the creatures of one's imagination. In these softer, but tenser days, when urban life pushes us more and more into the big pattern and denies us the need to know how to build a barn, train a horse, or when to plant a certain crop, our fingers, ears, and minds can still be fully absorbed. Puppetry can open up all the avenues. I think about my grandfather—the farmer, toolmaker, miller—and my father—the engineer, builder. Each made puppets for his son. My son is now making puppets.

PICTURE CREDITS

The following sources are repeated frequently in the list below and will, therefore, be referred to by the initials preceding their names.

AD — Photo by Arie de Zanger.
BB — Photo by Bil Baird.
BC — Baird Collection.
BD — Baird drawing.
EM — Ernest Maindron, *Marionettes et Guignols*, Paris, 1900.
MP — Puppet Collection, Munich City Museum.
PC — Picture Collection, New York Public Library.
PL — Photo by Peter Lacey.

CHAPTER ONE:
2-3—Peter Lacey Collection. 10-11-12—AD. 14—(left) BC; (right) Dr. Hans Purschke Collection; (lower left) BD. 15—(left) BC; (right) AD. 16—(top) Jurkowski Collection; (bottom) Percy Press. 18—(left) Jurkowski Collection; (top right) Guy Le Bolzer, *La Marionette*, Paris, 1958; (bottom right) Carl Schroeder. 19—BC. 20—NBC. 21—Albrecht Roser Collection. 22—Rufus Rose. 23—(top) Georges Lafaye Collection; (bottom) BD. 25—(left) BB; (right) Fred Schneckenburger. 26—(top) Norm Snyder; (lower left) WNDT/TV; (lower right) BB. 27—(left) PC; (right) EM.

CHAPTER TWO:
28-29—AD; puppet, Museum of the American Indian, Heye Foundation, N.Y. 32—(top) Smithsonian Institution; (bottom) AD; puppets, Museum of the American Indian, Heye Foundation, N. Y. 33—"Medicine Mask Dance" by Paul Kane, courtesy of Royal Ontario Museum, Toronto. 34—(top) Chicago Natural History Museum; (bottom) MP. 36—AD; mask, Museum of the American Indian, Heye Foundation, N. Y. 38-39—Albert A. Hopkins, *Magic*, Munn & Co., N.Y., 1911. 40—(top) AD; (bottom) J. Walter Fewkes, *Hopi Katchinas, U. S. Bureau of American Ethnology, 21st Annual Report*, 1899-1900, Washington, D. C., 1903. 42-43—PC.

CHAPTER THREE:
44-45—Madan Mahatta. 48-49—(top four pictures) BB; (bottom) Madan Mahatta. 51—BC. 52-53—Madan Mahatta. 54—Ernst Haas, Magnum Photos. 57-58—AD; puppets courtesy Indonesian Pavilion, N. Y. World's Fair. 59—AD; puppets courtesy Malaysian Pavilion, N. Y. World's Fair. 60-61—MP.

CHAPTER FOUR:
62-63—Miniature by Jehan de Grise from *Li romans du bon roi Alexandre*, MS 264, folio 76r., Bodleian Library, Oxford. 65—PC. 66—PC. 67—de Grise, op. cit., folio 54v. 68-69—(left) BC; (middle) V. V. Kallasha and N. E. Effrosa, *History of the Russian Theater*, Moscow, 1914; (right) Henryk Jurkowski. 70—(top) By permission of the Trustees of the Pierpont Morgan Library; (bottom left) Kallasha and Effrosa, op. cit.; (bottom right) Watercolor by Marcellus Laroon, the Elder, c.1690, British Museum. 72—Theatre Collection, Harvard College Library. 73—Peter Lacey Collection. 75—Kamil Bednar, *Johanes Doktor Faust*, Prague, 1959.

CHAPTER FIVE:
76-77—AD. 79-80—Marc Riboud, Magnum Photos. 82-83—Courtesy Turkish Government Information Agency, N. Y. 84—BC.

CHAPTER SIX:
86-87—AD. 88-89—Cruikshank illustrations from *The Tragical Comedy or Comical Tragedy of Punch and Judy*, Cambridge, 1926. 90—Princeton University Library, photo by Willard Stark. 92—Cruikshank, op. cit. 94-95—By courtesy of the Trustees of the Tate Gallery, London. 97—(top) Cooper Union Museum, N. Y.; (bottom) Frontispiece from *A Second Tale of a Tub, or the History of Robert Powel the Puppet-Show-Man*, London, 1715. 98—(top) BC; (bottom) Painting by A. G. Descamps of "A Polichinelle Street Show," c.1850, Victoria and Albert Museum, Crown Copyright. 99—BC. 101—PC. 102—Musée Gadagne, Lyon, photo by J. Camponagra. 103—Drawing by Lorentz from *Polichinel, Ex-Roi des Marionettes*, Paris, 1848. 105—Drawing by Duranty from *Théâtre des Marionettes du Jardin des Tuileries*, Paris, 1863. 107—(top left) MP; (bottom left) BB; (right) Musée Gadagne, Lyon, photo by J. Camponagra. 109—BC. 110-111—EM. 112—Index of American Design, National Gallery of Art, Washington, D. C. 114—EM. 115—Culver Pictures.

CHAPTER SEVEN:
116-117—AD. 120—B.C. 121—Bruce Davidson, Magnum Photos. 122—Drawing by Mario Vellani-Marchi from Orio Vergani, *Colori di Sicilia*, Edizione Radio Italiana, Torino. 123—AD. 124—PC. 127—MP. 129—*Vanity Fair*, Copyright 1963 by Condé Nast Publications.

CHAPTER EIGHT:
130-131—AD (BC). 133—From painting sequence "The Hundred Children," Ming Dynasty, British Museum. 134—(top) Victoria and Albert Museum, Crown Copyright; (bottom) Marc Riboud, Magnum Photos. 136—Cooper Union Museum, N. Y. 137—AD. 138—(left) BD; (right) Woodcut by Torii Kiyomasu I, Metropolitan Museum of Art, Dick Fund, 1949. 139—Consulate General of Japan, N. Y. 141—*Masterpieces of Japanese Puppetry*, Charles E. Tuttle Co., Tokyo, 1958.

CHAPTER NINE:
142-143—EM. 144—Otto Kunze Collection. 145—Ivo Puhonny Collection. 146—"Il Parlatorio" by G. A. Guardi, Civici Musei Veneziani D'Arte E Di Storia, Ca' Rezzonico, Venice. 147—PC. 148—(left) PC; (right) Cooper Union Museum, N. Y. 149—(top right) PC; (bottom) EM. 151—(left top and bottom) BB; City Museum, Prague; (right) BB; City Museum, Munich. 152—EM.

CHAPTER TEN:
154-155—All MP, except middle pictures of first two columns, p. 154: both AD. 158-159—Musée Gadagne, Lyon, photo by J. Camponagra. 160—AD. 161—BD. 163—(top left) BB, puppet from Moscow Central Theater; (top right) BB; (bottom) Tatterman Collection. 164-165—Austrian National Library. 166—(top four) BB; (bottom left) BC. (bottom right) BB. 169—(left two) BB; (right) Doris Boer-Puhonny Collection, Hamburg. 170-171—(left) PC; (middle) Otto Kunze; (right) BC. 172—Dr. Jan Malik, Prague. 173—(top right) Dr. Jan Malik; (top left and bottom) BC. 174—Ivo Puhonny. 175—Kunstgewerbemuseum, Zurich. 176-177—F. J. McIsaac, *The Tony Sarg Marionette Book*, N. Y. 1921. 178—(top two) BC; (bottom) Courtesy R. H. Macy Co., N. Y. 179—BC. 180—PC.

CHAPTER ELEVEN:
182-183—Felix Klee. 186—Kunstmuseum, Bern. 188—(left) Drawing, Alfred Jarry; (right) Xanti Schawinsky. 189—(top) Otto Kunze; (bottom) BD. 190—Andre Tahon, photo by Alpha-Omega, Hollywood. 191—Jean Loup Temporal. 192-193—Georges Lafaye. 195—(1) Albrecht Roser; (2) Fritz Herbert

Bross; (3) Fred Schneckenburger; (4) Angus McBean; (5 and 6) Ove Alstrom, Marionetteatern, Stockholm. 196—(top left and right) Adam Kilian; (middle left and right) BB; (bottom right) BC. 197-198—Norm Snyder. 199—(left) Moscow Central Theater; (right) Central Puppet Theatre, Prague, photo by Milon Novotny. 201—PL. 204—Dr. Hans Purschke. 206—(left) Harro Siegel; (top and bottom right) Dr. Hans Purschke; 207—(middle) Baisil Milovsoroff; (all others) Dr. Hans Purschke. 208—(1) Central Puppet Theatre, Prague, photo by Karel Stoll; (2) Central Puppet Theatre, Prague; (3) Panstwowy Theater, Warsaw; (4) Panstwowy Theater, Gdansku; (5 and 6) Tandarica Theater, Romania; (7 and 8) Allami Babszinhaz, Budapest.

CHAPTER TWELVE:
210-211—AD. 213—(top) BD; (bottom) BB. 214-215—(1 and 4) Vernon Lewis; (2 and 5) Nat Messik; (3) Frank Capra Productions; (6) PL. 217—Augustus Theodore. 218—Nat Messik; 219—(left) Nat Messik; (right) BC. 220—BB. 221—AD. 222—Guy Le Bolzer, La Marionette, Paris, 1958. 223—Nat Messik.

CHAPTER THIRTEEN:
224-225—Don Sahlin. 226-227—PC. 228—William Ireland Duncan Collection. 229—BC. 230—Frank Paris Collection. 231—Metro-Goldwyn-Mayer. 232—(top) Baisil Milovsoroff; (below, left and right) Don Sahlin. 233—Baisil Milovsoroff. 235—(top) Nat Messik; (bottom) CBS. 236-237—George Zimbel. 238—BD. 239—Roberto Lago. 241—CBS. 242—NBC. 243—Del Ankers. 244—(left) BC; (right) John Hugelmeyer. 245—(top) AD; (middle) Meher Contractor; (bottom) Roberto Lago.

BIBLIOGRAPHY

BOOKS

ALTHERR, ALFRED, *Marionetten*, Zurich.
ARNOTT, PETER D., *Plays Without People*,
Bloomington, Ind., 1964.
BENEGAL, SOM, *Puppet Theatre Around the World*,
New Delhi, 1961.
BLACKHAM, OLIVE, *Shadow Puppets*, New York, 1960.
BOAS, FRANZ, *Primitive Art*, New York, 1951.
BOEHN, MAX VON, *Puppen Spiele*, Munich, 1929.
BUCH, JOSEPH and ALFRED LEHMANN,
Das Puppentheater, Leipzig, 1923-31, Vols. 1-4.
CHESNAIS, JACQUES, *Histoire Generale des Marionettes*,
Paris, 1947.
COVARRUBIAS, MIGUEL, *The Island of Bali*,
New York, 1942.
DEMENI, EUGENE, *Kukli Na Stzene*, Moscow, 1949.
DURANTY, M., *Théâtre des Marionettes du Jardin
des Tuileries*, Paris, 1863.
EFFIMOVA, NINA, *Adventures of a Russian
Puppet Theatre*, Birmingham, Mich., 1935.
FEDOTOV, A., *Anatomie Loutky*, Prague, 1953.
GERVAIS, ANDRÉ, *Marionettes et Marionettistes de France*,
Paris, 1947.
GROPIUS, WALTER and LASZLO MOHOLY-NAGY,
Die Buhne in Bauhaus, Munich, 1924.
HADAMOWSKY, FRANZ, *Richard Teschner und Sein
Figurenspiegel*, Vienna, 1956.

HOPKINS, ALBERT A., *Magic*, New York, 1911.
INVERARITY, ROBERT BRUCE, *Art of the Northwest
Coast Indians*, Berkeley, Calif., 1950.
JONSON, BEN, *Bartholomew Fair*, New Haven, Conn., 1963.
JOSEPH, HELEN HAIMAN, *A Book of Marionettes*,
New York, 1920.
KALLASHA, V. V. and N. E. EFFROSA, *History of
the Russian Theater*, Moscow, 1914.
KENNARD, JOSEPH SPENCER, *Masks and Marionettes*,
New York, 1935.
KRAFFT, LUDWIG, *Munchen und das Puppenspiel*,
Munich, 1961.
LAGO, ROBERTO, *Ya Viene Gorgognio Esparza*, Mexico, 1944.
LE BOLZER, GUY, *La Marionette*, Paris, 1958.
MAGNIN, CHARLES, *Histoire des Marionettes en Europe*,
Paris, 1852-62.
MAINDRON, ERNEST, *Marionettes et Guignols*, Paris, 1900.
MALIK, JAN, *Narodni Umelec Josef Skupa*, Prague, 1962.
MALIK, JAN, *Puppetry in Czechoslovakia*, Prague, 1948.
McISAAC, F. J., *The Tony Sarg Marionette Book*,
New York, 1921.
McPHARLIN, PAUL, *The Puppet Theater in America—
1524 to Now*, New York, 1948.
McPHARLIN, PAUL, *Puppetry Yearbook, 1946-47*,
New York, 1947.
MIGNON, PAUL LOUIS and JEAN MOHR, *J'Aime les
Marionettes*, Paris, no date.
MILLS, WINIFRED H. and LOUISE M. DUNN,
Marionettes, Masks and Shadows, New York, 1927.
MURRAY, MARGARET, *The God of the Witches*,
New York, 1960.
NETZE, HANS, *Das Suddeutsche Wander Marionettentheater*,
Munich, 1938.
OBRAZTSOV, SERGEI, *The Chinese Puppet Theatre*,
London, 1961.
OBRAZTSOV, SERGEI, *My Profession*, Moscow, 1950.
PURSCHKE, HANS R., *Liebens Werte Puppen Welt*,
Hamburg, 1962.
RINGELNATZ, JOACHIM, *Kasperle Verse*, Berlin, 1954.
SAND, MAURICE, *The History of the Harlequinade*,
London, 1915.
SIYAVUSGIL, SABRI ESAT, *Karagoz*, Istanbul, 1951.
SPEAIGHT, GEORGE, *The History of the English
Puppet Theatre*, London, 1955.
SZTAUDYNGER, JAN; HENRYK JURKOWSKI, and
HENRYK RYL, *Od Szopki Do Teatru Lalek*,
Lodz, Poland, 1961.
TANIZAKI, JUNICHIRO, *Some Prefer Nettles*,
New York, 1955.
——————————, *Der Puppenspieler*,
Jahrhaney 1-3, Bochum, Germany, 1930-33.
——————————, *Punch and Judy*,
Cambridge, England, 1926.

PERIODICALS

The Marionette, Florence, Italy, 1918, Vol. 1,
Nos. 1-6, 1918.
Opera News, New York, Dec., 1951,
"The Marionette Opera" by Otto Kunze.
Theatre Arts Monthly, New York, July, 1928,
special issue, "The Marionette."

INDEX

Page numbers in *italics* indicate illustrations